Critical Issues in Clinical Practice

Critical Issues in Clinical Practice

Jennifer Clegg

SAGE Publications
London • Thousand Oaks • New Delhi

First published 1998

SAGE Publications Ltd
6 Bonhill Street
London EC2A 4PU

SAGE Publications Inc.
2455 Teller Road
Thousand Oaks, California 91320

SAGE Publications India Pvt Ltd
32, M-Block Market
Greater Kailash – I
New Delhi 110 048

British Library Cataloguing in Publication data

A catalogue record for this book is available
from the British Library

ISBN 0 8039 7554 6
ISBN 0 8039 7555 4 (pbk)

Library of Congress catalog card number 98–61165

Typeset by Mayhew Typesetting, Rhayader, Powys
Printed in Great Britain by Redwood Books,
Trowbridge, Wiltshire

Contents

Preface

The late twentieth-century clinician faces dilemmas daily. Whether to support or resist the women-only respite care hostel sought by Asian carers; why parents may object to their child being given facilitated communication and how to construct a response; or how to think through the dilemmas presented by a group of staff who seek your support while under police investigation for abusing clients. Some personal solutions which satisfied me at the time are proposed, but of course this book is not really concerned to give 'correct' answers: our perspective on appropriate responses will inevitably change as the moral horizons of our culture change. The book concerns the development of useful ways to consider clinical dilemmas and contemporary issues, and the identification of new directions for research-related practice.

It is addressed primarily to clinical psychologists, both experienced professionals and those in training, and to social scientists in search of fruitful dialogue with clinicians. However, Chapters 4 to 8 on ideas underpinning particular approaches to practice are also likely to be useful to research-minded psychiatrists, speech and language therapists, nurses and social workers.

The text is organized by five key themes. Firstly, that contemporary issues are illuminated both by *histories of the present* and by detailed examination of twentieth-century sources of *intersubjective meaning*. Theories of meaning generally fall into two main groups: a set variously described as pragmatism, social constructionism or activity theory, all of which draw on closely connected ideas; and a second set concerned with interpretation, described by philosophers as hermeneutics (and by the *Psychologist* as Herman Ewtix). The bulk of the text depends on concepts drawn from social constructionism; Chapter 6 is devoted primarily to hermeneutics. Working out how to develop and apply *critical thinking* to the contemporary issues illuminated by history and meaning is the central theme of the book, an activity carried out by *reflective researcher-practitioners* whose thinking is influenced by and enacted through the *human systems* with which they engage. These five themes are represented throughout the book, which tackles a number of contemporary topics from diverse positions: a summary of their contribution within each chapter is provided at the end.

The first three chapters introduce most of the concepts used throughout the text. Chapter 1 explores models of clinical practice and the relationship between academic and clinical psychology; the second considers the nature of explanation, the third charts the influence of the postmodern culture which we all inhabit. Readers unaccustomed to reading philosophy may wish to skip Chapters 2 and 3 initially, referring back to them once the philosophical concepts covered have been encountered through discussion of more obviously clinical material. However, I hope that initial unfamiliarity with the ideas will not prevent too many people from opening these chapters: they discuss, and hence open the possibility of addressing, conceptual differences between psychologists which preclude the possibility of debate as long as they remain unexamined.

Chapters 4 and 5 consider the way that psychologists use time and culture. Chapter 4 exposes our ignorance and hence misuse of past ideas: drawing on past work without any systematic method results in ideas being recruited to wholly incommensurate causes. It exposes the doggedly Newtonian assumptions – about time being linear and continuous – employed by most psychologists, assumptions which prevent us from noticing or conceptualizing non-linear changes. Systemic family therapists are lauded by many writers as one of the few exceptions to this rule, but other ways that past information can usefully be brought into clinical practice are explored as well. Chapter 5 unscrambles the conceptual muddle which the terms 'culture' and 'community' have created in clinical psychology, using ideas from geographers amongst others to expand our conception of social space. It is concerned to understand forces supporting social fragmentation, and to expand our concept of solidarity without adopting the mirage of communitarian politics. It advocates the creation of unity within diversity, rather than diversity for its own sake, while acknowledging that many contemporary dilemmas arise because people are members of more than one community: difficulties arise when each depends on a different value system. The chapter concludes with practical discussion of ways to work with cultural difference; models of our own cultural identity; how to work with translators in clinical settings; and what working in the community might really mean.

Chapters 6 and 7 concern the creation of meaning. In Chapter 6 this is through interpretation, through understanding and exploration of embodied meanings – for example, through disability or disfigurement – and through the co-construction of new narratives during therapy. Chapter 7 concerns the central importance of clinically relevant research for all practitioners, building on the argument put forward in Chapter 1. It focuses on five different qualitative techniques not because I dismiss quantitative approaches, which carry powers of persuasion unmatched by most qualitative studies to date, but because these are already familiar to clinicians or can be accessed readily. The range of different qualitative techniques, and the types of questions to which they can be applied, remain less well known: they are also more easily applicable to research into intersubjectivity.

Chapter 8 considers clinical ethics theoretically, politically and practically. It reviews different traditional and contemporary theories to show that utilitarian and rights-based statements cannot be put together in an intelligible argument, because they conflict conceptually. It draws on MacIntyre's virtue theory to give one account of the way ethical theory could affect practice. The book concludes in Chapter 9 by drawing themes together and offering some predictions about the future shape of services.

Whenever possible these ideas are fleshed out with clinical and other examples, indented within the text for clarity. Most of the clinical examples derive from 20 years of practice during a period which has seen considerable change in psychologists' perspectives on the ethics of case description. All recent material derives from research projects or clinical intervention where expressed permission to use the material for research and teaching purposes was given: names and other identifying details have been altered. When I have used older material from clients I cannot contact, I have pursued Davis's recommendations and gone for 'thin description'. Not only have personal details been changed but key identifiers have been left out, while occasionally other material from different cases has been added to further obscure and protect the individual. This provides what is sometimes termed a vignette, which I understand must originate in personal clinical experience but may be somewhat narrativized. A few useful illustrations suggested by colleagues were also narrativized in this way.

My project is to move clinical psychology away from narrow adherence to particular therapies. I do not want to restrict my work to a single umbrella, where to reject behaviourism is to limit one's options to psychodynamic theories (although it may satisfy some curiosities to know that when working therapeutically, rather than as a general applied psychologist within the NHS, my main resource is systemic family therapy). I want to explore pluralism and complexity yet develop coherence and integrity within this multiverse; to revisit the idea that psychologists are intellectuals who use psychological expertise in its widest sense to support people who are disabled, confused or ill. More positively my project is to build or reinforce various bridges – between psychology and philosophy, history, geography; between clinical psychology and the academy. There are others interested in this too. I am aware of round table discussions in Manchester and London which foster real dialogue about transcultural issues and about old and new ways to work with challenging behaviour. I know of imaginative conferences to debate the effect of bringing qualitative research into clinical training and hence into clinical psychology. No doubt other people are also developing spaces where ideas can be exchanged, efforts that should bear fruit in new and creative forms of practice.

While I was working on this text various people gave me generous help, believing that something new might emerge: it is dedicated to their optimism regardless of its achievement. Nottingham Healthcare NHS Trust has been a significant source of support through its continuing willingness to fund the academic half of my post. I am grateful to clinical psychologists in training at Sheffield and Leicester Universities and to colleagues in the Department of Learning Disabilities at Nottingham University, all of whom provided lively fora where I could try out some of the ideas presented here. I am also happy to acknowledge the influence of members of the BPS History and Philosophy Section, whose annual conference I value immeasurably.

Detailed input came from individuals – the many who commented on drafts, and my partner who ran our household almost single-handedly for three years. I thank Dot MacKinlay for letting me use her vast experience of children and her ideas on therapeutic narrative; Susan King for careful comments, familiarity with continental philosophies, and ongoing encouragement; Gillian Hughes, Emma Meldrum, Dawn Reeve, John Cromby and John Robertson for close and careful readings of chapters; and Richard Lansdall-Welfare for reading two chapters, for proffering new books before even he had read them, and for lively and intense engagement with many of these ideas. Thanks also to Penny Standen and the late Ann Craft for enabling me to take a meta-perspective on the process of book-writing, for faith in its relevance and concern for its progress; and to Ziyad Marar and Jim Orford for careful, constructive feedback that shaped and clarified. Finally I thank Jonathan Hill, who read every chapter on numerous occasions with unflagging enthusiasm, and claimed to enjoy spending night after night talking about their content over dinner.

1 Clinical Psychology and its Critics

New ideas are being introduced into all parts of our lives at an ever-increasing pace which makes it difficult for any practitioner to keep up. Alongside this accelerated turnover of ideas comes increasing competitiveness: between different types of practitioners, between clinical specialties, and between academic and applied scientists. This chapter creates a vantage-point from which to view new ideas as they come over the horizon, one which may allow practitioners to cease feeling so besieged. I consider clinical psychology from three perspectives: the relationship between academic and clinical psychology, three different schools of practice in clinical psychology, and criticisms of clinical practice from within and outside the profession.

Academic and Applied Psychology

Danziger's (1990) influential history of psychology is based on a systematic review of publications in applied and basic psychology journals. Focusing on psychology's construction of its subject matter the account ends in 1935, by which time the direction of applied psychology was set. Danziger demonstrates that psychologists marketed their ideas to applied settings from the beginning of this century, showing how applicability was built into the subject well before an accepted body of knowledge had been developed. The main site of applied psychology at that time was education, but Danziger's examination of the relationship between academic and applied psychology is relevant for clinicians.

One example is the way that psychology changed from providing research reports about individuals to reports about groups. Education officers in the USA and Britain wanted information which classified groups of people and evaluated the outcome of various policies. This created pressure to investigate groups and to analyse the results statistically, while psychology had initially published information about individuals. Danziger traces the way that the change to writing about groups rather than individuals occurred initially in applied journals and subsequently in academic journals. This was a lasting change, only recently challenged by Billig's (1994) provocative article suggesting that single case histories and individual reports be given much greater weight in psychology.

The term 'applied science' apes the natural sciences, suggesting that what is being offered to practical settings derives from university research. Danziger shows that the direction of influence was the other way:

> In actual fact, 'applied' research usually relied on its own practices with little or no help from 'pure' research, and 'pure' research either continued in complete isolation or adapted the practices of 'applied' research, contributing little but technical sophistication and a more abstract terminology. (1990: 190)

Danziger shows how meeting the needs of educational administrators in Britain and the USA meant that psychology grew much faster in these countries than in Germany.

However, attempts to make mental testing applicable beyond education showed the difficulty of generalizing across human contexts. The paradox which continues to run through psychology was exposed. Scientific respectability depends on creating distance between psychological and commonsense accounts, by imposing the objectivity of laboratories and statistical analyses. However, relevance requires similarity between contexts of investigation and contexts of application. Applied psychologists seek to narrow the gap between these contexts while academic psychologists act to maintain or enlarge it. This tension makes it unlikely that psychology and the people it studies can develop a stronger alliance.

Danziger's history suggests that the baleful influence of applied psychology was to turn open systems into closed ones, so that social environments mirrored the assessment situation or laboratory more closely. Thus the outcome of psychological procedures became more predictable. An example is the adoption of educational practices which mimicked those used in intelligence testing, so that timed tests became a routine component of school life with consequent improvements in the accuracy of their predictions of scholastic success. That this had little effect on whether those tests could predict success beyond the school walls received scant attention. Another example of the imposition of laboratory conditions on natural environments came later, when behavioural psychologists turned hospital wards into the closed environment of a token economy. Danziger uses such evidence to argue that psychology became and remains an administrative science which addresses the agenda of managers but offers little help to individuals who want to understand themselves or their social world. He feels that psychologists hardly realize what has been excluded from psychology to create its current narrow focus, arguing that social and cultural commitments need to change before the discipline can become receptive to this knowledge. His remedy lies in developing alliances with people who will use psychological knowledge to emancipate themselves, rather than use it to control others.

This history illustrates differences between the interests of employers and the knowledge/resources which applied psychologists can or should provide. Producing an appropriate product is a powerful force guiding the selection of investigative and clinical practices, a force which contributes to many of the ethical dilemmas experienced by clinicians (Kent and McAuley, 1995). As it is the smallest profession in the British National Health Service, many believe that clinical psychology will wither if it fails to develop its public image in the age of the sound-bite. Other psychologists feel that we should stay at the periphery of powerful institutions. For them the belief that such institutions always work against the interests of the individual means that psychologists will be compromised by joining or co-operating with their administrators. A bipolar dichotomy, with adapt-or-die at one end and never compromise at the other, needs exposing if we are to be able to consider when or under what circumstances it is useful to do one or the other. Such questioning can release us from unnecessary constraints.

The division between academic and applied psychology is most clearly seen in the USA where there is a split between intellectually driven training at universities which value research, and professional schools of clinical psychology which are oriented to practice. While this division has not occurred in Britain, there is nevertheless considerable distance between those who value research and those who regard it as an irrelevant and stressful aspect of their training which they vow never to repeat. This is sometimes played out as rigour versus relevance. The issue was exemplified by clinical and academic psychologists taking different perspectives on the actions of a forensic clinical psychologist in a British case of murder.

Rachel Nickell and the Forensic Psychologist

In July 1992 a 23-year-old mother called Rachel Nickell was murdered by being stabbed 49 times in front of her two-year-old son. This occurred during daylight in a public park where the police found no forensic evidence to lead their enquiry. The brutality of the murder engendered considerable media and public pressure to find her killer. After a search and local enquiries failed to produce any leads, the police decided to obtain the assistance of a clinical psychologist. This psychologist advised the police about the sort of person who killed Rachel, based on offender profiling. This professional was described in TV and newspaper accounts as also having acted as a consultant to the police during an undercover operation. Following this, a man was brought to trial for this murder, and acquitted. The trial judge described the undercover operation as misconceived and reprehensible, while other clinical psychologists and an FBI specialist in offender profiling criticized the psychologist's judgements in a number of areas.

The case became even more unusual when two academic professors of psychology separately wrote articles for national newspapers criticizing the clinician for having gone beyond the research evidence. Both professors also provide offender profiling services to police forces, and were therefore expert in the interpretation of the information. This also made them competitors.

The case is still under discussion, and some of the details publicized by the media may yet be questioned by the psychologist at its centre. Whatever its outcome, it serves to illustrate how new institutional pressures on psychologists can turn stresses into rifts. Market-orientation and the pressure to generate income for both university departments and NHS trusts have become significant factors only during the 1990s; such pressures inevitably create subtle threats to the integrity of any psychologist's decision-making. Combined with equal pressure to demonstrate relevance, external forces may have pushed the practitioner in this case too close to relevance at the expense of rigour; they may also have encouraged his competitors to make their criticisms public. This is not to say that debates and critiques should be silenced, but that it is easier to resist such pressures if we perceive them and understand how public disputes are located within their web. That in turn facilitates the development of alternative positions where debate can spring from intellectual and ethical considerations instead.

Three Approaches to Clinical Practice

The Scientist–Practitioner

This model of British and American clinical psychology was developed at a founding conference in Boulder, Colorado, held in 1949. Given the phenomenal changes which have occurred in the following five decades of academic and applied psychology, it is remarkable that most course directors still regard it as the appropriate description for clinical practice (Miller, 1995; O'Sullivan and Quevillon, 1992). Developed during the positivist and empiricist era of social science when psychology's admiration for natural science was aptly described by the term 'physics envy', spokespersons for clinical psychology adhere to it ever more strongly in the positivist managerial environment of 1990s health care.

Barlow et al. (1984) summarize the main intention of the original model as ensuring cross-fertilization between research and practice. This is achieved by building research into practice because there is so little dependable knowledge about psychological distress. It also ensures that clinical experience generates relevant research questions for academics, and brings in health service funds for new research into these areas. The originators were sure that suitable graduates who can balance both roles would be found easily. Yet by the early 1980s it was becoming clear that the majority of clinicians did no research; since most postgraduate dissertations in clinical psychology were described as using obsolete methods on trivial issues, this was perhaps to be expected. Of greater concern is the knowledge that most practitioners also consume no research. They describe clinical experience and conversations with peers as influencing their practice rather than research papers.

Barlow et al. suggest that the problem lies not with the scientist–practitioner model but with its expression in practice; they identify two areas for change. Firstly, that clinicians in training rarely work with practitioners who carry out research and so have no role-models, a problem which should gradually change as more research occurs. Secondly, that experimental psychology was not an appropriate model for clinical research and so of course there had been problems in carrying out clinically relevant research of interest to clinicians, problems which newer research techniques such as single case studies and time-series could overcome.

The hope that new investigative techniques will solve the problem of a putatively research-based profession which neither carries out nor consumes research is often voiced. Researching clinicians intermittently provide anthologies of user-friendly research designs and analytic techniques to enable psychologists to engage with the research agenda (for example, Barlow et al., 1984; Parry and Watts, 1989). To date they seem to have had little effect on research output, which continues to involve only about 10 per cent of the profession. Pilgrim and Treacher (1992) ascribe this to psychology still being a 'pre-paradigmatic discipline', presumably expecting many problems to be resolved when this perpetual adolescent finally comes of age.

Nevertheless, the criticism made by adherents of the scientist–practitioner model must be taken seriously: if clinicians do not consume research, how do they update themselves? If most clinicians switch procedures and approaches not because of systematic and reasoned thought, but because they are responding to marketing pressures, clinical psychology is in danger of following 'what is in vogue or what new charismatic leader . . . happens to be most visible or is giving the most workshops' (Barlow et al., 1984: 35). This is an alarming strategy for a profession dealing in human distress.

Clinicians such as Pilgrim and Treacher (1992) and Harper (1994) criticize the scientist–practitioner model for providing technocratic solutions to existential problems, and also for assuming that 'facts' are non-problematic and that the possessors of power are justified in using them. These link to general criticisms of positivist science in academic psychology voiced by Gergen (1994) and Shotter (1993) amongst others. Accompanying this criticism should be a re-evaluation of the Venn diagram (Figure 1.1) beloved of clinicians who are trying to encompass the complexity of clinical practice.

To make a successful move away from a positivist, empiricist version of clinical psychology to one which incorporates human interdependency and complexity, we must question the validity of a descriptive model derived from mathematics and logic. Creating models which are interactive, haphazard and which incorporate the huge diversity of contexts in which clinical psychologists now work will support reconceptualization of many issues.

One such issue in need of reconsideration is the hegemony of adult mental health as the paradigmatic form of clinical practice. Adults with

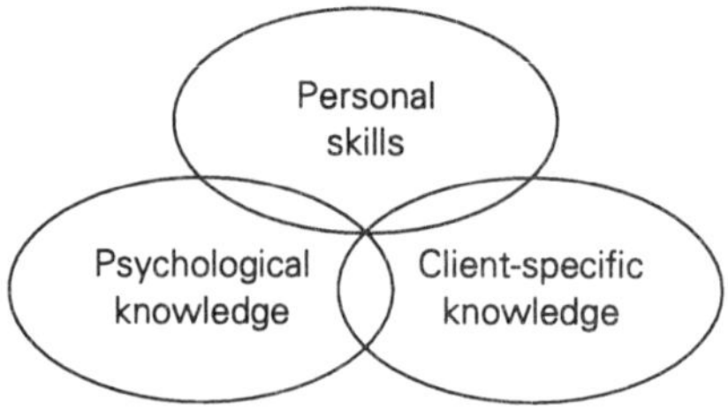

FIGURE 1.1 *A timeless representation of clinical psychology*

mental health problems remain the single biggest client group but they no longer dominate the total agenda. The majority of British clinical psychologists now specialize in work with clients outside adult mental health: people who have complex difficulties associated with physical and/or intellectual disabilities, childhood, old age, substance misuse or physical illness. This broader client base must lead to some reconceptualization of the subject matter of clinical psychology.

One response to criticisms of the scientist–practitioner model could be to shift away from the preoccupation with science, which originated in the 1950s and 1960s, towards a more open-ended model of the researcher-practitioner. This is an approach which clashes with few of the recommendations made by the American 1990 National Conference on Scientist–Practitioner Education and Training for the Professional Practice of Psychology (Belar and Perry, 1992). If one replaces 'science' with 'research' the component skills and knowledges of such a practitioner lie in five areas:

1 knowledge of assessment, research and intervention with individuals, groups and organizations;
2 an understanding of the strategies and tactics of applied work, primarily establishing working relationships; problem conceptualization; awareness of personal issues in the delivery of clinical services; analysis of risks and iatrogenic issues; informed consent and other ethical and legal considerations; learning how to supervise and teach others;
3 ensuring that practice is research-oriented, and research practice-oriented;
4 application of knowledge in practical settings through core experiences which are broadly based, supervised closely and provide practical experience of the isues taught in section 2;
5 integration of education and training throughout all aspects of the learning experience.

The move towards a more open intellectual agenda associated with the term researcher-practitioner rather than scientist–practitioner retains the virtues of the old scientist–practitioner model, in bringing in research funds and in making dialogue between academic and clinical psychology at least possible, if not inevitable. It also maintains some pressure on practitioners to think, read and debate rather than just sway with the tide. However, this adapted model still focuses on intellectual skills, failing to theorize the skills-in-action of a good clinician: that is more effectively covered by the next approach.

The Reflective Practitioner

Schön's (1987) important contribution to modelling complex behaviour in professionals builds on the scientist–practitioner model while criticizing it. A positivist view of science which places technical rationality at the core of professional practice is the basis of the scientist–practitioner approach, most status being accorded to professions closest to pure science and to practitioners within each profession who carry out classical quantitative research.

These values are questioned by Schön, who believes that solving particular problems using known techniques is only a beginner's skill. The transformation of a morass of conflicting ideas and difficulties into a set of problems for which some solutions exist is a complex skill shown by experienced practitioners; they also generate new hypotheses which allow them to experiment with problems which have no known solutions. Experienced people cannot usually describe this process of multilevel reasoning: if asked to describe what they do they quote rules learned as trainees which they are clearly not following. Schön argues that expert practitioners can easily be identified and agreed by peers in any given situation, with consensus focusing upon personal qualities such as wisdom, integrity and intuition. Research-based knowledge is accessed during this process, but it is combined with knowledge of other cases which bear some similarity and with subjective, emotional perceptions about the particular therapeutic relationship or context. This stands in sharp contrast to a rational technical approach, where experts are people who have acquired the most knowledge.

Schön's thesis is that the expert's personal qualities should not remain mysterious, that they can be studied and the opportunity to acquire them provided for students and practitioners alike. He gives examples of reflective practice for a number of professions. Teachers are initially asked to learn something for themselves and to reflect on the processes and curiosities which helped them to master the topic, then they are encouraged to generalize this approach to their pupils. Incorporating knowledge of self as learner with theories of cognitive development should assist them to understand what may confuse children, to develop insight into ways in which their thinking may be different. Teachers are also encouraged to consider the degree to which the setting inhibits listening and reflection. Experimenting with new ways to adapt environments so that concentration on both sides is maximized is a component of practice given equal importance to curriculum planning and the teaching process itself.

An outline of a course in counselling psychology that Schön developed (with Argyris) fleshes out the idea of reflective practice in Schön's text, both in its description of the students' difficulties and also in its narrative about the development of the course itself. Students were taught two different models of human exchange. The first was overcontrolling, unilateral and devoted to 'winning' the negotiation, while the second was open-ended, jointly controlled, risk-taking and oriented towards growth. All favoured the second model and believed that they used it, and were shocked to discover that various frailties led them to depend on overcontrolling strategies during actual discussions and role-played counselling situations. Having confronted their dependence on the first model they spent a semester jointly discovering ways to change the meanings they create, and the strategies they employ, during interaction.

Students encountered a number of problems which they needed to overcome. They feared looking incompetent and losing control: defensive protectiveness prevented them from offering or receiving positive criticism. They were angry when asked to imitate an expert performance, even though they recognized that they had mastered part of a skill but could not yet construct it as a whole. Prerequisites for student learning were reflection-in-action during the sessions, establishing joint responsibility for the outcome of the course, and constructing a virtual reality where students lowered the expectations of success with which they beat themselves.

Is this just another way of talking about theory–practice links in clinical psychology? Schön says not, arguing that the question itself is rooted in the model of technical rationality, since it implies that what is being applied is the psychological knowledge developed in universities. He notes instead that professionals nominate as expert practitioners peers who exhibit personal qualities of wisdom and intuition. The idea of reflective practice cuts across the theory–practice axis, making personal knowledge and interaction as important as command of technical skills.

Writing from a North American perspective, Schön describes the growing power of the model of technical rationality as inhibiting acceptance of the reflective-practitioner model. Amongst other pressures this demands increasing numbers of publications, supporting conservative methodology since publication occurs more easily and quickly in standard experimental journals. Because research into process is unpopular with funding agencies and difficult to publish, the dominant model encourages defensive practice, restricts innovations in practice, and limits the development of new ways to educate university students in intuitive performance skills.

On the other hand reflective practice has inherent weaknesses of its own. Describing skills-in-action rather than knowledge, its main value is also its main limitation since it does not distinguish a clinical from a counselling psychologist, an architect or psychiatrist. Nor does it narrow the gap between applied and academic aspects of the discipline to develop better debates. Thus the model falls short of being sufficient in itself, requiring the addition of discipline-specific knowledge to be combined with the reflective-practitioner's artistry-in-action.

Hoshmand and Polkinghorne (1992) developed some of these ideas to argue that clinical psychology needs a new epistemology of practical knowledge, which develops criteria and standards for judging the value of knowledge held by experienced clinicians. It should also develop methods which help clinicians to systematize their experiential knowledge, to protect them against being unduly influenced by the most recent case they have encountered. Such an epistemology might bridge the gap between academic and applied psychology, although commentators on this position paper felt that additional ideas and work would be necessary.[1]

The reflective-practitioner approach is most commonly applied to work at an individual level, and is most commonly discussed in the context of verbal therapies with non-disabled adults. The model itself gives little consideration to an individual's opportunities or disadvantages, nor does it describe ways to work preventatively rather than reactively. Some practitioners advocate approaches where fundamental social change has a prominent place on the agenda: the third school of thought provides such a model of practice.

Community Clinical Psychology

Danziger and others have called for a new approach to psychology. This is exemplified by taking an interest in lay accounts and concern to create a psychology which supports people rather than a psychology which subjects them. Shotter's (1993) dialogic view of psychological practice maintains that a distant, interpretive approach merely maintains power relations. The psychologist should be willing to be influenced by the relationship, and aim to produce accounts or plans of action which have been constructed collaboratively. Such idealism is difficult in practice when clinical psychologists are working with people who are extremely distressed, when some boundary is an essential component of personal survival in a stressful job. Nevertheless, the political point is well made and there clearly are circumstances where such an approach to practice is appropriate.

Collaborative work alongside community members was initiated in the USA as long ago as 1966. In Britain its main sponsor is Jim Orford: he brought out the *Journal of Community and Applied Social Psychology* (co-editing it with Stephenson) in 1991, and published a useful summary of the theory and practice of community psychology in 1992. By far the most political branch of clinical psychology, it has much to contribute to a dialogue with academics seeking social relevance in research, and many of its exponents maintain a foot in both camps. Aiming to stay as close as possible to everyday social environments, it often transcends boundaries between the different applied spheres of clinical, educational, criminological and occupational psychology. Community clinical psychologists assume that most psychological support is provided by ordinary people to one another and that their task is to facilitate such processes. This may be done by information-sharing, or by lobbying for resources or changes which tackle the roots of the difficulties people experience.

The practice of community clinical psychology involves proactive networking in a community to identify the problems which a group feels it has. This is a vital first step if psychologists are to avoid the traps of imposition and paternalism into which professionals fall so easily. It can demand the skills of a neighbourhood action co-ordinator, union activist or business manager, and Orford notes that the natural development of community clinical psychology may lie with social and community workers, health visitors and GPs, and neighbourhood co-operatives. While the purpose of working preventatively to promote psychological well-being in a population is clear, many psychologists are uncomfortable doing work for which they are not well qualified. They argue that their skills lie in therapy and that these should be complemented by other professionals who carry out community work. Unfortunately most settings do not fund such preventative work, and unless relatively powerful practitioners either do it themselves or argue strongly for it to be done, we run the risk of maintaining a system where the victim is expected to do all the changing.

A multilayered community project developed in a London housing estate is a good example. Intent on reducing high rates of depression and suicide amongst women in the locality, Holland (1988, 1992) offers individual psychotherapy as the kernel of a larger whole. This includes facilitating an awareness-raising group where women discuss those issues which contribute to their depression, such as poverty or violence in the home; and training and managing a group of peer-counsellors. She also contributes to neighbourhood action groups which address problems such as poor street lighting or dangerous roads. People move between different parts of this project according to the personal and emotional resources they have available.

Community psychologists enact an implicit model of an ideal society towards which social change is aimed. This may be difficult to express and harder still to agree, and represents a limitation of this approach which is explored in Chapter 5. Moreover community psychologists often fail to live up to their own high ideals, the majority of their research papers still reporting individual interventions or perspectives. Wertsch (1995) describes some of the cultural influences which maintain these practices and make it difficult for us to break out from them, not least the individual–society opposition which frames Western understanding of the human condition. He and others argue that reconceptualization is required which identifies social action as the unit of analysis rather than individual skills or attributes, enabling us simultaneously to think about persons and their sociocultural contexts. As he observes, these ideas are difficult to pin down into concrete realities because they challenge so many of our current ways of construing the social world. Nevertheless, this is the change he and others seek.

The Relationship between These Three Approaches

A profession has been defined as having four essential elements (Salmon, 1994): administrative structures which oversee training, registration and promotion to senior grades; a body of knowledge which is coherent and differs from other knowledges; live assessment of skilled performance in developing formulations relevant to a client's or clients' problems and carrying out an intervention; and a distinct group of people for whom these skills are appropriate. The three models of practice discussed relate to three of these four elements of professionalism.

The scientist–practitioner, reworked here as the researcher-practitioner, describes an evolving body of knowledge specific to clinical practice which is in dialogue with academic psychology. Despite having its roots in a scientific conceptual system which many question, the researcher-practitioner idea must remain at the centre of clinical psychology if practice is to remain creative and original. The reflective-practitioner provides important insights into skilled performance by members of the profession, and describes ways that supervisors can transmit their experience more effectively. Adherents of this approach have proposed ways to narrow the gap between research and practice by developing an epistemology of practice, rebalancing the relationship so that clinicians can take an equal role with researchers in developing clinical psychology. Finally, community clinical psychologists question the utility of treating people who have been damaged by their social environments. They have redefined clients to include people who are likely to benefit from preventative or supportive intervention; they also move beyond the individual, extending the focus of intervention to the societal level.

Yet this description reiterates the Venn diagram criticized earlier for being too ordered, too mathematical to describe the fluidities and varieties of clinical practice. It suggests that once somebody can colour in each circle they have become a clinical psychologist who need strive no further – a bleak vision of practice. What is missing from the tripartite model is any conception of time. The model needs to encompass the unfolding development of each clinician, every branch elaborating and interacting with our chosen contexts of practice and intellectual preferences.

A Word from our Critics

The headline KEEPING THEM DOWN ON THE FARM introduced a short review of Trent's (1994) history of state schools for the mentally retarded.

Admiring the punning title, it was natural to assume that the iniquities of the medical profession would once again be laid bare. My initial surprise at finding psychologists included in the criticism led to reflection on the utility of external scrutiny: it helps professionals to balance the pressures and cultural changes which impinge on practice.

This section aims to support such reflection by drawing on five texts which criticize clinical psychologists from a variety of standpoints. Two were written by clinical psychologists: Pilgrim and Treacher's (1992) book is concerned with the analysis of power, illustrated by the authors' practice origins in therapy with non-disabled adults experiencing mental health problems; while Gambrill (1990) discusses a skills-based perspective rooted in cognitive psychology. Two recent observations come from a psychiatric iconoclast (Szasz, 1994) and from a historian of services for people with learning disabilities (termed mental retardation in the USA) (Trent, 1994). The final source is Said (1994): Professor of English, Palestinian commentator and cultural critic, his views provide an invaluable perspective on professional life in the postmodern era.

Difficulties at the Researcher–Practitioner Interface

Gambrill (1990) notes that clinicians do not distinguish weak from strong evidence. Her complaint is exemplified by student essays which cite informal clinical experiences reported by lecturers alongside the results of five-year research projects. She does not suggest that clinical experience is less valuable than formal research but that clinical case studies require systematic thought and reading to construct them into an argument which advances knowledge. This work is absent from discussion of the interesting conundrum encountered in yesterday's clinic. The challenges involved in developing an epistemology of practice have already been outlined in the discussion of Hoshmand and Polkinghorne's (1992) position paper. Reporting *ad hoc* experience alongside systematically constructed information as if these forms of communication carry the same authority displays conceptually muddled thinking. Schön (1987) found that many trainees are confused by the switches teachers make between different types of discourse during supervision sessions, laying the foundation for this to be a problem amongst experienced professionals as well.

Perhaps more alarming are articles submitted to journals by qualified psychologists which cite workshop leaders as if their words carry great authority. It is not uncommon for charismatic clinicians to write a text describing their own practice and run workshops based on it without ever submitting the ideas to detailed scrutiny. When a clinical psychologist cites such workshop material as evidence, their training has failed on two counts. It has not provided conceptual positions from which the person can assess new ideas critically, and it has failed to persuade them that measured reflection and debate are vital protections against forceful gurus with ephemeral therapies.

Gambrill argues further that clinicians do not think deeply about new ideas which raise important challenges to existing thinking, preferring to seek superficial similarities which allow them to incorporate the new position into old ones. Her general point about the difficulties professionals experience in thinking independently is supported by Said, and by Billig's (1987) advocacy of reading and reflection rather than the constant doing which has come to represent most forms of psychology, clinical psychology in particular. Seeking superficial similarities to nullify a critique can be seen in the exchanges between Hastings and Remington (1994a, 1994b) and Clegg (1994).

On the other hand, practitioners complain that academic psychology does not provide them with a secure intellectual base. But why should it? This complaint was raised by Pilgrim and Treacher (1992), who said that the diversity of options with which trainees are confronted merely adds to their confusion. The charge is based on the rational-technical view of psychology which derives from the very scientist–practitioner model which they challenge, since it implies that ideally there would be an authoritative body of psychological knowledge which practitioners merely absorb and use.

Clearly it is not that simple. Pilgrim and Treacher raise the issue because students feel uncertain, apparently hoping for a solid footing which does not exist. Yet academics have little idea what situations and problems the users of psychological services face: they need to hear about them both from clinicians and from users themselves if debate about useful psychological knowledge is to be joined. There has to be a recognition that alliance between the academic and applied branches of the discipline is the way forward, that it takes time to develop and that it will only prove useful if there is a willingness to try some of the recommendations which emerge from it.

Finally, practitioners complain that research and researchers, not insightful clinicians, dominate the profession and the subject. This is linked to the previous two issues, since clinicians who do not acquire habits of clear thinking and expression cannot communicate their insights to the wider intellectual world. However, it is equally true that without an epistemology of practice there is little opportunity for clinical knowledge to influence psychology as a whole, and so experimental research papers become the only way for practitioners to join in public debate.

A number of factors suggest that this situation could change. Clinically inappropriate methods from experimental science are under severe challenge, both from new methods which facilitate the systematic analysis of case material and from changing epistemological perspectives which show what different approaches to psychological knowledge can contribute.[2] A few academics are also becoming interested in the real difficulties which practitioners and service users face, keen to find out how useful social constructionist ideas are in practical arenas (Gergen, 1994; Shotter, 1993). These changes create a rare opportunity to develop a bidirectional dialogue between applied and academic psychology which could nourish both.

Professionals are not Altruistic: They Adjust their Interventions in Changed Social Contexts according to the Dictates of Self-preservation, not Concern for their Clients

This criticism is based on the assumption that power is central to human relations and underpins behaviour. Encapsulated in Foucault's (1980) binary term power/knowledge, it has forced many intellectuals to reflect on their motives, and underpins many current critiques of clinical practice (e.g. Boyle, 1994a; Smail, 1995a). However, other philosophers argue that individual power and instrumental analyses of human experience are too narrow, that they ignore conflicts between competing views of 'moral goods' to pursue a single argument.[3]

Describing the criticism that professionals abuse power as too narrow does not of course dismiss it. Trent summarizes two historical positions to contextualize his argument. The revisionist position is that we are entitled to judge past actors by present standards. The alternative new humanitarian perspective views past responses to social problems as mostly sincere efforts to devise rational responses, given the political and social realities of the time. His summary of the output of historians from these two camps shows that they focus on different topics. Revisionists write about issues which seem very distant from our current sensibilities, such as the eugenics movement and past prison policy on corporal and capital punishment: new humanitarians discuss changing social policies on poverty or the development of nursing, topics which have a less problematic connection to current thinking.

Trent places himself firmly in the revisionist camp, suggesting that earlier this century professionals in the USA used people with learning disabilities to ensure their institutions and thus their power grew larger, and they maintained their strength by setting the research agenda. His accusations focus on sterilization as it was constructed and reconstructed through the first half of this century in state schools across the USA. He records the appalling abuse of mass sterilization, but balances it against the objections to it made by principled men and the care which staff gave to multiply disabled children who would otherwise have starved during the Depression. It seems then that the accusation of self-interest is a partial one: we should take it seriously when considering which service developments to promote and support, but it is not a comprehensive condemnation. The important lesson arising from this critique is to understand the setting conditions for such abuses of power, and to consider which ethical principles and sociocultural conditions enable psychologists and others to perform in the least self-interested fashion.

Said (1994) describes the way that intellectuals can be confused and neutralized by being given power, a position endorsed by Gambrill (1990), Pilgrim and Treacher (1992) and particularly Shotter (1993), whose chapter 'Power on the margins: a new place for intellectuals to be' also describes a variety of routes towards solidarity with clients rather than separation.

Paths away from self-interest and power-broking are open to clinicians: one suggestion is that research and intervention should be grounded in the experiences of the people we claim to help and results checked with them. While it is impossible for practitioners to stand outside the service, professional bodies can support work which is more rather than less ethical by promoting and honouring such practices.

Clinical Psychology Supports a Psychomedical rather than an Environmental Understanding of Human Distress

This criticism, which goes beyond clinical practice to psychology as a whole, has its roots in the traditional focus on individuals to the exclusion of other levels of analysis. Ecological theories have been developed but generally marginalized (e.g. Bronfenbrenner, 1977; Vetere and Gale, 1987) partly because they focus within rather than across levels and because they theorize stability and maintenance, not disequilibrium and change. In order to move this agenda forwards, human scientists need to confront the arbitrary lines drawn between psychology, sociology, anthropology and politics. Some Europeans are dismantling these boundaries (Doise, 1986; Moscovici, 1993; Valsiner, 1995) which are also addressed by the community psychology movement in the USA (Levine and Perkins, 1987) and Britain (Orford, 1992).

While critics of individualistic psychologies make many salient points, it is illuminating to read their alternatives. Szasz's (1994) apparently liberal critique of overcontrolling professionals contains many right-wing opinions expressed in hyperbole. His views include the ideas that 'Bedlam is now everywhere, making our streets and our parks both ugly and unsafe' (1994: 168), that most patients want to get back into institutions and that mental illness is a mask for idleness. The Protestant work ethic is also promulgated by Trent (1994), who eschews cultural diversity in his discussions of ways to support people with learning disabilities:

> None would argue that there are no needs particular to some person with intellectual disability. Yet, most needs of people labelled mentally retarded are the same as those of people not labelled mentally retarded: meaningful work and economic security, fulfilling personal and community relations, dignity and a measure of control over one's life. (1994: 274)

Trent also appears to believe that supporting the development of a range of fulfilling relationships is an easy matter not requiring the interference of professionals. However, a decade of community projects has so far achieved little change in the isolation of which people with learning disabilities complain,[4] and Trent goes on to contradict his own position later in the book. Observing that clinicians do not confront the reality that people who have learning disabilities or mental health problems are unproductive in a production-oriented environment, with social and communication difficulties which make them vulnerable to exploitation, he implies that professional interference may be necessary after all. This modified position, that the support of specialist staff is necessary for people with learning disabilities to achieve fulfilling lives, is a topic over which the British campaigning group Values Into Action is equally ambivalent.

When community policies were planned in the 1970s very little was known about bullying and abuse. Optimism was high that tolerance would flow from increasing social contact between community members and people who had been concealed in asylums. Sadly, most of the people with learning disabilities living independently in both Flynn's (1989) Manchester sample and Halpern et al.'s (1986) New York sample reported victimization or harassment in the previous 12 months. The presence or absence of such bullying played a major role in determining their life satisfaction. While none of Flynn's sample thought the experiences sufficiently bad for them to want to return to their former institution, this is a problem which is not going away.

All people who behave unusually, look different or have disabilities are at increased risk of bullying at school, of physical and sexual abuse in childhood, of exploitation at work, and of being suborned into law-breaking. Jealousy also seems to be an issue, suggesting that the scramble for limited resources is an important setting factor in bullying. This has been amplified in 1997, a year which saw the introduction of a political campaign in Britain to identify, shame and hound 'paedophiles' from town to town. Not only is this an extraordinary response to a social problem, it spills over into the lives of the different so that each street gang can declare that somebody with a learning disability looks like a paedophile and start a reign of terror.

It appears then that critics of individual psychomedical approaches support community living and integrated schooling as articles of faith, not knowing how societies can incorporate their weakest members without hurting them. This is a point which families make and professionals ignore. The ethical challenge for psychosocial interventions is to go beyond simple mantras of the 'institution bad/community good' type and show how the relative success of particular demonstration projects such as that of Brown et al. (1992) can work on a larger scale.

Lack of Self-reflection Contributes to Clinical Thoughtlessness

Rorty (1991) argues that we need to reflect on ourselves before we can create new forms of human solidarity with people who are pained or humiliated. Szasz (1994) notes that when definitions of both help and harm are problematic, professionals are more likely to impose treatments on unwilling people; while Gambrill (1990) observes that lack of clarity about our own skills and motives makes it difficult for professionals to resist the rhetoric of certainty created by their organizations, which typically oversell the feats of members.

TABLE 1.1 *Presentations to annual conferences of the British Psychological Society's Division of Clinical Psychology (%)*

	1988	1989	1990–93	1994
	n = 71	n = 29	No annual conferences	n = 20
Professional issues	21	42	–	40
Managerial or occupational issues	9	30	–	10
Psychological concepts and interventions	70	21	–	50

Information analysed from the abstracts of papers published by the BPS. My classification was as follows:
'Professional issues' are discussions of psychological practice in the National Health Service: included were papers focusing on the professional society itself, on trainees, supervision, stress, or assessments of skills and competencies.
'Managerial or occupational issues' concerned investigating the staff and clients in a hospital ward as if they were a single client or customer and gearing intervention accordingly. These include papers on evaluation, planning, quality assurance, morale, and debates about the possibility/desirability of combining clinical and managerial responsibilities within a service.
'Psychological concepts and interventions' were descriptions of difficulties, treatments or conceptual frameworks underpinning intervention; also comparisons and evaluations of treatment effectiveness.

There are two responses to these criticisms. Firstly, personal reflection within supervision has long been argued to be the most effective defence against abuse of vulnerable people by psychodynamic therapists, although it now appears to be a less effective bulwark than people hoped. It has also been criticized as a conservative strategy which inhibits creativity. Schön (1987) provides a valuable discussion of ways to support the development of thoughtfulness amongst reflective-practitioner students by using group settings in preference to individual supervision. Both provide important counterweights to the potential for abusing clients by meeting one's own needs rather than theirs.

The second response is a more general one concerning the difficulties of clinical practice and the need for some degree of self-care. People do not reflect upon their actions critically when self-efficacy is low: we need to increase helpful feedback and identify problems which have a reasonable probability of change in order to support greater reflectiveness. This is made more difficult in a constantly changing postmodern culture where shifting agendas produce huge lurches in the new direction, not balanced debate. An example of such a huge change of direction can be seen in British clinical psychology in the late 1980s. Reflection and self knowledge were thought to be important topics, but this resulted in a navel-gazing conference where psychological concepts themselves received little attention (summarized in Table 1.1). Following that agenda change there were no clinical conferences for the next three years, no doubt the outcome of multiple factors: nevertheless it is interesting to speculate whether the prospect of listening to an 'intellectually arid profession' (Mair, 1989a) was one contribution.

We berate ourselves for lack of thoughtfulness and misuse of power. To confront these difficulties squarely we need to follow the same self-care advice we give to other people who work in areas where change is difficult to measure and harder to see.

Western Culture Militates against Intellectual Development

Said (1994) describes three pressures which challenge the intellectual's will. The first is specialization. Here authority is associated with increasing narrowness which, he believes, kills curiosity and excitement and shuts out topics such as literature, history or anthropology which could contribute to an original stance. A referee for the *British Journal of Clinical Psychology* exemplified this by asking that reference to Eagleton's (1983) *Literary Theory* be removed from a review article because it is not a psychology text, even though Eagleton's clear exposition of postmodernism was germane to the whole paper. Linked to this is the second pressure of the cult of the certified expert, where the arguments of people outside the appropriate group are not refuted but ignored.

The final pressure on professionals is the inevitable drift towards power and authority with experience, towards being engaged ever more closely with people developing the policies to which we may object. Said avoids naively conjuring a golden age where independence was assured, since the only way to achieve that is to have independent finance. Instead he suggests that by remaining alert to these processes and pressures we can obtain a measure of control over their impingement on our thinking and decisions.

Said notes that professionals are becoming more narcissistic. He warns that public displays of assent and subsequent apostasy divorce intellectuals from the people and the debates which are important. Worse, these frozen positions stop the organic evolution of understanding, both for the intellectual and between intellectuals and clients. Such positions may be religious creeds, or political statements of rights, or professional methods. Recent statements for and against normalization, behaviourism, or gentle teaching are examples of this process: perhaps most irrelevant was the fierce debate which raged about the terms people use to refer to clients now described in Britain as people with a learning disability.

> The hardest aspect of being an intellectual is to represent what you profess through your work and interventions, without hardening into an institution, or a kind of automaton acting at the behest of a system or method. (Said, 1994: 90)

Conclusions

This chapter set out to create a vantage-point from which to view the burgeoning information and ideas that practitioners receive. Providing past and present perspectives on the relationship between academic and applied psychology may help both sides to approach dialogue with more realistic expectations of the other, as I believe that both are necessary to a study of human experience which intends to yield better lives. In describing how the three major approaches to the practice of clinical psychology relate, I intend to help practitioners clarify their own position, and identify both common ground and differences between their own stance and those espoused by others. Finally, confronting criticisms both within and outside psychology throws into focus some of the external forces which do and should constrain us.

Subsequent chapters in this book gather together new knowledges and topics relevant to clinical practice. In order to explore them through the lens of this introduction, it is necessary first to agree on some terms and rules of debate. These are discussed in the next chapter.

Summary

Contemporary issues about clinical psychology concern elucidating and considering the relationship between it and academic psychology; the degree to which research on individuals may be accepted as providing information about human experience that is as relevant as information from group studies; and the ethical posture we as clinicians take towards the clients we purport to help. Finally, the debate between three different models of what comprises clinical psychology practice (that is, the researcher-practitioner, the reflective-practitioner and the community psychologist) continues. All have virtues and shortcomings, and none incorporate time considerations to describe how clinicians enact their jobs at different points in their careers nor how they reflect upon themselves differently from time to time.

These issues were illuminated by *histories of the present*. Danziger's analysis of the origins of academic and applied psychology suggests that there has been relatively little mutual influence between these traditions. For example, there is little evidence that applied psychologists use the insights of their academic colleagues to solve real-world problems; if anything, the exigencies of practice have become incorporated into academic research designs. An informal survey of clinical psychology over the past 50 years gave another perspective on how the goals of practice have evolved. Trent's (1994) history of services for the 'feeble-minded' introduces the question of whether histories should be revisionist (judging past actors by present standards) or new humanitarian (a more sympathetic approach to past responses to social problems, by viewing them within their own contexts). His revisionist history helps us to see how professional self-interest can be a strong factor, but his criticism is partial: Trent also documents those clinicians whose actions kept vulnerable people alive during the Depression and whose principles prevented them from becoming involved in the abuse of mass sterilization.

These contemporary issues were briefly illuminated by discussion of *intersubjective meanings*. Although these are not strongly represented in this chapter, it introduces criticisms of 'fact' in the human sciences because the 'facts' inevitably incorporate many aspects of power: power expressed by those who fund research, those who carry it out and those who turn it towards various positions. For example a research committee could fund investigations into, say, the role of violent videos in the lives of people who commit violent acts, as opposed to the role of videos in providing socially excluded people with an affordable pastime. Both studies would produce results but they would not be socially neutral: each set would be imbued with socially created meanings and effects. Similarly, our conception of the subject matter of clinical psychology would shift if we ceased seeing adult mental health as the paradigmatic practice from which all other specialties deviate.

Although each model of practice has shortcomings, I prefer to think about the clinician who takes a stance on these contemporary issues as a *reflective researcher-practitioner*, that is, as somebody who continues striving to combine personal awareness with therapeutic practice and psychological research. Including the epistemology of practice in the remit of research journals would mean that the wisdom and empathy of experienced clinicians no longer need be ignored. The difficulty of combining reflectiveness and research within practice are acknowledged: few clinicians succeed in living out these ideals and the connections between research and practice are therefore hard for the learner to see. We also need to heed the warnings of philosophers and psychologists that we can only increase solidarity with people who have been pained or humiliated by reflecting upon ourselves and our compassion.

In addition to clarifying how and to what end one practises clinically, it is also vital that *critical thinking* skills develop. These are discussed later but were introduced here by questioning the way that action is prioritized over reading, thinking and debate in clinical practice. Critical thinkers can differentiate weak from strong evidence, and can engage deeply with new ideas so that old frameworks do not swallow up and neutralize fresh insights.

The final theme concerns context: what role *human systems* play in these contemporary issues. Shifting intellectual frameworks and research practice in the physical and social sciences suggests that goals of clinical psychology created 50 years ago are overdue for renewal. Another relevant stance is taken by community clinical psychologists who seek to change social contexts in preference to 'treating' people whose environments cause damage and distress. Finally, Said's observations about Western culture sapping the will of intellectuals provide a useful warning to us all.

Notes

1 Four short commentaries on Hoshmand and Polkinghorne (1992) were published in *American Psychologist* (1993) 48: 56–60.

2 For changing techniques of analysis, see Lovie and Lovie 1991. For discussion of the range of qualitative methods relevant to clinical practice see the special issue of the *Journal of Community and Social Psychology*, 4 (1994), edited by Henwood and Pidgeon.

3 Taylor (1989); his approach is elaborated at length in Chapter 8.

4 Reviewed by Clegg (1993).

2 Thinking Straight

Explanations of human experience are problematic: they come in many different forms and their heterogeneity inhibits comparison and debate. Psychologists attack one another's methods vehemently because it is easy to undermine a piece of research by criticizing the way the information was obtained: it is much more difficult to debate the content or appropriateness of the topics studied. Recent exchanges on the relative merits of qualitative and quantitative research continue this focus on method, an interest sometimes described by the derisory term 'methodolatry'. By contrast, rethinking subject matter or theoretical positions tends to be a minority pursuit whose apparently arcane nature puzzles many clinicians.

To promote debate about content rather than method, we need to explore the background to conceptual differences. We also need to work out how different positions can be evaluated if we are to avoid slipping into weak liberalism where all positions are given equal value. People can then enter into 'living dialogue', discussion which creates new understanding out of the combination of common ground and some understanding of the source of difference. The alternative is to continue to hold sham debates where people merely talk past one another. A clinical example about the way that different assumptions underpin different interventions may illuminate these ideas and the vocabulary required to describe them.

> *Susan is 28 years old with a moderate learning disability; she shares the interests of many young women – clothes, pop stars, soap operas. Able to talk about her feelings at times, she lived in a small hospital but wanted to move out into a supported environment elsewhere. She explored the possibility of an adult foster-placement, but the woman matched with her withdrew when Susan became clinging. Following that disappointment her friendship with Jane, one of the nursing assistants, became problematic. Susan would follow six inches behind Jane while she was working and would protest when Jane tried to leave, shouting and hanging onto her clothes; after Jane had left, Susan would often break things in the house or barge into the kitchen and stuff food into her mouth until she vomited. This behaviour gradually escalated until a particularly distressing end-of-shift tussle between them resulted in Jane's clothes being torn, prompting the referral.*

The model most likely to inform an intervention in this case would be the cognitive-behavioural approach, but attachment theory might also be considered.[1] Figure 2.1 compares them.

	COGNITIVE-BEHAVIOURAL	ATTACHMENT THEORY
Theoretical framework	A model with a universal set of rules	A culture-related theory with interlinked propositions
View of history	Rarely drawn on in practice	Important to understanding situation and working with client
Ontology	Realist	Modified realist: a real social world internalized and subjectivized
Epistemology	Phenomena can be measured externally by an observer gathering data, although subjective self-report is also important, perhaps using a tape-recorded diary	Accessed mainly by self-report, amplified by observation and description of meetings, greetings and partings
Type of explanation	A reductive approach where explanation is based on functional analysis	Uses a classificatory explanation, drawing also on mentalistic and teleological approaches
INTERVENTION		
(a) individual client	Main focus, group or individual sessions aimed at understanding, recognizing and expressing emotions soon enough, so there is no explosive loss of control	Individual therapy to help client to understand and explore feelings, with possibility of therapist becoming attachment figure, but this may not be the only focus
(b) enmeshed carer	No specific role	Substantial support given to help enmeshed carer make sense of their experience and avoid repetition by clarifying emotional boundaries
(c) staff team	Rarely recorded in descriptions but most clinicians will explain, asking staff to acknowledge and support more controlled expressions of emotion, e.g. shouting or banging doors	Told problems are rooted in insecurity; client needs acknowledgement of emotions, information about staff shifts and holidays to cope with changes, and other staff will need to reassure her

FIGURE 2.1 *Comparison of the intellectual background to two possible interventions*

Two points of similarity could be sites for methodological discussion which might help psychologists from both orientations to understand each other. First, both the cognitive-behavioural model and attachment theory take the client's report of their emotions as the main focus of work; both also advise staff to acknowledge and support the client's efforts to express their emotional world appropriately.

However, there are so many differences it is no wonder that clinicians find debate difficult. Examples of differences in the respective interventions suggested by this analysis are neglect of the enmeshed carer's emotional life by cognitive-behavioural theorists, and failure to consider the potential for group support by attachment theorists when these difficulties are quite common amongst people with learning disabilities. One way to equip ourselves to address those differences is to understand what theories and assumptions influence us, explicitly or implicitly, and what types of explanation we accept as being valid. That understanding enables people to identify for themselves which positions are non-negotiable, and which could be adapted without undue compromise to their intellectual integrity. Doise (1986) noted such pragmatism to be the sort of creative and fruitful psychology often found amongst clinicians: it seems worth taking time to understand the language a little better.

Theories – I

Einstein is reported to have said the following to one of his colleagues in Berlin:

> You make experiments and I make theories. Do you know the difference? A theory is something that nobody believes except the person who made it, while an experiment is something everybody believes except the person who made it.[2]

Others have said that theory helps us to endure our ignorance, and that there is nothing as useful as a good theory. Such aphorists challenge the criticism that theory is an abstract activity divorced from practice, arguing instead that theory supports and enhances practice. Yet theory is a confused idea in social science: Layder (1990) observes that the term is employed in at least four different senses. For him 'theory' is used to describe the presuppositions people make about the nature of knowledge, such as whether they favour thinking and reading as the most important way to understand the world, or whether they prefer to go out and experience it first. It is also used to describe preferred stances such as humanism, behaviourism or normalization even though these are not encapsulated in particular theories or, as in the case of behaviourism, eschew the idea of theory altogether. Others use theory to describe large discourses or systems of thought such as feminism, Marxism or constructionism. These carry with them perspectives on the nature of reality and how we come to know about it, but are portmanteau positions gathering together a number of slightly different and at times competing theoretical statements. Finally, social scientists use theory to describe their assumptions about research, for example about the nature of the relationship between researcher and researched, or the degree to which accounts from participants can be taken at face value without articulating them against any other sources of information.

Such differences inevitably create barriers to discussion because these different orientations to theory contain premisses with no systematic relationship between them. In turn debate fails to satisfy people because the meanings are rarely all accounted for and proponents try to understand each other while discussing different entities. Layder suggests that first we must hold metatheoretical discussions: these should identify the implicit frameworks hampering debate and enable participants to have more fruitful exchanges.

If different uses of the term 'theory' create one set of problems, implicit theorizing within psychological thinking presents even greater hazards. Soyland (1994) shows how the metaphorical child theorized in developmental psychology has not remained the same entity throughout the twentieth century, although most developmental psychologists debate their respective positions as if s/he is the same. Yet this child changes, at one moment passing through psychosexual stages where they may or may not be able to control the bidding of their low urges; at another driven by the genetic unfolding of cognitive abilities; at another shaped by social relations which are primary prompts to development itself variously cast as behavioural, emotional or cognitive. Soyland shows how developmental theories are incommensurate. They cannot disprove each other because they discuss different conceptual children.

If the theories describe different entities, how do any of them overtake others? Soyland argues that this occurs through rhetorical moves rather than – or as much as – evidence. He suggests that Freud's influence can be traced to his powerful ability to engage readers, predicting the way their thinking would resist his perspective and then making them responsible for overcoming their 'resistance'. Soyland provides a similar analysis of rhetorical moves made by theorists of the emotions. He is not suggesting that psychology can do without rhetoric; on the contrary he acknowledges that powerful argument and metaphor are essential to the creation and extension of meaning. His thesis is that readers need to be aware of the subtle ways we become enrolled into particular discourses. Without that insight we may prefer one theory over another because we are attracted to the hidden aspects of human experience it describes, rather than because its content, evidence or argument is convincing.

A further source of confusion can arise from the terms 'model' and 'theory'.[3] Used interchangeably by many psychologists, models are best used as simple analogies where the relationship between the idea and the entity need not be close. An example is ethological psychology where human behaviour was modelled on observational studies of animals. Treating human territoriality as if it corresponds to territorial display in primates is a model that makes no assumption about other aspects of human behaviour mapping onto that of apes. The model will not be abandoned even if disconfirming evidence mounts up, so long as it continues to be fertile in generating new research questions. By contrast, theories are complex expositions of interrelated ideas that correspond to information we have about the world: disconfirming evidence therefore mounts a serious challenge to them. Newell and Simon's (1972) proposal that people be viewed as limited-capacity information processors is an example of a model, while Bronfenbrenner's (1977) ecological approach to psychology is an example of a theory. Few psychological theories have been proposed or accepted by the academic community in the last decade, reflecting a shift away from grand theoretical statements often described as a defining feature of the post-modern era.

Classical philosophers used two metatheoretical concepts to discuss their ideas: ontology and epistemology. Ontology describes one's set of beliefs about the nature of reality: interest in different aspects of reality results in moral, physical and social ontologies being highlighted by different philosophers. Ontological debates running through psychology are often found in discussion of biology versus social experience; as Brown and Stenner (1995) observe, this replays the mind–body problem first discussed by Descartes. In academic psychology it was exemplified by the debate between Lazarus (1984) and Zajonc (1984), who discussed the relative primacy of either cognition or affect in our experience of emotion. The success of Lazarus's argument for cognition may be judged by the centrality of cognitive psychology and of cognitive-behavioural treatments within the subject, but their debate is nevertheless one based on premisses derived from outdated Cartesian dualism.

Clinical disputes based on ontological differences include whether it is most salient to focus on the impact of genes on the experience of somebody with Down's syndrome or on their treatment as someone stigmatized by society. The genetic argument is often dismissed unthinkingly by psychologists as 'the medical model' and therefore not worthy of debate, but cannot be so simply dismissed. There is considerable interest in the experience of embodied disability, not least among those who experience it, and it deserves proper attention. Similarly, does evolutionary theory provide the greatest insight into people who experience depression, or is it more useful to focus on and change their relative poverty or history of abuse by others? It will be impossible to hold a debate between Gilbert's evolutionary perspective on depression and that held by community psychologists without acknowledging that there is a fundamental difference in the assumptions each side makes at an ontological level. In the example about Susan given above, it is difficult for cognitive-behaviourists who subscribe to a realist ontology to debate ontology with attachment theorists whose interests follow the subjectivization and internalization of social experience.

Taylor (1989) notes that people who decry ontological debate, by saying that they just want to get on with life, make an implicit moral decision that greater good accrues from action than from reflection. It is likely that clinical psychologists and other NHS practitioners will be oriented more towards action than reflection, since they occupy jobs focused on intervention; however clinical psychologists' position bridging the academy and problem-solving makes them well placed to engage in both action and reflection. Most important for thinking straight is understanding and acknowledging the relevance of ontological assumptions: the barriers that unquestioned beliefs place in the way of living debate. Taylor argues that there are three axes of moral ontology, those concerning respect, dignity, and what gives meaning to life. He asserts with some force that the social evils of the twentieth century can be traced to exclusive concentration on one of these axes, while ignoring moral goods deriving from the other two.

Unscrambling the principle of normalization shows how Taylor's approach to moral ontology can illuminate practical matters. Most normalization values cluster around his respect axis: this makes it easier to see both its contribution and its limitations. Normalization derives from a value he terms the affirmation of ordinary life, an idea that can be traced back to the Enlightenment but which has always been impossible to define. Taylor's triaxial approach to moral ontology allows us to acknowledge the goods normalization has brought while inviting us to move beyond binary debate for or against it. Instead he proposes a reorientation to incorporate goods deriving from his other two axes of moral ontology, in this case aspects of rights and citizenship, and whatever draws the meaning of people's lives into debate.

Taylor's argument for unifying or umbrella ontologies which encompass different perspectives is echoed in physics where Bohm (1980; Bohm and Hiley, 1993) discusses the way that different entities can be understood as belonging to one conceptual world. He uses light to describe moving beyond the traditional division into wave and particle to see how holograms transform our understanding of the phenomenon, because each region of a hologram contains enough information to make the whole image and that image becomes sharper, not more complete, when more information is sent. Bohm argues for an unbroken wholeness in the physical world based on two orders, the explicate and the implicate.[4] The explicate world is the world which unfolds before us, following causal laws framed by the theory of relativity; pursuing the hologram example, it is the final image unfolded from the transmitted information. The implicate world is the world of contexts, obeying acausal principles where information is yet to be unfolded: it is described in quantum physics by concepts such as the Uncertainty Principle.

Bohm's argument is that we remain concerned with the explicate order of physical causality while what is really important is the implicate order of acausality. Layder (1990) extends Bohm's ideas into social ontology to describe cultural factors which influence us in ways we barely recognize, or may not recognize at all, but which nevertheless are the medium in which we exist. A parallel development has occurred in psychology where Buddhist ideas of conscious and unconscious thought have been explored in an attempt to develop a unitary conceptualization of human experience (Claxton, 1994). These perspectives take the realm of the unconscious or acausal out of the exclusive hands of various schools of psychodynamic and existential psychology, as do recent explorations of non-conscious rather than unconscious processes within cognitive psychology (Brewin, 1988; Loftus and Klinger 1992). Their inchoate, abstract nature makes such ideas and assumptions difficult to research. However, the implicit task set by Bohm, Layder and Claxton is that of constructing theories that merge causal and acausal, conscious and non-conscious processes within a single ontology. We are asked to go beyond the fragmentary, to dare to imagine how our ideas could encompass all of human experience.

If ontology describes the assumptions we make about the nature of reality, epistemology concerns how we know what we know. It often describes the methods or approaches that are warranted as providing knowledge about reality.[5] Whether reading and thinking are sufficient to produce insights about the nature of the world, or whether it is necessary to collect information through direct experience, is an epistemological dispute discussed above. This debate, between rationalism and empiricism, emerged in the seventeenth and eighteenth centuries but remains with us to form a significant distinguishing feature between various disciplines and various researchers.

Questioning how we 'know' something is often ridiculed as armchair philosophizing which encourages useless navel-gazing: surely it is obvious that there is a ground we can walk on and a chair we can sit on? Yet such issues rapidly become key topics for debate in clinical practice. How do we know whether a client is worse or better? Do all the people who spend time with that person agree on their improvement or deterioration? Research shows that baseline observations can be misleading even when definitions are tightly controlled, inter-rater reliabilities on a variety of problem behaviour checklists being notoriously low.[6] Moreover, what information would tell us anything useful about this individual? Is it possible to understand them from observation alone, or should we access their subjective experience before deciding whether they have improved or deteriorated? Other relevant dimensions are time and culture: can we discover everything we need to know about this person from currently available information, or should we amplify this with historical and contextual knowledge?

Mrs Curry has not spoken for five years, lives in a unit for people with long-term mental health problems and has started to show stereotyped hand and finger movements. It may be tardive dyskinesia, a treatment-related movement disorder which carries its own politics: some lawyers have used it to challenge the medical right to prescribe psychotropic medication to one person for long periods. Keen to replace a medical with a psychological model of care we might not look into Mrs Curry's background, which records that she spent the first 20 years of her working life operating a weaving-loom in Lancashire. This does not prevent her having tardive dyskinesia but does suggest an alternative hypothesis, that failing sight and understanding have led her to repeat threading movements that were deeply ingrained. Clearly, how we 'know' what we know about Mrs Curry's stereotypy – that is, whether we rely on observation alone or whether we delve into her history – is fundamental to the way clinicians respond.

This first section has summarized arguments about thinking straight that flow from classical philosophy and theories based on it. Theories which revolve around ontology and epistemology are usually characterized as realist because they assume that various techniques of scholarship will produce information about a real world. Both interventions discussed for Susan have realist components, albeit a subjectivized version in attachment theory. A second set of theories take a different perspective.

Theories – II

A major challenge to a natural science or classical view of psychology comes from acknowledging the centrality of people to the study of people. Our own histories and perceptions shape the way we appraise ideas and interventions, and habitual metaphors and analogies influence the way we construct ideas about the social world. Even more important than the subjectivity of the researcher, however, is that of the people who participate in human studies. They transform the experience uniquely, bringing their own histories and interpretations to bear on the enterprise and on their attitude towards us. Not only do we need to reflect upon the contribution our own views and relationships make, we also need to take into account the degree to which psychological knowledge informs participants' understandings of themselves, which they in turn use to describe their experiences to us. A reflexive stance towards the subject of psychology is essential.

Nietzsche rejected the idea of reality, suggesting that all we can ever know is the constructions that people create about the world. Whether such constructions bear any relation to a 'real' world is unknowable and therefore irrelevant. Anti-realist approaches are sometimes derided as relativist on the grounds that they dispute the notion of reality itself, making knowledge relative to the perspective of the knower. This criticism is disputed by Rorty (1991): he defends the position that to say we cannot know reality is not to say that it is not there. He argues that it is striving to find out about reality that is fruitless. Rorty observes that in order to go about our lives successfully we only need to know the representations which we and other people make about reality. Rorty goes on to cite Nietzsche's view that clinging to objective reality is based on fear of losing our culture, that it is a test of human character to adopt a relativist view of knowledge – a test few would want to fail, thus making a powerful rhetorical move to recruit us to the anti-realist position.

Anti-realism is also sometimes described as pragmatism, but this term carries many meanings which threaten to confuse. Pierce (see Mounce,

1997) and William James (1907) are regarded as the co-founders of contemporary pragmatism, but their version was far from the positions espoused by either Nietzsche or Rorty. Haack (1992) identifies two broad styles of pragmatism: reformist and revolutionary. The reformist version was described by James and developed by Mead (1934), by Vygotsky (1962) and by Bruner (1990) into a set of ideas often described as social constructionist or as based on activity theory. These authors seek the meaning of concepts within their practical application, acknowledging the legitimacy of traditional questions and accepting a quasi-realist view of truth. Haack contrasts this reformism with the revolutionary version of pragmatism described above by Rorty, which acknowledges no legitimate epistemological questions about the relationship between our knowing and a real world. Haack suggests that the reformist version of pragmatism contains the most interesting epistemological work. More recently Shotter (1993) suggests that a non-systematic but situated form of realism can be incorporated into his version of social constructionism; while from the other direction Layder's (1990) concept of realism approaches the anti-realist position by including aspects of constructionist thinking. As in all the most fruitful debates a simple bipolar dichotomy, realist/anti-realist, has become a dimension on which many different positions can be found.

Latour (1987) moves beyond the realist/anti-realist dichotomy to suggest that soft information hardens more or less into scientific or sociological truth by associational networks within an intellectual community. These networks develop among allies recruited after conference presentations, by persuading relevant communities such as client advocacy groups of the value of your position, and by getting information published in peer-reviewed journals. Members of such networks are open to being influenced by new work: however, it gains authority either by being linked to previously established strong facts, or establishes technical authority by introducing investigative techniques which in themselves break new ground. Latour notes that there are some scientific facts which are disputed by no one and so it is reasonable to treat them as true for current purposes. Gambrill's (1990) criticism that clinicians often fail to distinguish between weak and strong facts seems to have much in common with Latour's thinking.

More recently, Deleuze and Guattari's (1994) powerful exposition of constructionist philosophy follows Haack's revolutionary wing of pragmatism, to focus on creativity and question any idea of truth. They describe how a new idea needs a new field to be cleared so that it can flourish and be fertile. This was the sense in which Soyland discussed the way successive developmental theories have laid out and then painted a different picture of the conceptual child. Deleuze and Guattari treat ideas within their own realm of influence or plane, organically connected to neighbouring ideas but presuming no relationship with ideas distant from them. For those conversant with the Internet, such a web-like approach to philosophical concepts has been characterized as hypertextual. Deleuze and

Guattari suggest that ideas are evaluated not by teachers writing 'true' or 'false' in the margin but by readers finding the ideas interesting, remarkable and significant. We may return to dormant concepts, such as Berrios and Porter's (1995) return to the idea of 'will' in psychiatry, but we always do so by playing them out on a new stage. Thus Anderson and Goolishian (1988) were among the clinicians who moved family therapy beyond a focus on technique to reconceptualize it as conversation, one which stays alive and meaningful through the co-creation of fresh ideas and perspectives.

Certainly the right to be original must be earned. Karmiloff-Smith (1992) has made a bold attempt to recast developmental psychology by going outside the dualisms which normally stifle it. Clearing out old dichotomies such as nature/nurture (or at least almost managing to), implicit/explicit representation and domain-specific/domain-general development, she develops the alternative idea of representational redescription. This idea is used to shape chapters that construe development quite differently, to see the child in turn as linguist, mathematician and psychologist. Soviet psychologists were similarly bold in their invention of activity theory earlier this century, developing central concepts to drive a new psychology for a new society which tackled the individual–society antinomy head-on (Brushlinskii, 1987).

These approaches to theory make serious assaults on the timorous habits of psychology. They may not stand the test of time as new conceptualizations: it is possible that these ideas are complex elaborations of epistemology rather than a new approach to theory. Whatever their final classification, it is clear that they demand creativity and reflexivity, skills rarely taught or celebrated as we stolidly embed research in the footsteps of our predecessors. Mair (1989b) is one of the few clinicians to risk discussing creativity within practice. Although the attempt falters somewhat in the middle this does not destroy his argument that creative thinking is a vital component of clinical practice, one which involves exposing yourself and taking risks.

Explanations

> An encouraging breakthrough for London Underground communication skills has been spotted at Holborn. 'We apologise for the fact that there are delays in all areas of the Piccadilly line tonight,' read a blackboard message yesterday. 'This is due to the late running of trains.' (*Guardian* Diary, 12 December 1996)

Adequate explanations are accepted as useful and valid when they provide new information that is coherent with the theoretical perspective we adopt. However, to be adequate, explanations themselves must follow some coherent logic. It is easy to see that this tube explanation is tautologous or circular: it is not an adequate explanation because one idea – late trains – is used to represent both the thing to be explained and the explanation. It is less easy for people to see the tautology in clinical explanations, yet it is often there. If, for example, a decade of behavioural teaching states there are only four possible reasons for somebody exhibiting challenging behaviour, including attention-seeking and demand avoidance; and if researchers then ask staff why they think these people are being difficult, the 'result' showing that staff believe challenging behaviours to be caused by attention-seeking or demand avoidance discovers nothing new. Such research merely demonstrates that staff have learned which new ideas are accepted about challenging behaviour. While the authors argue that it tells us how staff see clients, an alternative argument – that the result demonstrates how influential behavioural explanations are in this context – is at least equally plausible.

An explanation is generally regarded as the answer to a why-question: popular wisdom expects that only one explanation for a phenomenon is possible, but this is rarely the case. Explanations distinguish the thing to be explained from the thing that does the explaining, but they require attention to who asked the question, what it was aimed at, and who gave the answer. For example, why did my son have to die? may request consolation rather than information; why do powerful men rely on spin doctors? may ask for information but also seeks justification. Explanations of human experience have to take into account the knowledge and perspectives of the questioner if they are to satisfy. A journalist might be seeking a general answer to the question of political advisers, while an MP whose power had been reduced by that adviser might accept the principle but want to hear why that particular adviser survives. Explanation in human affairs is necessarily complex: it is difficult to reduce events or incidents to their barest essentials without also stripping them of important layers of meaning.

Throughout the twentieth century changing views of scientific explanation and challenges to the idea of science have perplexed psychologists. Valentine (1992) observes that we are not always clear about what our accumulated facts are evidence for, that there is little agreement about what a psychological explanation looks like. She identifies seven distinct types of explanation commonly found in the social sciences:[7] these are summarized in Figure 2.2 and their application to the individual provided in the Appendix (p. 213).

Not all classification schemes are explanatory: merely giving a phenomenon a name is insufficient to qualify as an explanation. However, it becomes an explanation if it avoids circularity and conveys additional information. So it would not be an explanation to say that somebody pokes their eyeball because they have stereotyped behaviour: that would simply be to name the event. It would be an explanation to say the person was *classified* as partially sighted; partial sight introduces a number of additional pieces of information to the questioner, including the knowledge that pressure on the eyeball provokes visual sensations that the person cannot obtain any other way.

REDUCTIVE	Classificatory Correlational Causal
CONSTRUCTIVE	Functional Neurophysiological
EMERGENT	Teleological Mentalistic

FIGURE 2.2 *Summary of Valentine's types of explanation*

Most explanations in social science use *correlations*, they are probabilistic; such explanations imply imperfectly understood determinism. Skinner was an exponent of these explanations, which he regarded as sufficient in themselves, requiring no further theorizing. However, while most clinicians hear the dictum 'correlation does not imply causation' at some point in their training it is curious how often it gets forgotten. An example is Hastings and Remington's (1994a) statement that people with profound disabilities engage in stereotypy because they are left alone with nothing to do. Baumeister countered this common belief as long ago as 1978 by observing that the reverse is at least equally likely, that staff leave the person and stimulate others because their attempts to engage clients who display stereotyped behaviour fail. Having to depend on correlational information is one reason why psychological explanations are difficult to understand and communicate.

Hume's three conditions for deciding that A caused B were that the relationship between cause and effect requires close association, the same order of events, and that they occur together on every occasion. *Causal explanations* were powerful in classical science: the apple falls because of gravity, the moon goes around the earth because of gravity. However, since most human events are probabilistic it is rare to find a truly causal explanation in psychology, and our concern to be scientific also ignores how dissatisfied physical scientists became with such explanations: for example, they do not explain why the apple fell today rather than tomorrow. Most mature sciences now consist of mathematical statements of functional relations between a number of factors, rather than the identification of one overriding cause. Explanations of human experience can rarely be reduced to such mathematical statements.

Valentine believes that *functional explanation* offers psychology 'an autonomous level of description' by analysing processes or operations within an infinite variety of possible systems. Although the idea of functional explanation is most often associated in clinical settings with behaviourism, it may underpin equally cognitive psychology or structural family therapy. Functional explanations move beyond why questions to say what the action or experience achieves. Clearly there are many possible variants, not all of which will satisfy all audiences. To the degree that cybernetics is accepted as the origin of many of these types of explanation, a conceptual link exists between the cognitive-behavioural and attachment theory approaches outlined earlier as ways of working with Susan. One limitation of functional explanations is the lack of a historical dimension: they describe present events, often with the support of a flow chart, but rarely encompass wider temporal contexts.

Recent clinical applications based on functional analysis incorporate multiple perspectives and different types of explanation into flow diagrams which usefully integrate multidisciplinary interventions in complex situations. Examples are a set of planned interventions for somebody who occasionally starts fires (Clare et al., 1992), and a systemic analysis of the cultural and family tensions that led a Kenyan to kill his uncle soon after the family moved to London (Cohen, 1997). Such multimodal formulations of complex behaviours often combine a variety of types of explanation and possible theoretical positions. These require conceptual vigilance if the final formulation is to avoid falling into the many traps associated with eclecticism, if it is to offer a meaningful account that has internal consistency and conceptual integrity.

Somewhat surprisingly, Valentine's second example of a constructive rather than a reductive explanation is one using *neurophysiology*. She describes the complexity of the relationship between psychology and physiology and the various positions different people have proposed. Although arguments at the level of cell biology are usually considered reductive, Valentine prefers to follow Deutsch (1960) in seeing them as two separate and complex systems that have a relationship with one another. This is because it has proved so difficult to establish secure relationships between psychological experiences such as language and neurophysiological processes.

Valentine's final two types of explanation are teleological and mentalistic. *Teleological explanations* describe intention by reference to a future event. An example is to say that somebody who felt his family was not listening to him brandished a knife to ensure he would be taken seriously. Describing actions in terms of reasons rather than causes is a form of explanation used by ordinary people. An example of teleological psychology is the seminal book on plans and purposive behaviour by Miller et al. (1960). Teleological explanations are recommended by philosophers such as Feyerabend (1993) and psychologists such as Shotter (1993), who argue for frameworks that allow academic explanation and lay understanding to merge.

Finally, *mentalistic* explanations came from a radically different approach to psychology, that of early German psychologists concerned to develop understanding rather than causal prediction and control. Such explanations depend on the assumption that all people have shared responses to the same experience, an assumption which may break down when significant differences exist between individuals. Valentine criticizes such explanations for falling into the hermeneutic circle: since the interpretation of events is based on existing understanding, there is no opportunity for innovation and the development of new ideas cannot be accounted for. However, hermeneutic writers dispute this perception of their position, arguing that it derives from a mistranslation of original German texts.

As is clear from Figure 2.2, another way to understand differences between people derives from their use of diferent types of explanation: reductionist, constructive or emergent. Reductionist explanations assume that complex actions are entirely made up from lower-level phenomena: for example that there are core emotions which map onto physiologically distinct events, and that complex emotions are mere combinations of those core sensations. Unfortunately no general agreement has been reached about those core emotions nor the physiological sensations associated with them. Valentine's constructive explanations describe phenomena in terms of more abstract or higher-order constructs, mainly concentrating on functional aspects of human experience or explanations about points of contact between two major systems. Finally, emergent explanations assume that at a certain level of complexity new forces come into play which are not observable when working at the individual level alone: family therapy and community psychology both use emergent explanations.

Valentine cautions against evaluating one type of explanation according to the criteria of another, showing how difficult it can be to hold debates between positions. It is also important to avoid the mistake of comparing 'our' ideals with 'their' realities. This is more commonly seen in political or ideological disputes: for example, Protestants criticizing what they see as barbaric actions by Islamic fundamentalists while remaining blind to atrocities carried out in the name of Christianity in Northern Ireland. Similar criticism of the failures of 'their' research from the pinnacle of 'our' theory, rather than from acceptance of the practical exigencies that compromise the usefulness of the research based on our theory too, can be found amongst psychologists as well.

While clinicians may feel little need for metatheoretical knowledge as long as there is widespread agreement on conceptual foundations, such knowledge provides a helpful perspective on various conceptual positions during periods of rapid change. In order to hold meaningful exchanges, people need to create shared understanding. Pitfalls and possible misunderstandings outlined here have concerned the relationship between mental and physical events, between knowledge available to introspection and tacit knowledge, and between belief states and tacit understandings which are not integrated with those beliefs. However, the list is endless: most of us have to struggle hard to have any chance of understanding the perspective of others.

Conclusions

It is vital that clinicians grow more accustomed to engaging in theoretical debates and question any suggestion that greater good accrues from action than from reflection. There is considerable change in the air and we must be able to distinguish the radical from the valuable from the trivial. As is exemplified in the next chapter, some people take up positions with little understanding of how little they differ from existing stances, while others oppose them unaware that they are employing many assumptions used by their opponents. In particular the stale behaviourism–psychotherapy dichotomy shows signs of weakening in the face of increasing theoretical complexity: the conditions for renewal and regeneration are in place. What is required is conceptual creativity and boldness, skills rarely discussed or explicitly fostered during training.

There are three major reasons why naturalistic, reductive explanations are inappropriate to psychology: the reflexivity of participants and researchers, the inherent complexity of social phenomena, and the contestability of many of its concepts. Theorizing interpretation is one of the key tasks of an anti-realist approach to social science, as is taking an ethical position toward its goals. Rather than prediction and control, some argue that psychology's project should be practical, in other words developing understandings that allow people to alter their own circumstances, or it should be critical with the intention of increasing their liberation.

Summary

Metatheoretical debates about what we know and how we know it is a key *contemporary issue* felt throughout the humanities and human sciences. Such fermenting ideas create a degree of uncertainty even when people are not aware of its source, as is clear from the conceptual confusion expressed by some trainees. One way to avoid uncertainty is to refuse debate by settling upon one position and ignoring alternative ideas, but that way lies stagnation and a fragmented profession. In this chapter metatheoretical differences were discussed to provide a framework for understanding and evaluating ideas, so that clinicians may identify common ground with others as well as differences. Philosophers reviewed here argue that attempts to create conceptual unity which encompass multiple perspectives are both possible and worthwhile, although difficult. This flies in the face of contemporary fragmentation and competition between single-interest groups, each demanding their rights; the position is developed over subsequent chapters.

A *history of the present* was summarized in Soyland's conceptual child as it changed during twentieth-century developmental psychology. His analysis of the relevance of rhetoric in establishing the superiority of one theory over another is offered not as evidence that all is talk and there can be no dependable truth; rather it helps us to identify the role rhetoric plays in our assessment of theories, and in the way others assess our proposals. Elegant argumentation is not all there is, but it is a component of intellectual work we neglect at our peril.

Theoretical positions describing *intersubjective meanings* are central to this chapter, where creating the conditions for living dialogue was a theme continued from Chapter 1. These include holding initial metatheoretical discussions that enable participants to develop rules about recognizing and reaching agreements, and considering for ourselves what rhetorical moves we find most persuasive. Intersubjective meanings in theory-building, explanation and therapy can be enhanced by turning bipolar dichotomies into multiple dimensions, a concern described by the somewhat hackneyed phrase 'moving from either/or to both/and'. This ability is useful in debate, supervision and in interventions such as family therapy. Both Burnham (1993) and Jones (1993) show how it gives all participants room for manoeuvre, neither generating conflict nor requiring anybody to abandon strongly held positions.

Discussion of the *reflective researcher-practitioner* focused most on the reflexivity of the people who are the subject of psychology. Psychology is shared and published and discussed to such a degree that research participants must be changed by that knowledge – either because they accept and incorporate it or because they reject some ideas which they believe are ways of viewing the world held by the researcher. That makes it impossible for psychology to accumulate a body of knowledge about 'memory' while the phenomenon remains unchanged, because the ways teachers and parents and learners remember material inevitably changes in response to the ways psychologists conceptualize and study it.

However, this chapter above all addresses *critical thinking*, because debate cannot start until participants both reflect and acquire a shared language. Even the term 'theory' carries multiple meanings, and it is in the realms of implicit theorizing that the most violent disputes occur because the ideas are not open to scrutiny. Three different ontologies or assumptions we make about different aspects of our world (social, physical, moral) were explored theoretically. Psychologists are familiar with problems associated with separating mind from body, an issue some resolve by considering the person as an entity which acts: this combines body, thought and intention through the addition of time. Layder extends this argument to consider how opposition between individual and society can be brought within one social ontology so that cultural factors of which we are barely aware can nevertheless be made present within our assumptions. Finally, Taylor argues that moral decisions require that different positions be balanced against each other, rather than that one should be pursued to the exclusion of others: unification if not conceptual unity.

How we know what we know connects with the assumptions we make about what it is to 'know reality' and to what others assume about the world and themselves. It also derives from the way we think about theories, theory-building and models, and from the types of answers we accept as explanations. This chapter emphasizes how vital it is to be able to recognize and understand the assumptions behind different sorts of explanation, not only so that we can hold debates which employ different types of explanation but also so that we can recognize what sort of explanation of a phenomenon makes sense to the person we are talking to. Five different explanations commonly accepted by the scientific community were outlined, grouped as both reductive and constructive. Two emergent ones that incorporate more complex phenomena into their assumptions were also discussed. These are more commonly found among the general public and move beyond the individual to incorporate aspects of the wider social community, and are the types of explanation preferred here.

All of these activities depend upon *human systems* where people enter into debate with good will, striving towards the Ideal Communicator (Habermas, 1992) who joins debate to forge a new position which goes beyond their current view. Such efforts are of course destroyed by individuals who are not used to negotiating their ideas with others. These people pursue a type of intellectual imperialism, treating opponents as objects rather than fellow persons (Buber, 1958). By attempting to impose their views without adapting or changing them in any way, such individuals create a defensive environment where nobody learns anything: that would need to be addressed before intersubjective meanings could evolve. Finally, and perhaps most important, this review of the development of intersubjective meanings summarized the way that knowledge is created amongst research communities. It is intended to enable clinicians to add their contribution to it, a concern developed later in the book.

Notes

1 Attachment theory has been misused by psychologists writing about Gentle Teaching, who airily talk about bonding but not the consequences of repeated loss of attachment figures in institutional settings, nor do they consider the possibility of insecure or ambivalent attachments ocurring. Clegg and Lansdall-Welfare (1995) provide a more detailed exposition of attachment-based interventions that address enmeshed carer–client relationships. A critique of Gentle Teaching itself is provided in Chapter 3.

2 Cited by G. Holton in A.F. Heath (ed.) *Scientific Explanation*. Oxford: Oxford University Press, 1981, p. 11. I am grateful to Norman Wetherick for providing both the quotation and the reference – and also for doubting its veracity, since witty and profound remarks tend to be attributed to men like Einstein.

3 The British Psychological Society hosted a conference to discuss this, one of the few occasions when prepared papers were circulated beforehand and discussed in detail by a small invited audience (Chapman and Jones, 1980). I am drawing on a number of those papers in this paragraph, for which Thines's review chapter provides a good introduction.

4 Bohm uses a thought experiment to illustrate the implicate order. With two glass test-tubes of different sizes, we may half fill one with a clear viscous fluid and suspend the other inside it. Their sides do not touch. A drop of ink is then introduced into this fluid and the two tubes rotated in opposite directions; the ink will spread into a thin strand and then disappear from sight altogether. If the

direction of rotation is reversed the strand and then the drop will reappear. A further drop introduced while the tubes were being rotated could create the illusion of one drop moving from place to place rather than two drops appearing and disappearing. This then describes how the *explicate* order of apparent causality may be observed which is underpinned by an *implicate* order where entirely different processes dictate the movement of the ink-drops.

5 The following brief outline of epistemology is based on MacDonald and MacDonald (1995) and on Dancy and Sosa (1992). MacDonald and MacDonald focus primarily on explanations pertinent to cognitive psychology, while the Dancy and Sosa text is philosophical.

6 An example is Newton and Sturmey's (1991) demonstration that the Motivation Assessment Scale has an inter-rater reliability of only 0.18. The low reliability of this and other scales assessing challenging behaviour in people with learning disabilities is reviewed in Clegg (1993).

7 The following description of the different types of explanation is heavily dependent upon her excellent and acclaimed text, to which the interested reader should refer for amplification.

3 Postmodern Culture and its Influence

During most of the 1990s British politicians tried to close down debates by asserting that they knew 'the fact of the matter': simplistic rhetoric that clearly illustrates the intellectual environment of the time. Simultaneously, however, emerging debates in the human sciences made it much more difficult to establish and sustain truth claims. This chapter explores the cultural tensions experienced by human scientists as we work to create 'truths' that are both conceptual and practical.

Said (1994) notes that people who provide ahistorical accounts tend to oversimplify opponents' positions into caricatures; he also describes re-reading and reinterpreting canonical texts as a vital part of academic renewal. This exhortation made me read for the first time the original 1970s reports of the Head Start project, alongside Tizard's seminal description of the first community care project in Britain for children with a learning disability. In both I found thoroughness and farsightedness which explains the powerful positions they have attained in the learning disability 'canon': the experience also made me question psychology's implicit belief that anything written more than a decade ago is worth neither time nor trouble.

Since history provides some understanding of the origins of contemporary complexity this chapter opens by tracing themes in the two main positions that came to influence post-Christian Western thinking, the Enlightenment and Romanticism. Necessarily a selective account, it forms a springboard into the second section which considers how current clinical psychology comprises and contains postmodern practice, since postmodernism is a reaction to these great traditions. The third section explores how these cultural contexts influence two particular interventions and the debates that surround them, while the final section identifies four emergent topics whose development could shape future clinical practice.

Two Influences on Western Thought[1]

The Enlightenment

Descartes and Locke were the Enlightenment's precursors, Rousseau and Voltaire its main proponents. The title describes their intention to shed light on the dark places of medieval life: some thought this had been created by the Church, which dominated intellectual life at the turn of the eighteenth century, others that the whole period was encrusted in unthinking, dogmatic superstition and cruelty.

Some important principles developed by Enlightenment thinkers have influenced psychology throughout its history. Reason was valued above all: Enlightenment philosophers generally approached the creation of knowledge ahistorically. They believed that the world was arranged in systems which awaited discovery, systems that were not particular to a place or group of people but existed universally. This love of systems extended to creative expressions too, an aesthetic expressed by classicism. Mozart's symmetry and perfect cadences conjured an ordered and predictable world, countering the florid music of previous eras that celebrated coronations or royal birthdays. Elegant and symmetrical cities and squares were built during this period, British examples being found in Bath and the new town in Edinburgh; in painting, classical buildings and still life became popular themes.

As the Enlightenment developed, reason gave way to a new focus on sensory experience, forming the basis of empiricism. Science became increasingly powerful, because it held that observations of the world can be safe from self-interested interference in knowledge-production. Facts would emerge from the analysis of these observations, and such knowledge was expected to connect into the universal systems which were believed to underpin the world.

Perceptions of humanity moved away from the priests' depiction of people who bear the guilt of original sin. Enlightenment philosophers viewed people as autonomous individuals: born with a clean slate, if they behave badly then society is the cause. However, this was not the wholesale rejection of religion it is sometimes portrayed: Davies (1996) observes that Renaissance thinkers would not accept the reason–religion dichotomy, suggesting that by the end of the seventeenth century the churches had reformed in various ways. Their idea of a God, recast as the Great Clockmaker in charge of this ordered universe, stood alongside the humanist image of man at the centre of the universe.

Certainly, thinking for oneself without the guidance of others was highly valued: this self-determination supported the development of democracies where traditional authority could be rejected and debate could thrive. Concern for equality and universality follows from believing all persons to be both autonomous and equal, with ordinary lives based on work and family being accorded the same status as those of priests and kings. The Enlightenment emphasis on shared humanity created an ethic of beneficence, a duty to improve the lives of others and to relieve suffering, a view which continues to have a place in the minds of many twentieth-century clinicians. Consequentialist ethics – that the value of an act should be judged by its outcomes – is central to Enlightenment thinking, utilitarianism being its most common expression. As a movement to counter the more or less corrupt social and religious hierarchies that had held onto power and provided so few opportunities for social change, Enlightenment thinking had much to recommend it.

Twentieth-century expressions of these ideas can be seen in the growth of science and technology, but also in the arts and humanities. Enlightenment values encouraged musicologists of the 1950s to measure the plaster casts of dead pianists' hands and study sequences of photographs taken while pianists played, in the belief that these could reveal performance technique. Similarly, literary structuralists identified basic rules of composition, looking at the framework of a narrative or drama rather than its content or effect. These approaches to music and literature were mirrored by the development of mechanistic models in psychology and increasing numbers of ways to classify people by psychometric assessment.

Examination of Valentine's (1992) seven different types of explanation current in psychology shows that most (classificatory, correlational, causal, functional and neurophysiological) are based on Enlightenment assumptions. This version of psychology is concerned with prediction and constructs itself as a science, accepting that systematic forms of information such as classification schemes or neurophysiological ratings are valuable. By referring to information considered to be universal, they make no assumptions about the subjective life of anybody involved – not the client, nor the carer nor the psychologist. Enlightenment thinking supports research that deludes itself with the belief that psychologists do not affect social situations. As Danziger (1990) demonstrates, this played an important part in the subject's development in Britain, Germany and the USA.

Romanticism

> Philosophy will clip an Angel's wings,
> Conquer all mysteries by rule and line,
> Empty the haunted air, and gnomed mine –
> Unweave a rainbow, as it erewhile made
> The tender-personed Lamia melt into a shade.
>
> From 'Lamia', by Keats (1973)

Keats's complaint that science unravels rainbows and strips them of their beauty was written early in the nineteenth century. He and other Romantics challenged Enlightenment beliefs, suggesting that both human communities and human happiness were destroyed by the pursuit of wealth and technological power. Although Enlightenment philosophers had declared ordinary human experience to be important, critics observed that friendship and mutuality got very low priority once they came into conflict with industrial society's need for a mobile workforce. Davies observes that 'in retrospect it seems extraordinary that so many of Europe's leading intellects should have given such weight to one human faculty – reason – at the expense of all others' (1996: 578); early in the nineteenth century the

Enlightenment was described in a dictionary as a period of shallow and pretentious intellectualism. In seeking to replace Enlightenment reason with subjectivity, Romantics focused on fulfilment, intimacy and particularity. They revered ordinary living, expressing this in idealized rural paintings of pretty cottages and abundant gardens, or musical celebrations of childhood.

Romantic expressionism underpinned the national life of many countries during the nineteenth century. The human particularities manifested in folk music and other traditions created symbols that were used by nation states such as Norway (Grieg, Ibsen, Munch) and Ireland (Yeats, Joyce) as they emerged in the late nineteenth and early twentieth centuries. These and other countries asserted their nationhood as much through culture as through battles or politics, laying the seeds of twentieth-century nationalistic conflicts which Billig (1995) and Ignatieff (1994) struggle to understand.

Valentine's last two types of psychological explanation, teleological and mentalistic, are primarily Romantic ideas which depend on subjectivity. Their main psychological expressions are humanism and pragmatism. Both were described in 1907 by William James, often credited as the founder of British and American schools of psychology (and, incidentally, brother of the writer Henry James); but humanism did not really develop in the USA until the late 1950s. It needed hermeneutic and existentialist psychologists to move there from Europe following the second world war for significant development to occur.

Humanism's main exponents in psychology have been Maslow, Allport, Rogers and Kelly. Maslow (1954) described humanism as a third force which could counter psychoanalysis and behaviourism, and these psychologists' agenda was to produce a human science which was both about people and for them. Thus they studied positive human experiences such as choice, altruism, dignity, uniqueness. Rogers's ideal of self-actualization and Maslow's hierarchy of need (1954) still underpin many psychological arguments, for example, in Newman and Beail's (1994) article on needs assessment.

Humanism is fundamentally weakened by its individual perspective; it is unable to theorize interdependence and has difficulty conceptualizing variations in cultural identity. Layder (1990) criticizes the way that humanist theories regard individual accounts as unquestionable, leaving no room for social and environmental influences of which the person is unaware. He also feels that when they reject the naive objectivism of positivist science, humanists wrongly reject all forms of systematic or rigorous enquiry. Valentine (1992) criticizes humanism for failing to define or evaluate core concepts such as altruism. In addition, she joins others in viewing the goal of self-actualization as self-defeating, since the resultant 'human potential' movement in the USA has become a narcissistic ideology which promotes what it seeks to avoid. However, Valentine's main criticism is of humanism's origin in hermeneutic understanding, which she regards as logically circular.

Both Layder and Valentine see humanism as having played an important role in promoting subjectivity within psychology, particularly in the early stages of an investigation. However, unadulterated humanism provides an incomplete account of human experience. By contrast, pragmatism and its more recent reincarnation within social constructionism focuses on the way that ideas are used in practice and on how implicit cultural pressures are brought to bear on our actions. The main characteristic of social constructionism is the rejection of research into individual skills; it is replaced with the exploration of socially negotiated and shared understandings. Although the idea has been elaborated at various points this century, many psychologists date its recent development from Gergen's (1985) paper. In the last decade there has been substantial growth in interest and publications in the area, McNamee and Gergen (1992) probably being the constructionist text most familiar to clinicians.

The Enlightenment–Romanticism Dialogue

Understanding the tension between these two movements is not merely esoteric; it reveals the ideas that support different positions in psychology. Although contemporary thought questions the usefulness of debates that are organized around binary opposites or dichotomies, recognizing such dichotomous arguments and understanding why postmodern discourse questions them can help to clarify different positions. In turn that understanding enables practitioners to move beyond dispute to identify common ground between themselves and others.

Taylor (1989) argues that nineteenth- and twentieth-century cultures became confused about the meaning of life once religious certainties were displaced, although Romantics have always been concerned to develop spiritual aspects of life in secular ways. Richards (1997) provides historical evidence that psychology's role at the end of the nineteenth century was to replace religion in providing moral guidance to unruly students in the USA.

An alternative solution to the meaning of life can come from striving towards artistic truth, the main strategy Romantics applied to the problem. Artists have seen a considerable change in status over the past 200 years, from artisan to paradigm human being. No longer paid poorly to entertain the rich, not only is their work well paid but their modes of life are revered: biographies of artists have never been so popular. This suggests that many people seek answers to existential questions in artistic work.

It is tempting to associate Enlightenment thinking with science, and thus with cognitive and behavioural psychology, while seeing Romanticism as underpinning the arts and psychotherapy, but that is too sweeping and stultifying. As Deleuze and Guattari observe: 'Nothing positive is done, nothing at all, in the domains of either criticism or history, when we are content to brandish ready-made old concepts like skeletons intended to intimidate any creation' (1994: 83). Yet there is continuity. Taylor (1989) provides a useful analogy about the world of ideas: he considers intellectual life to be like a hard-boiled egg sliced longways, some slices rolled forwards and others back by time and culture. A cross-section through these misaligned slices represents a theory or body of work that draws on some old and some new intellectual frameworks; such a cross-section could also represent a point in time when competing frameworks at different levels of development are being simultaneously employed within any given discipline.

To return to artistic endeavour, Bartók's music may be described as Romantic because it expresses the music of a particular set of people; however, his development of new systems of rhythm and tonality, his printing on the music how long to the nearest second a piece should take to perform, and his total lack of interest in the difficulties experienced by his piano pupils clearly show the influence of Enlightenment values.[2] Freudian theory crosses the boundary between Enlightenment and Romantic thinking as well, and has acquired canonical status in a number of quarters, from literary theory to philosophy and feminism. Among constructionists there is a surprising absence of critical reflection about psychoanalysis.[3] As a major statement about subjective life it is a Romantic theory, but Freud's structured psyche and its putative universality are conceptions clearly derived from the age of reason.

Such contemporary analyses challenge the dichotomy between the Enlightenment and the Romantic movement, showing how elements of both can co-exist in one body of work. The energy that is created from debates between or combinations of two different positions can be highly productive: Davies (1996) notes that the four countries where the Renaissance flourished first were those where Catholics and Protestants co-existed. The period that followed in this century is often described as modernist. Exemplars – such as Stravinsky, T.S. Eliot, Kafka and, in psychology, William James and Jung – produced work of enormous importance and durability, but which few could understand because extensive cultural knowledge is necessary to interpret their meanings. Such intellectual elitism made them poor makers of meaning for the majority of the population. Modernism was also criticized for having failed to prevent the massacres of the two great twentieth-century wars.

More egalitarian modernism came after the second world war, from poets such as Auden and Neruda – the latter intended to create a 'poetry smelling of urine and white lilies' – and from dramatists such as Brecht who removed many of the barriers that classical theatre erected between audience and players. Influenced by such egalitarian values, mental health services developed therapeutic communities that dismantled traditional barriers between professionals and residents, while Neill's (1968) experiment at Summerhill brought these ideas into education. Bateson (1956) headed the reaction against the critical language of psychoanalysis and psychological individualism to form the basis of systemic family therapy.

Meanwhile, Enlightenment thinking fuelled first behavioural then both cognitive and cognitive-behavioural psychology. Their ahistorical search for universal rules fitted the post-war scientific *Zeitgeist* perfectly; their focus on concrete recommendations and rejection of abstraction was consistent with political moves away from elite intellectualism. Functional flow diagrams arising from these analyses lack contextual, relational and historical dimensions, while the absent psychologist was not yet regarded as a significant omission. The rift between 'artistic' and 'scientific' psychology grew apace.

Social science debate between Romantic and scientific ideas was joined first in sociology. Studies of the research process showed how 'hard' scientific research teams construct an understanding of what is permissible evidence and how it is to be recognized, challenging previous beliefs about the brilliant lone scientist who discovers facts about the world (Latour and Woolgar, 1979). Applying these ideas to psychology it became clear that a number of different social constructions were contained in its experiments. As well as the knowledge-constructing process among team members in the physical sciences, and between them and their wider scientific community, there are two further complications: the participant inevitably makes their own sense of the task, often using psychological ideas to do so, and their participation is further mediated by social exchanges between them and the researcher. This knowledge is then further constructed in textbooks. Morawski (1992, 1994) illustrates how textbooks contrive to smooth the paradox at the heart of psychology: we can only cast ourselves as knowledgeable experts by creating a separation between us and the people we study. It takes skilled writing to depict 'subjects' as confused and inefficient thinkers who are gullible or biased or in need of psychological expertise, while making first-year undergraduates feel they are members of the 'knowing experts' group.

Currently, tensions between these ideas are played out methodologically, as are most disputes in psychology. Layder (1990) and many other qualitative social scientists argue that because all human systems are open, they cannot be replicable; thus description and explanation are the only possible outcomes of human enquiry, which should draw on both quantitative and qualitative approaches. Moscovici (1993) questions the Enlightenment view of human beings as free and independent thinkers who may associate with whom they like, aligning himself with many constructionist thinkers in promoting societal influences and the interdependence of people. However, Shotter (1993) suggests that the Enlightenment's values should not be replaced but displaced: we need to make way for new ideas without losing the age of reason's concern for rigour and for the emancipation of ordinary people.

Postmodernism: Glorying in the Cacophony of the Fragmentary?

Scientific psychology is regarded by many as having excluded itself from late twentieth-century culture, donning a corset of such rigidity that it is left barely able to breathe in the new atmosphere of the approaching millennium. Some have reacted to this by moving beyond the constraints of classical psychological thinking to explore a wider agenda, incorporating sociology, philosophy, religion, literature and politics within the cultural context of postmodernism. Richards (1997) uses his history of psychology to argue that it may now be time for psychologists to re-examine the traditional opposition between their subject and religion. However, postmodernist concern to combine different ideas in different ways contains both its energy and its downfall. When postmodernism rejects the past and fragments time into a series of perpetual presents, Gergen (1994) has criticized it as Romantic anarchism: long on rhetoric but short on social transformation.

Postmodernism simultaneously eschews and incorporates elements of Romanticism while maintaining a primary focus on play, performance and participation (Brooker, 1992). Some clinicians write about postmodernism as a framework one can choose to employ as if it were any other theory (e.g. Hoffman, 1992) but this is unhelpful, since what postmodernism encapsulates is the social environment through which we all move (Lyotard, 1984).[4] We cannot choose whether or not to live in a postmodern culture, we can merely notice some of the ways it affects us and act to amplify or minimize those effects. Described as a decentring of knowledge which focuses on social heterogeneity, and on the local and practical, it questions modernist abstractions based on ideas of deep and surface structures, high and low culture.

Postmodernism is often a local and specific reaction rather than a unitary force in its own right and so it is a difficult idea to communicate. The channel-hopping adolescent's fascination with contextless images piling one upon the other gives a picture of postmodernism, random concatenation being valued as a strategy that kills the old and creates a new world. However, images may also be brought together in a more thoughtful way to present a multifaceted consideration of complex events. Paintings from a particular decade are contextualized by being presented alongside a montage of TV film showing key events of the time, interspersed by advertisements; similarly paintings of the metropolis gain added perspective by being displayed next to town plans and comments from contemporaneous writers about their experience of urban life. Postmodernism describes a rejection of modernism's search for pure, basic, central truths: bringing together many perspectives is one of its defining features.

Postmodernism questions all 'grand narratives' and major theoretical statements about the world, and also questions assumptions such as the idea that society is progressing. Debates that compare binary opposites are seen as reductionist, failing to provide the understanding which can be gained when approaching topics from non-hierarchical and multiple vantage-points. A current focus of such concern in psychology is finding ways to move beyond the Cartesian mind–body dualism which pervades our thinking.[5]

Michael (1991) suggests that three aspects of postmodern culture are particularly relevant to psychology: the accelerated turnover of ideas, the transgression of traditional boundaries and the consumption of spectacle. The accelerated turnover of ideas is clear in many branches of academic and clinical practice. The constant cloning of images and ideas makes all statements out of date as soon as they are made – a 1995 study of British government documents describing clinical audit in the NHS yielded 62 different definitions of the term[6] – while rapid global communication means that a small number of ideas acquire enormous influence. For example, course materials published by Britain's Open University had a significant influence on the design of community services in St Lucia for people with learning disabilities. One implication of this accelerated turnover of ideas is that the psychologist's role as intellectual innovator for health services has been usurped, since most staff now have rapid access to new ideas through computerized literature searches.

Accelerated turnover meant that the modernist systems of structuralists quickly spawned post-structuralism.[7] In literature this re-created interest in the text itself rather than in classifications of types of stories or interpretations of the author's intention – the so-called 'death of the author'. Post-structuralism underpins the technique of discourse analysis in increasing use in academic and clinical psychology,[8] where it is used to identify the functions of various pieces of language irrespective of any putative intentions of the author. Its main clinical applications have been to challenge diagnostic labels (Boyle, 1994b; Harper, 1994) and to deconstruct power within multidisciplinary meetings (Marks, 1992).

Meanwhile, feminist critiques shifted agendas in many fields of enquiry. For example, although the rewriting of history by representatives of totalitarian states had been widely criticized, feminist historians argued that accounts should be revised to include the women whose lives had been ignored. With such rapid transformation in values, distinguishing principled histories from inappropriately politicized ones is far from easy: it rests in part on some demonstration of integrity through the inclusion of all relevant sources. As long as revisions are not merely based on sources that fit particular biases, then reinterpreting the past makes a major contribution to societal change. It also demonstrates how rapidly ideas we regard as foundational can be overturned.

The accelerated turnover of ideas seen in manufacturing industry, where customers are manipulated by techniques such as product differentiation (different nappies for boys and girls), can also be detected in the proliferation of therapies for marginally different types of problem. Just as there seem to be different natural remedies for every specific complaint, where pains in the big toe joint seem to need a different unction from pains in the thumb joint, so books about psychological treatment of specific conditions emerge. Bold claims about newness and differentness are made but the same set of ideas is often recycled, with very minor alterations and with little context. Clinicians with no interest in history or context have no way to distinguish or evaluate these proliferating therapies.

Boundary transgression is Michael's second aspect of postmodern culture: Foucault's work at the interface of history, psychology and philosophy is an influential example illustrated by Rabinow (1984). Used effectively it creates synergy between ideas or positions to the benefit of each: examples include joining the perspectives of psychiatry and psycholinguistics (Leudar et al., 1987), or articulating ideas from Russian and American developmental psychologies (Valsiner, 1987). Nevertheless it has disadvantages. Researchers have to master twice as much material, and evaluators need to have much more knowledge themselves before they can discuss or critique it. The supposed creativity of postmodernism can be merely the playground of incompetence: anyone who has sat through amateurish attempts to incorporate graphic design, film and music into academic conference presentations knows this only too vividly.

The iconoclastic nature of boundary transgressions inevitably brings power struggle into debates about knowledge. One aspect of such skirmishes is played out in debates about how to carry out debate, and about how to recognize valuable work: many people argue that change will not occur if they tamely accept the language and metaphors that structure the status quo. Thus feminists, disability activists and people writing about gender and ethnicity challenge the words people use and the texts that are accepted as contributing to academic debate. Some of these challenges are carried out originally and elegantly; others descend into polemic from which little light emerges.[9]

Michael's third point about postmodern psychology concerns the consumption of spectacle. Perhaps 'moral panic' about the satanic abuse of children and people with learning disabilities had its roots in spectacle. The current moral panic appears to concern both children and adults who behave in anti-social ways: society does not believe that the police can stop criminals from committing crimes, but does hope that professional services and therapists can stop disturbed people from disturbing them. Miller (1996) discusses the way that not only the media but professionals are fascinated by tales of misdeeds, yet show little interest in hearing about interventions that produce positive change. When problems occur they are clearly laid at some individual's door. When problems disappear, it seems that in Britain at least most professionals attribute this to whim, 'it just happened', showing no interest in their colleagues' efforts at all.

Baudrillard's (1988) view that culture is divorced from reality and exists in hyperreality – that is, in media images and computer communications – makes a similar point, since many extreme spectacles are film images rather than lived experiences. Terms like hyperreality can feel like ideas that are only important to computer enthusiasts, with little bearing on the complex world of clinical practice. But Baudrillard argues that high-profile scandals such as Watergate were themselves fabrications which served rhetorical-political purposes by injecting a sense of political morality into that culture. He argues that power is exercised in pre-scripted scenarios such as the Watergate trial, rarely in real events. Harvey's description of Reagonomics as economics with mirrors is another vivid illustration:

> A sketch on the back of a napkin by a little-known economist called Laffer purported to show that tax cuts were bound to increase tax yields (at least up to a certain point) because they stimulated growth. . . . So was the economic policy of the Reagan years to be justified . . . even though it brought the United States several steps closer to international bankruptcy and fiscal ruin. The strange and puzzling thing is that such a simplistic idea could gain the purchase it did and seem to work so well politically for so long. Even stranger, is the fact that Reagan was re-elected when all the polls showed that the majority of the US electorate (to say nothing of the majority of eligible voters, who did not vote) disagreed fundamentally with him on almost all major issues. . . . Strangest of all is how such a President could leave office riding so high on the wave of public affection, even though more than a dozen senior members of his administration had been found guilty of serious infringement of legal procedures and blatant disregard for ethical principles. *The triumph of aesthetics over ethics could not be plainer*. . . . A tough but warm, avuncular, and well-meaning person who had an abiding faith in the greatness and goodness of America, built an aura of charismatic politics. Carey McWilliams . . . described it as the 'friendly face of fascism'. (1989: 328–9, emphasis added)

What has this to do with clinicians? It provides a perspective on the new culture of health services, where government will is communicated by images and rhetoric. Where auditors publicize examples of waste but give less prominence to the cost of carrying out those audits, even though in the UK the Audit Commission's administrative costs were reported to have increased at three times the rate of inflation in 1994–5.[10] It is communicated by the focus of enquiries. In the 1970s and early 1980s British committees of enquiry into health and social services concerned the failings of hospitals or other organizations; by the 1990s virtually all concerned the mismanagement of individuals by individual clinicians (the enquiry into Ashworth Hospital (DoH, 1992) being a notable exception). In many ways this hyperreality runs in parallel to service delivery and has little direct impact on real exchanges between clients and professionals nor the development of new ways to understand and explain human distress. However, increasing systems of scrutiny, inspection and risk management create a blame culture which has very real consequences on the well-being of staff (Schaefer and Moos, 1993).

Postmodernism may be summed up as an intellectual environment which is alternately confusing and creative. Full of energy and new ideas, problems arise because the criteria for evaluating them are unstable. It is a reaction, a transitional state within which we are currently positioned. Where there are new ideas, postmodern disdain for the author produces real dangers. An example is Epston and White's (1989) treatment of problems by externalizing the symptoms: it is frequently divorced from the reasoning of the originators, so that therapists with little or no understanding of the thinking behind the treatment have heard that the latest treatment for encopresis concerns talking about 'sneaky poo' with the family. Authors have no control over such decontextualization of their ideas, and can only point out the dangers: that externalizing the symptom is one possible treatment for a variety of family problems, not necessarily appropriate for all cases of encopresis nor limited to it; that it needs to be accompanied by many other moves associated with family therapy such as avoidance of scapegoating, striving to create alliances with all members, and so on; and that a treatment such as externalizing could be unethical if there is a possibility of abuse within the clinical picture. This demonstrates Shotter's point, that in questioning the role of Enlightenment rationalism we need to beware of throwing out rigorous thinking and respect for participants in the process.

Harvey (1989) suggests that postmodernism's unreal mirror has cracks in it, cracks which make it possible to move beyond the postmodern era in four ways: by focusing on becoming rather than being, seeking unity within difference, challenging image-making with narrative, and confronting the aesthetics of style with ethics. The rest of this chapter brings these issues home in two ways: by examining two controversial interventions to clarify how aspects of postmodern thinking have unnecessarily muddied the debates, and by exploring some emerging topics that could underpin a new agenda for practice.

Clinical Practice in Context

Clinical psychologists in training often complain of being overwhelmed by new theories and interventions which all seem to carry equal weight. When there are few agreed concepts or approaches that help them to make sense of the rapid expansion in ideas, people run the risk of being swayed by the next ideology to be promulgated by charismatic workshop leaders. I will describe two clinical interventions with people who have a learning disability to show how postmodern clinical practice means that creative and potentially interesting ideas appear, but that sometimes they get overwhelmed by excessive boundary transgression and contemporary confusions.

Gentle Teaching

Gentle Teaching (McGee et al., 1987) blends a number of different ontologies and perspectives and so it is a difficult position to assess: its primary claim to be a non-behavioural approach has been challenged frequently. Gentle Teaching is a good example of the way that accelerated turnover of ideas in clinical practice makes it very difficult to evaluate the worth of any of them as they combine and recombine. It has been promulgated in Britain largely through workshops. These are often held in hospitals with the injunction to 'bring out your worst' so that the charismatic hero-innovator can demonstrate how to work with the most shocking and difficult clients. Successes are videotaped. The consumption of spectacle was never clearer: criticisms of the hero-innovator model of organizational change seem to have been forgotten. The consumption of spectacle has also been involved in rhetoric surrounding Gentle Teaching, which has not been slow to imply that it offers hope in circumstances where carers have been driven to control people through brutal care practices.

Some clinicians accept Gentle Teaching ideas from these workshops rather than from critical reading. Perhaps their naivety about the financial imperatives operating on workshop leaders are understandable given professional desperation to find ways to work with people who are destructive and aggressive. Nevertheless, 'whose interests does this serve?' is a useful question Foucault urged us to pose when trying to identify implicit power issues, such as those that underlie interventions lacking the warrant provided by systematic research evaluations.

Behaviourists such as Jones and Connell (1993) describe Gentle Teaching's advice to block, ignore and redirect aggressive or destructive actions as constructional behaviourism revisited. McGee et al.'s assumption that all persons are the same, and thus that staff should apply the same rules of conduct to all of the clients they work with, is also an expression of the basic positivist philosophy which supports behaviourism. Apparently there is no necessity to adjust one's approach according to any specific difficulties the person may experience: for example, the autistic phenomena of being overwhelmed by touch or confused by extensive demands from other people are not thought to be relevant. Nor apparently does one need to know anything about visual impairment before using Gentle Teaching with somebody who has little or no sight.

Casual misuse of the attachment theory concept of 'bonding' by using it outside its intellectual context exemplifies boundary transgression. The suggestion that initial intensive contact between a careworker and an avoidant client will necessarily result in any sort of emotional connection must be challenged. Gentle Teaching recommends that such a bond is developed by holding sessions which last continuously for two hours on first meeting and are repeated in intensive teaching sessions during the next five to 10 days. Following the person's interests and choices is recommended so long as their choice does not include moving away from the teacher, this not being an option: it is assumed that the person has to be taught the value of human presence and that staff are entitled to teach this. Thus while the approach gives a high profile to the development of an ethical stance or posture towards the individual, eschewing punitive techniques because they compromise client–caregiver communication, their ethical thinking does not extend to this policy of imposition.

Jones and Connell (1993) question whether Gentle Teaching has created 'much ado about nothing'. It rode on the tide of an idea whose time had come, the movement to create non-aversive behavioural interventions.[11] They suggest that Gentle Teaching's most important contribution may not be to change the clients but to humanize a social environment that brutalizes clients and carers alike. Perhaps staff find it easier to face the intractable actions of their clients when they feel they are doing as much as possible to accept the clients as human.

Facilitated Communication

Facilitated Communication is another intervention focused on relationship-building which has generated debate.[12] Basically this involves a facilitator devoting many hours a week to create a relationship with a person, with the intention of supporting their communication both physically and emotionally. However, there is no suggestion of overriding the client's wishes in this approach.

The most commonly discussed version of Facilitated Communication concerns supporting the weight of someone's hand while they direct it themselves towards letters on a computer keyboard. For example, Carol is a woman described as having a profound learning disability who seemed to discriminate neither shape, colour nor sounds; yet apparently through facilitation she became able to analyse speech into its component letters and type it onto a keyboard. This strategy seems likely to be most helpful to people whose cerebral palsy or other motor disorder affects their ability to control movement; it may assist people whose emotional problems include difficulty initiating action, as occurs in some people with autism. However, boundary transgression encourages people to take ideas out of context and to use them uncritically. Developed in education with severely autistic children, Facilitated Communication's rapid application to people of all ages and types of learning disability has presented major difficulties to investigations into its efficacy.

Moreover, Facilitated Communication's rhetoric shows elements of an ideology, not merely an intervention on which one can draw. When Emerson (1994) described Carol's progress and was asked where her proficiency in written language could have been acquired, she suggested that perhaps Carol had learned by reading the road signs which she passed each day. Surely only believers can take such an assertion seriously – and 'believers' is the rather revelatory term that Emerson and some other exponents of Facilitated Communication use, generally by presenting and publishing in non-academic environments. Since cult-like ideologies inhibit if not prevent dialogue with other perspectives, it becomes difficult to explore the benefits and limits of this approach.

Three tensions present in current clinical practice are being played out on the site of Facilitated Communication, one methodological the other two political. The apparent methodological dispute is between quantitative and qualitative approaches to human research. Claiming that people with disabilities will not respond to being tested, exponents argue that experimental evaluations of the technique wrongly suggest that clients are unable to communicate. Experimentalists counter that since none of the messages make sense when the facilitating non-disabled person is blind to the question, a safer assumption is that helpers are influencing the communication, however unconsciously. Exponents feel that Facilitated Communication works and that experimental science fails them and their clients. Stale debates then exchange incompatible 'evidence' arising from a dichotomy which, when expressed this way, is unresolvable. Thus Jacobson et al. wrote on behalf of the American Psychological Association's science working group on Facilitated Communication:

> Since its introduction in the United States only five years ago, FC has become the eye of a growing storm of controversy. . . . Is the facilitator unwittingly selecting the letters that spell out the message? Or, is it true that FC can unlock hidden intellectual competence and reveal a massive misunderstanding of human potential . . . ?
>
> More confounding, however, is that, in the absence of scientific evidence of its validity and effectiveness . . . and in the face of objective research findings clearly identifying widespread, systematic facilitator control of typed content, FC has become ubiquitous in special education and adult services for people with developmental disabilities . . . FC serves as a case study in how public and, alarmingly, some professionals, fail to recognize the role of science in distinguishing truth from falsity and its applicability to assessing the value of treatment modalities. (1995: 750–1)

Strong language, showing great faith in scientific method as the sole pathway to truth. Yet political tensions mount, arising from the complex difficulty of who is the client: the individual with learning disabilities or their family? Facilitated Communication plays an important role in providing people with learning disabilities with an independent voice, if it can be said to be their voice, and so was likely to become a focus of concern for families whose own voice was disempowered by Facilitated Communication. The dispute reached a higher pitch when Facilitated Communication got embroiled in controversies about that most spectacular of 1990s clinical concerns, disclosure of sexual abuse, creating a critical issue about who was the author of such a disclosure.

Claim and counter-claim led some parents to demand that Facilitated Communication be banned. Jacobson et al. (1995) report that of five dozen allegations of sexual abuse made through Facilitated Communication in the USA, only two proceeded to trial: they do not give comparative figures for the probability of successfully prosecuting a carer for sexual abuse against somebody with a learning disability who can speak, but they are likely to be very similar. People with a learning disability tend to make very poor witnesses: it is not necessarily Facilitated Communication that is on trial with these figures. Nevertheless, exponents argue that poor technique is responsible for questionable disclosures, a problem which can be solved by restricting its use – in other words by professionalizing – thereby crystallizing the second political dimension, that of the huge resource implications of Facilitated Communication.

The Facilitated Communication debate has focused on sexual abuse, ignoring the legal dictum that hard cases make bad law. What this obscures is that both exponents and opponents are attempting to legislate on mutual interdependence and interpretation, essential components of all human experience for which little legislation can or should exist. There are parallels with therapeutic relationships, where ethical practice needs to be to the fore and consideration needs to be given to protecting people who feel they hold the weak position within such relationships, but such oversight generally comes from the organization and from therapeutic supervision, not from legislation. While one hears reports of certain states in the USA outlawing behaviour modification, it seems unlikely that all attempts to influence the behaviour of others by responding warmly, by ignoring them or by shaping their behaviour towards different goals has been stopped by the passage of such statutes. Attempting to determine what appropriate communication is for the majority, by extrapolating from legal concerns about exceptional situations, is the wrong direction to take.

Disputes about both Gentle Teaching and Facilitated Communication mask a vitally important issue: both interventions are starting to conceptualize interdependence and challenge Western assumptions of autonomy and individual selfhood. These are issues of fundamental concern to many social constructionists, and practitioners should be contributing to the debate. It will be unfortunate if the postmodern cacophony surrounding both techniques turns the joint agency that people with disabilities need into a problem. Most people who come into contact with human services have problems associated with a paucity rather than a surfeit of relationships and communication, and what is needed is greater clarity about ways to address their isolation. Clinical psychologists should be working to clarify what these interventions are doing and why there is such a diversity of views in Britain and the USA. It will be useful to draw more extensively on the European literature summarized by Dosen (1993) where there seem to be far fewer concerns about the concept of joint agency.

Conclusion: Emerging Themes

Working in postmodern culture requires us to be alert, so that we can create new ways to harness chaos productively while challenging the tendency towards fragmentation and incoherence. Keeping the transitional nature of this culture in focus will also be useful, since it reacts to the past with little forward movement. The choices we make as intellectuals and clinicians will contribute to the closure of postmodern culture and the development of a new cultural plane.

Living and working in a series of perpetual presents has been a powerful postmodern theme. In clinical practice this is seen most clearly in minimal history-taking and sometimes a refusal to explore the background at all, justified as rejection of the medical model. Perhaps the relative unpopularity of attachment theory as a conceptual base was influenced not only by feminist readings but also by its strong emphasis on history. Yet clinical intervention is oriented towards change, and so it demands a time-frame which includes past, present and future experience. And although clinical research is rarely longitudinal, much of the most influential work does include the fourth dimension – time – in prospective studies. Harvey's suggestion that one of the cracks in the mirror of postmodernism is a shift in focus from 'being' to 'becoming' is an important issue.

Narratives challenge the snapshot postmodern world of images. Sharing them with others is a powerful way to generate understanding and commitment. Stories are spun out in time and require a move beyond the present; they can challenge images made from concatenations of events and provide a different measure. There is growing interest in narrative forms as vehicles for therapeutic discussion and the creation of personal change, rendering traumatic events less terrifying and evolving a degree of control for their victims. Disability services increasingly focus on narrative histories as ways to change the present and understand the future, since people may not be able to comprehend the emotions evoked by the death of a close relative without some understanding of their own life-span.

Many clinicians acknowledge variable modes of human agency by working at multiple points in society and striving to include a political dimension in their work.[13] The 'KIDS' project (Dale, 1992) moved outside standard models of service to create a resource centre for children with special needs, their parents and their siblings, intended to empower families by offering a range of choices. Similarly Holland's (1988) combination of individual psychotherapy, awareness-raising, peer-counselling and neighbourhood action in an estate-wide project has already been described as a seminal example of community psychology (see p. 10). When considering the difficulties experienced by one individual, consensus-building discussions about what is the problem, in how many people does it partially reside, and what intervention would make the most sense to the people asking for help may be the crux of many clinical interventions.

Postmodernism's emphasis on multiple understanding may be its most important contribution to the comprehension of clinical problems. By moving away from stages and linear hierarchies to encompass multimodal phenomena and multiple routes towards similar ends, practitioners can reconsider concepts of change and development. However, the problem of multiple approaches is that they tend to fragment so that one can no longer grasp any event or phenomenon. A current example is that of the rapidly changing conceptions of community and culture. We are becoming more conscious of diversity amongst the different social groups, and within them of the changing identities constructed by first-, second- and third generation immigrants; but much of this raises an implicit challenge to community care assumptions developed during the 1980s. Harvey's suggestion that we should strive to identify unity amongst diversity is one theme which should focus thinking about clinical practice in community settings.

The last major theme to emerge from the cracks in postmodernism is the necessity to promote ethics. This is essential to support the turn towards subjectivity and joint agency while acknowledging the interference with knowledge-creation against which Enlightenment thinkers fought. To use Shotter's (1993) phrase, the issue can become one of power, of 'who shall live in whose reality?' Caring is not a simple matter: routines can become punitive and carers' and parents' needs can become destructively enmeshed with those of the identified client. Professionals can lose the ability to deal with all parties ethically, prioritizing the client while scapegoating parents or staff. Senior clinicians will sooner or later find that their organizational responsibilities conflict with the needs of a particular client. Taylor argues that pluralism becomes untenable when tracing moral issues through to their conclusion. Safeguards need to be built into services, and professionals need to find ways to construct and review their own ethical frameworks.

Nevertheless, we do need to keep a weather eye on the political agenda. As social scientists fret over metaphysics and measurement error (is there a juvenile crime problem or was it created by the research that the Reagan–Thatcher governments were willing to fund? See Griffin, 1993), there is growing concern that divided intellectuals give governments licence to do as they please. If we are to succeed in changing the relationship between psychologist and client, to emancipate and contextualize rather than to individualize and dominate, then clinicians need a strong political voice, not a fragmented one.

Summary

The *contemporary issue* explored in this chapter concerned a positivist political climate in which clinical services operate: here facts are assumed to be unproblematic, individualism is the most important level of analysis and professionals practise within a culture where blame and the threat of legal proceedings grows ever larger. It is a culture that operates in hyperreality, that is, through impressions communicated via the media rather than through reason or logic. This occurs in an intellectual climate where there is considerable chaos and creativity, accompanied by questioning how to establish truths that are accepted as such within this community at this moment. The context is difficult to pin down because it contains all the virtues and vagaries of the postmodern culture that we all inhabit, but it has a number of recognizable elements. These are that play, participation and performance are as important as conceptualization; that the conjunction of multiple perspectives gives a closer approximation to human experience than the identification of single, core concepts or theories; and that postmodern culture is characterized by the accelerated turnover of ideas, the transgression of boundaries, and the consumption of spectacle.

Contemporary culture was discussed by drawing a *history of the present* where differences between the Enlightenment and the Romantic periods were sketched to reveal tensions inherent in postmodern culture. Many modern and postmodern thinkers have combined aspects of both periods during the twentieth century, but recognizing the origin of the various positions can provide clarification. There continue to be groups who defend poles of binary oppositions such as science/art, but it was argued that social science will benefit most from researchers and practitioners who accept that both the creative imagination and rigorous method are necessary: the imagination to take us beyond what is currently known into new planes of activity, rigorous methods helping us to minimize bias and selectivity.

The limitations of postmodern montages were emphasized: this is an arena where *critical thinking* is crucial, otherwise incompatible ideas can be thrown together in the play of incompetence. Bringing many ideas together requires that we are familiar with them all and with their contexts of meaning – a tall order. Limiting the number of planes of understanding being sampled is one way to ensure that ideas are not just tossed together in meaningless heaps. The ideas of cultural commentators who suggest ways to bring postmodern culture towards closure, and identify means to counter its worst effects, were also reviewed. Most important of these are the insertion of time into fragmented postmodern accounts, so that there is a focus on becoming and narrative rather than image-broking; pushing beyond the celebration of difference to identify areas of unity, doing so without recourse to previous impositions of power that silenced voices; and confronting the aesthetics of style with ethics.

Critical thinking helps to identify the *human systems* impacting on both Gentle Teaching and Facilitated Communication, making them controversial interventions at the moment. It also enables us to go beyond the specifics of those disputes to see that both could make a useful contribution to the development of interventions based on *intersubjective meanings*, techniques that clinicians need urgently if individualism is to give way to socially constructed approaches to practice.

Notes

1 This section is based primarily on Taylor's (1989) seminal history, *Sources of the Self*, leavened by consideration of Shotter's (1993) ideas. Music and painting are the primary illustrations used although many other approaches would have been equally appropriate.

2 Gillies, M. (1990) *Bartók Remembered.* London: Faber and Faber.

3 People whose use of Freudian ideas influences constructionists include Lacan

and feminists such as Kristeva and Grosz. Some psychologists refer to the psyche as if it is an understood and undisputed concept amongst constructionists (see Faulconer and Williams, 1990).

4 His book *The Postmodern Condition: A Report on Knowledge* was translated into English at that time. Extracts and discussion of Lyotard and other writers on this subject are contained in Brooker's (1992).

5 The group of authors whose productions go under the jokey pseudonym 'Beryl Curt' (1994) have been working to integrate or enfold (to use Bohm's ideas, outlined in Chapter 2) mind and body into a new psychological agenda. Nevertheless, constructionists such as Sampson (1996) admit to finding it very difficult to move beyond this dichotomy. Perhaps we expect too much. Deleuze and Guattari describe every immanent plane of understanding as holed, letting through the fogs which surround it. Thus each new immanent plane must constantly reconstitute the chaos it had to ward off, just as to think about reflexivity begs the question of who is the subject of this reflection at the same time as the question is seen to be unanswerable.

6 Reported at Forging Ahead, a national audit office conference held in Sheffield in 1995.

7 Most commonly associated with Derrida: see Eagleton (1983) for a description of this and other movements.

8 The technique was described by Potter and Wetherall in 1987.

9 Burman's (1994) recent attack on Bowlby and attachment theory is but one example. Claiming that Bowlby's work 'Naturalises class and cultural privilege' (p. 85), she perceives the constant contact between mother and child valued by early attachment workers as a sexist plot. Yet by criticizing a 1950s statement of a theory by 1990s standards, to such a degree that very few 1950s theories would withstand her scrutiny, Burman's critique loses enormous force; in addition it ignores the degree to which mother–child interdependence is valued by many women, for example those of Asian origin, and thus her critique itself expresses the perspective of the white middle-class majority.

The really notable feature of critiques such as this, often based on theories used and developed by clinicians, is the anachronistic focus on original statements. There is no reflection on the sociocultural context of the time, nor interest in more recent developments and expositions.

10 Reported in the *Guardian* newspaper, 24 August 1995.

11 See for example LaVigna and Donnellan (1986).

12 See Biklen (1990) for a positive statement; Wheeler et al. (1993), for the 'anti' position derived from experimental psychology; and a review of the full debate in a set of articles edited by Taylor (1994).

13 This is reviewed in detail in Clegg (1993).

4 Past Events in Present Time

> In the Iranian religious centre of Qom, during the last years of the Shah, the clocks were resolutely set at a different time from that observed in the rest of the country. Qom hours were holy, and the years were naturally counted on the Islamic calendar. The devout of Qom were on God's time, as calculated by religious men, while the Shah and his government inhabited a dubious time zone ruled from Greenwich and a calendar devised by Christians. A third calendar, based on Iranian imperial history, also did battle for the possession of time.
>
> Iran in those days showed particularly clearly the political and cultural importance of time. The question of who owns time, who defines it, lays down its uses and qualities, and distributes it to human beings is fundamental. Fundamental, but not easy to debate because ideas of time are so often taken for granted.[1]

Some postmodernists say we live in ahistorical times. 'Year Zero' has become a favoured term amongst management consultants who focus on present and future actions, the origin of ideas and practices apparently having no bearing on current concerns. Most behavioural and cognitive-behavioural psychologists take a similar stance,[2] developing interventions from functional analyses or accounts of the immediate content of thought: current strategies to address current problems.

The perfunctory interest in historical matters taken by psychologists is consistent with this trend. Although its history is regularly taught to undergraduates, this rarely extends beyond teaching to include the serious business of doctoral research and journal publications. Introductions to research papers superficially acknowledge the contribution that past ideas make to current concepts, but generally these are shallow in both time and domain. They cite few studies older than the previous decade, pressure on journal space ensuring that only a narrow range of the relevant literature is discussed.

An implicit ideology that psychological science is rationally evolving and history only reveals irrelevant and defunct ideas means that courses on the history of psychology can only 'retrace the steps by which the pinnacle of the present was reached' (Danziger, 1994: 469). Psychologists who study their history are usually limited to public relations, writing 'ceremonial' chapters in introductory textbooks while making no real contribution to the subject. Danziger contrasts the situation in psychology with two examples, physics and economics. Physicists take scant interest in history, leaving it to be studied by professional historians in separate departments for the history of science. This results in a high standard of historical research, which is ignored by the practising physicists who could use the information most effectively. By contrast economics is ignored by history of science departments, its history being actively studied by specialists from within the discipline.

In concluding that history in the human sciences should follow the lead of economics rather than physics, Danziger describes the way that the subject matter itself changes. There are two major forces shaping psychology: previous studies that influence our understanding of our own experience, and changing technological and cultural values. These can be seen in current memory research, where the phenomenon studied has as much resemblance to that which Ebbinghaus (1885, discussed in Richards, 1996) studied as does the conceptual child conjured by Freud and Bruner (1990) respectively. Ideas and terms from previous research colour the understanding of remembering and recall on which participants draw; they were taught by teachers whose educational practices were influenced by that same knowledge; and they were brought up in a culture that is ceasing to value memorized facts, since pocket calculators and computers reduce our dependence on a somewhat fallible rote memory. The net result is less use of this ability and less observation of it as a skill, a personal and cultural experience of remembering very different from that experienced by people a century ago. Psychologists need to keep all these changes in mind when comparing and combining the results of research studies with different cohorts.

Postmodern fragmentation and the waning of North America's dominant influence on psychology increase complexity and generate ever-multiplying positions and perspectives. Yet we continue to discuss these in terms of traditional antagonisms between different psychological groups – psychodynamic versus behavioural, realist versus relativist, more recently qualitative versus quantitative – which draw on a dichotomous approach to argument. This in turn derives from traditional metaphysical assumptions, which remain implicit in psychological discussion. As was outlined in the last chapter, twentieth-century thinkers such as Deleuze and Guattari have created and refined alternative philosophies which branch in a number of directions instead of being limited to binary oppositions. The subject of psychology has been decentred, distributed across many conceptual planes of understanding.

Conceptual revolutions are difficult to understand from a contemporary stance alone. Clinical psychologists confused by too many competing ideas are likely to continue to be antagonistic towards alternative positions, stultifying debate. Danziger argues that historical knowledge helps to create cohesiveness out of all these schools of thought, a position endorsed by Jahoda (1992). History helps us to see where our central assumptions came from, so it enables us to ask whether those conditions still hold. Perhaps more important is its ability to engender a broad appreciation of issues, to contain fragmentation without stifling change. Adopting a historical perspective on practice provides much-needed integration to balance the fertile but chaotic forces of postmodernism.

This chapter considers what history is and how to distinguish competent from incompetent versions, and explores the conceptual moves necessary to work with a relativistic approach to past experience rather than remaining driven by Newtonian clock-time. The main clinical section uses these ideas to discuss how recasting the way psychologists consider past human experience and remembering can affect practice.

Constructing a History

Recent changes in learning disability services started in the USA when reforming projects such as Kennedy's Head Start were introduced in 1965 to interrupt cycles of disadvantage.[3] *Blatt and Kaplan's photographic essay 'Christmas in Purgatory' made a crucial contribution to creating a demand for change by displaying shameful institutional conditions in a national photographic magazine, and in a limited-edition book distributed free to influential people.*[4] *During the 1970s numerous official enquiries into the iniquitous living and working conditions concealed in institutions for people with learning disabilities in Britain*[5] *and the USA*[6] *confirmed the widespread nature of the problems illustrated by those photographs.*

Britain responded with two major initiatives. It established a pilot project – NIMROD – which introduced community care to Wales, a principality of approximately 2.5 million people; and the National Development Group (NDG) and the National Development Team (NDT) were established to support change throughout the country. The NDG was a policy-making body, publishing a series of reports and pamphlets. The NDT was an inspectorate drawn from a pool of health service professionals which visited services on invitation, providing reports which described how that service could change to attain the ideals laid out by the NDG.

The 1980s in Britain and the USA were characterized by the growth of psychosocial approaches to learning disability, fostered by the Scandinavian principle of normalization. Forward-looking rather than retrospective review meetings became the forum for planning client care, in an atmosphere of risk-taking rather than paternalism. Rapid service change away from congregate care to small community homes was simultaneously heady and de-skilling. The revolution necessary to create new services swept previous patterns of intervention before it. Countless hours were consumed drawing up operational policies which stated how community teams would work. Costs spiralled and policies shifted towards cash control, away from the previous focus on creating change in the lives of disadvantaged people. Funding was withdrawn from the NDG, leaving the NDT beached as a policy-implementing group receiving no intellectual renewal.

The 1990s have become dominated by 'rights'. However, concern to meet the rights of clients, carers and staff has created an associated growth in fear of legal proceedings. Community development projects stagnate and the pace of managerial change increases. Cost-benefit analysis and later risk analysis were transplanted from their business origins into the foreign soil of professional care. Administrative costs continued to spiral and opportunities for staff to learn new ways to work with clients disappeared. Instead professionals struggled to meet the requirements of European legislation, for example about back care for staff, while trying to make sense of quality initiatives and computerized databases. Managers set targets based on business standards for quality of service delivery, even though achieving BS5750 was estimated in 1994 to cost an average-sized service £14,000 to introduce and £3,000 a year to maintain.[7] It also increases bureaucracy and paperwork significantly, yet is introduced to services at the same time as an accompanying demand for annual 'efficiency' savings. The all-singing all-dancing information systems that will resolve all these problems seem to be constantly shelved until the next financial year.

The fragmentation of district health authority services into a number of NHS Trusts contributed to low morale in small professions such as clinical psychology. Absenteeism was rumoured to be met with crass management initiatives, such as introducing a local lottery and giving staff who had been at work all week one free entry. The story is probably apocryphal, but its rapid transmission highlights the increasing gulf developing between managers and health workers.

Brief historical sketches such as the one I have assembled are common in psychology, superficially respectable because the events selected are chronologically ordered and referenced. Clinical psychologists who have been involved in British services for the last 20 years would probably agree with most of it, none with all. It is certainly not a celebratory history; indeed it fails to record enormous improvements in living and working conditions that some clients and staff experienced. Nevertheless, it is flawed.

The account is primarily the view of a psychologist, coloured by professional agendas and fears. The threat to livelihoods faced by 1990s nurses and social workers in Britain who were exhorted to start their own businesses is ignored. It shifts across various levels of analysis: geographically between Britain and the USA with a brief mention of Scandinavia; intellectually between the research agenda and the academy one moment, changes in professional practice the next. The dilemmas of parents, who depend on endlessly changing services barely comprehended by the staff employed to run them, are ignored.[8] There is little political or financial context-setting nor amplification of the intellectual climate, although both have been profoundly affected by Britain's developing relationships within the European Community.[9]

Clearly, listing the key events which come to mind and placing them in chronological sequence does not make a history. Creating a convincing account requires a method and systematic exploration of a manageable topic. Berrios (1995a) describes a range of different historical approaches relevant to clinical services:

biographical
narrative

anthropological
sociopolitical
institutional
conceptual
iconographic

He argues that most histories of mental health and learning disabilities tend to focus on the biographical and the institutional – Trent's *Inventing the Feeble Mind* being a recent example of the latter – while Berrios advocates conceptual or semantic histories as more fertile.[10] An example is his history of the term 'hallucination' within psychiatry, which expanded beyond the visual to describe disturbances in any sense modality at a particular point in psychiatry's development.

All historical methods adopt either an internal or an external stance towards the topic at hand. An external stance assumes that histories can be written by an uninvolved, outside observer whose objectivity is assured. An internal stance assumes that all people, participants and researchers, change and are changed by observation and measurement.[11] In the latter view, just as a cool thermometer put into hot liquid to measure its temperature will affect the liquid by cooling it slightly and be affected itself by being warmed, so a historian may find her views changed by the information she encounters while carrying out historical research. Another historian may effectively create history by seeking out and archiving information not otherwise available, for example researchers who obtain oral histories by interviewing ordinary people: the resultant histories tend to differ from those that emerge from the study of official documents.

These different approaches to history can be used to develop a critique of my historical sketch. The account was not merely biographical but autobiographical, in that the time-span selected runs from a little before I took up employment and continues through each of the decades I have worked. Yet if we ask whether my professional career is sufficiently important to justify its use to structure an account, the answer would probably be negative. Furthermore, the account blurs this questionable autobiographical structure with sociopolitical, institutional and conceptual influences, doing justice to none of these approaches.

Of course history itself is no longer regarded as a monolith whose methods and narratives are unproblematic. Many accounts are criticized for reproducing gender, class and colonial power imbalances. Past historians are also criticized for their documentation of military and governmental power, expressed through laws and restrictions. Until recently they ignored power that operates through institutional structures, such as the assertion of medical hegemony through doctors' legal responsibilities. They also failed to identify powers that operate through the desires they inspire in people, however that is achieved, rather than by the actions they forbid.[12]

Berrios warns that blurring different methods or stances within one study results in a confused account of past events which is incoherent and unreliable. His conventionally modernist recommendation that histories should not blur genres is disputed by postmodernists, who argue that mixing different perspectives results in a closer representation of human experience. However, judicious combination is not the same as blurring: histories should be formed from coherent themes whose integration complements the focus of the account.

Problems arise when the topic of interest is the forum for incompetent information-gathering, where any mixture of methods will do: then the account must fail. As was observed in the last chapter, postmodern accounts of the 'multiverse' can be exciting and synergistic but they can also be the playground of the incompetent. Blending different perspectives doubles or triples the work required. Foucault's research has made a significant impact on social science[13] – as it did earlier on history and philosophy – because he was able to master enough of these three subjects to write and lecture on them all, an achievement few of us can match.

Blackman's (1994) description of Foucauldian research criticizes the idea of history as a monolithic backdrop; she prefers histories of the present to occupy a central position in all enquiry. Blackman recommends Foucault's 'archaeological' approach which she summarizes; this is not a method as such, rather an exposition of three analytic tools. The first explores why certain topics emerge as priorities for social and governmental concern at particular times; it may also describe the way these objects of study are made 'other' by being specified, differentiated or classified. Common objects of concern are the family, crime, or how to ensure adequate care for children born to people who are seriously disabled or disadvantaged. Boyle's concluding comments in her history of women's sexuality illustrate this well:

> The presentation of the professional literature on sexual problems involves the assumption – both explicitly and implicitly – that sexual 'dysfunctions' are scientific rather than social constructions . . . in terms of its individualistic and pathologizing theoretical framework, the professional literature helps to remove sexual complaints from their wider cultural context; in terms of the content and language of its classification systems, and the conduct and goals of its interventions, the literature can be seen to reflect traditional views of appropriate sexual conduct and may serve as one means of reproducing traditional gender relationships. (1994a: 116–17)

Foucault's second analytic tool examines how concepts used in research about these objects of study originate, suggesting that at certain points of social and intellectual convergence particular concepts acquire strength and gain widespread acceptance. Hacking (1995) argues that the elision of child abuse and child sexual abuse into one umbrella term is such a convergence, extending emotional responses to incest to a much wider set of cruel but arguably less abhorrent acts. The final tool of Foucauldian archaeology investigates strategies of regulation. Blackman describes this as going beyond the deconstruction of power to research the internal relations between objects of study and society.[14] She suggests that the strategy of regulation underpinning clinical psychology and psychiatry is an implicit valuing of the free, autonomous individual. People who fail to conform to this condition for full societal membership are subject to treatments or exhortations to transform themselves into the sort of person society requires.

Clearly, embarking upon a historical study or giving one a critical reading involves selection from a variety of methodological and assumptive positions. The final aspect to consider is its exposition. History as an art has long concerned itself with writing, seeking styles to complement the author's aims. Danziger's exploration of the relationship between applied and academic psychology before 1935 used a linear approach to its content,[15] reconstructing past priorities by a reading of all of the articles published in psychology journals of the period. However, he prioritizes topic over chronology in structuring his account, an approach that emphasizes the interwoven nature of academic, professional and political influences.

Examples are clearer than descriptions: I conclude this section by summarizing history by a historian. Simon Schama is amongst those who see history as an art which requires narrative gifts as well as intellectual coherence and purpose. His short history 'The many deaths of General Wolfe' (1990) makes a compelling read. Since war is a topic with few connections to psychology or clinical practice, it may be easier to see how he blends themes from a number of complementary histories in crafting his account. The following précis gives the flavour of an approach that is very different from writing familiar to psychologists:

> *Wolfe's command of troops at the Heights of Abraham in 1759 was regarded as one of the decisive battles between the French and the British in the formation of modern Canada. Remarkable because the British army's rear attack on the French encampment required that they sail upriver and scale an almost sheer cliff in pitch darkness; and because Wolfe died a tragic death that day in the teeth of victory. Schama starts with an eye-witness who paints the soldiers' perception of the General as he ordered them to climb the cliff, alongside the author's account of Wolfe's position as he went into battle. Lampooned by caricatures in newspapers because of his odd features and a previous attempt at landing which he had botched, Wolfe was losing control of his command. He was also running two races: against the onset of winter and against his own deteriorating health.*
>
> *Schama's second section is set a decade later in London, when a radical painting by a Pennsylvanian called West dramatized Wolfe's death on the battlefield. It recast events in heroic style, creating a fiction which was incorporated rapidly into the next generation's understanding of history. However, by painting the characters in contemporary clothes he outraged Sir Joshua Reynolds, who thought that a naturalistic portrayal robbed Wolfe's history of the universal significance associated with classical dress. This second death of Wolfe*

> *created a new version of Wolfe's history, but also established a new convention for painters and made West's career.*
>
> *Moving on a century, Parkman's radical account of the battle on the Heights of Abraham recast understanding of Wolfe again. He was an American who wanted to counterpoint unsympathetic British histories of the continent with a locally constructed account; his love for the clean air and open land made him sure that only a distinctly American voice would do. He wrote his major historical work* France and England in North America *in spite of chronic illness, just as Wolfe had fought his great battle in the teeth of physical pain. There were many points of resonance between historian and subject, not least that this great work became Parkman's lasting epitaph.*
>
> *The narrative is completed by another eye-witness account. The battle was ended and the French in retreat; the narrator found the dying Wolfe just in time to tell him that the day was won.*

What was the history Schama provided? It gave two examples, separated by a century, of American citizens using Wolfe's death to create new agendas. In describing the battle on the Heights of Abraham, the careers of two Americans were made to resonate with a distinctly American conception of the world: their accounts of history were themselves turning-points in history. By sandwiching those subsequent events between the direct language of soldiers who started and ended the battle, Schama's broad canvas provides emotional insight as well as information about the event. Thus he blends two different approaches to history which complement each other, blurring the power of neither. Schama leaves us to draw our own conclusion from his account: that each time Wolfe died, both history and culture were changed.

Relativity and the Psychological Past

> Channel 4's decision to squeeze Anthony Powell's 12-novel sequence into four handy two-hour chunks resulted in absurd feats of narrative compression, as characters were introduced, did their stuff, and met their sad ends within a matter of minutes, rather than volumes. Powell's preoccupation with the passing of years and the distortions of time become an absurd joke . . . [by contrast an] extreme experiment with narrative and mortality is currently being undertaken by Lars Von Trier, director of *Breaking the Waves*, who is shooting his feature *Dimension* at a rate of three minutes a year, to be completed in the year 2024.[16]

Contemporary film-makers take perspectives on time that escape psychologists: in the world of social science, Newtonian time largely rules. For Newton time is absolute, a contentless backdrop against which events and experiences are measured with no perceiver to complicate things. Psychological research to identify the cognitive factors which make people misperceive this 'proper' time exemplify the way that Newtonian assumptions still undergird psychology, although it seems somewhat bizarre that psychologists would regard a clock as something to which a person should adjust. Pleas for the human sciences to abandon nineteenth-century concepts and develop more relativistic ideas have been made, but subverted.[17] The notion that time itself exists, without reference to people or events, is encapsulated in language that refers to *the* past, *the* present, *the* future.

This contrasts with Einstein's view of time as malleable and flexible in itself, not merely acquiring these properties as a consequence of human perception and experience. Davies (1995) notes that Einstein liberated time and space from Newtonian limitations but did not combine the elements of his ideas into a coherent theory. Relativity uses the concept of motion to combine space and time, but does so in ways that are not entirely compatible: space-time in some circumstances prioritizes space and in others time. The familiar conceptualization of different aspects of light as wave (prioritizing time through motion) or particle (prioritizing space by permitting pinpoint location) illustrates this. While neither idea is 'really true', they are useful models that were in turn challenged by new physics which theorizes holograms.

The crux of a psychology of time based on relativity rather than on Newtonian physics is the connection between time and a perceiving individual. Just as arrows pointing North identify no particular place and directions need a point of reference to be meaningfully interpreted on a map, so concepts of past and future exist relativistically rather than as events or places that stand alone. It can be said therefore that there is a concept of psychological 'past', but not one of 'the past', because past can only be relative to the person's experience of time with other persons, events or places. Psychological time needs to change, to prioritize the experiencing individual over clock-time.

While relativity is a difficult idea for Westerners to use in practice, it is our Newtonian ideas of time that others find alien. Indigenous peoples of America, Africa and Australia use a subjective approach to time, connecting it with place and personal experience rather than separating time from events or moods as we do. An example of the implications of absolute versus relative time is the way that we think of ourselves getting older in years. Instead of referring to objective events such as birthdays as markers of ageing, relative time reverses the direction of this causality to suggest that physical/emotional maturation or deterioration are the important prompts inviting us to reflect on age and its implications. If relative time depends on human experience rather than on clock or calendar time, then we need to pursue this perspective in psychological intervention and in the judgements we make about change in others.

This may seem self-evident. Yet clinicians continue to ask clients or carers to estimate the frequency of a problem or distressing experience on weekly charts or diaries, or to estimate how often it has happened within the last three months. By doing so we show no interest in their relative experience of past events; rather we impose a Newtonian frame of reference on their experience and thereby distort it. This may be useful if it illuminates debate about how awful the problem seems when compared with how long it lasts, but all too often such information is used to deny the extent of the problem. 'Look, the chart says you only argued with your daughter for 10 minutes this weekend so it cannot be much of a problem, it is much less time than last month' pays no attention to the mother's experience. If the argument involved her being kicked on the shin and a door being slammed so hard that surrounding plaster fell off, she may have been so upset by it that its echoes remained with her for the rest of that day. Whether the argument was recorded as lasting 10 minutes or half an hour may make no difference to the intensity or degree of her distress: what she recalls is that her weekend was spoiled this month just like last month.

Einstein argued not only that time is relative but that it does not flow, it exists in blocks or timescapes: Charmaz applies this (see p. 75) to describe the way that people cope with chronic illness. Post-Einsteinian physicists also model the implications of applying the sub-atomic world to human experience: they suggest that human experience is not dominated by fragmentary streams-of-processing nor timescapes, but by parallel universes opening up at each decision-point or event for each person. This is the so-called 'Many Worlds' theory,[18] an organic conceptualization very similar to the constructionist approach to philosophy outlined by Deleuze and Guattari (1994). Apparently the stuff of science fiction, it allows us to conceptualize how people may 'jump' from one state or position into another without any continuity. It also explains how people in apparently similar social ecologies, such as a family or organization, can experience events so differently.

Slife (1993) has explored the implications of these ideas for both academic and clinical psychologists. His fascinating book traces the taken-for-granted presence of five Newtonian assumptions within psychology, arguing that we need to recognize and question their presence before it will be possible to recreate the discipline without them. Focusing on the way that psychologists have organized and interpreted change in human experience, he agrees with others that the main problem is treating time as an objective or absolute phenomenon. However, he suggests that the assumptions of universality, reductivity, continuity and linearity are equally problematic.

Universality and reductionism are basic assumptions in scientific enquiry, already discussed and found wanting in exploring some aspects of human experience. Universality concerns the search for laws that apply across times and cultures. An example is Bretherton's (1985) attempt to demonstrate the universality of attachment theory, in an account that in my view fails. Selectively quoting the three studies that agree with an attachment theory perspective, from anthropological research carried out over a 50-year span, is poor history and poor argument: more recent attachment theorists have abandoned the attempt to demonstrate that their concepts are universal. Reductionism assumes that a phenomenon is no more than the sum of its parts and thus they can be studied separately. The positive and negative tensions that arise when family members or work colleagues spend time together, tensions that influence their experiences and actions, are obvious examples of emergent phenomena.

Continuity assumes that time intervals are both uniform and consistent, that is, each hour is the same as the next hour and one hour follows another consistently – one cannot miss an hour. The uniformity assumption leads to longitudinal studies that treat two time-periods of, say, three months as if they are comparable.

> *A longitudinal research project with adults who have profound and multiple disabilities illustrates the problem. Their physical frailty means that winter is fraught with illnesses which are slow to clear. During this season their experience differs significantly from life in the autumn when they are generally healthier, and when student nurses on placement simultaneously disrupt their social world and make interesting excursions more probable. Traditional psychological research minimizes seasonal variation by adding controls that allow us to treat all time intervals as if they are uniform. Qualitative researchers argue that this strategy controls out of the research factors that are vitally important to these clients.*

Continuity assumptions underlie the question frequently posed when formulating a clinical problem: 'what is the process?', which makes it difficult to reply that there is no process. Discontinuous developments or change tend to be dismissed because they are difficult to understand. Sometimes they are linearized by assuming that what happened occurred in some speeded-up way, denying the possibility of instantaneous change even though this is a common phenomenon in the sub-atomic world. An example was described by Brown et al. (1992) in their quality of life project for adults with a learning disability. They report that when the client gains sufficient confidence to reflect on what they value, and chooses to learn (for example) to read; and when the right tutor and the right environment are found, some people make huge leaps in reading ability which cannot be explained by continuous processes. It is the very discontinuity that is exciting.

Linearity is Slife's final criticism, the assumption that past, present and future experiences have only one direction, from past to future. This results in past events being given primacy in most psychotherapeutic treatments of human distress; and in the assumption that interaction is a sequence of actions and reactions, such as turns in a conversation, rather than simultaneous communication made through mutual gaze or facial expression. Assuming that change and influence occur simultaneously across a psychologically connected group of people in family therapy is an example of a non-linear assumption supporting practice. Slife also cites Jung's account of a man who was describing his dream about a scarab beetle just as one flew into the consulting-room. Virtually every psychological theory treats coincidence as an event rooted in chance and without significance: Jung championed the idea that if people from many different cultures do think synchronicity is meaningful, it merits serious attention. John was concerned about a slightly different type of coincidence, but it still held explanatory power for him as he described the death of his wife, Ann:

> It has taken a long time to come to terms with it myself. You see before that I had lost my sister, I can't remember whether it was two or three month, I had lost my sister and then I lost Ann. You see, my sister was 59, Ann would have been – Ann was 59. I am coming up 59, so it doesn't give much light at the end of the tunnel, does it?

Slife is not erasing past experience from psychology, he recommends that we reorient ourselves with regard to it. Not only does the linearity assumption erroneously suggest that all events follow in a regular sequence, it also disallows simultaneity and the possibility that present experience may be as much influenced by future expectations as by past events. For example a clinician may believe that the ideas parents hold about their disabled child were constructed out of past events, perhaps the moment of diagnosis; by making this the main topic for discussion, really salient information can be missed: perhaps that these parents believe their child will not live beyond young adulthood. This gives them a very near-sighted approach to their child's future life, a stance they defend because it enables them to avoid the enormously difficult decision of who will care for their child when they die. Thus Slife takes a Heideggerian view that past, present and future are always represented in consciousness to some degree; the balance of power exerted by each will of course change according to circumstance but clinicians need to consider them all.

A few psychologists who employ non-Newtonian assumptions are termed anomalous by Slife, people whose ideas are liable to be linearized or in other ways brought within the fold of accepted pre-theoretical assumptions. Lewin, von Bertalanffy, Chomsky, Jung, Kohut and Bruner are his examples of anomalous theorists.[19] By assembling them he hopes to strengthen the challenge to current implicit understandings which none managed to sustain alone. Slife argues that we must identify and challenge all Newtonian concepts within psychology before we can move beyond them. The implications of this relativistic view of past events in psychology may be summarized as follows:

1 Time is a context-bound phenomenon.
2 Psychological events can occur outside linear time.
3 The past is always reconstructed from the vantage-point of the present.
4 We need methods that can identify discontinuities.
5 We should stop treating time as interval data and so cease aggregating different periods of psychological time, treating it instead according to ordinal assumptions.

Slife's fourth and fifth points relate to the research agenda, to which I return in Chapter 7. The second half of this chapter explores the implications for practice of time being context-bound, acknowledging that psychological events can occur outside linear time, and that past experience is constantly reconstructed during discussion and remembrance.

Reconstructing Past Events in Clinical Practice

Conceptualizations of memory and remembering are fundamental to the way we consider past experience. Cognitive models describe within-person processes, parallel strands of thinking or neural networks which support memory. Social constructionists emphasize human relationships because they shape the way that remembrance is expressed, discussions that lead us down one narrative line rather than another. A clinical example would be therapeutic concern to help people move from narratives of victimhood to tales of survival. But clinicians also need to bear in mind that our understanding of memory and remembering is itself coloured by social experience, by previous research, and by cultural changes which affect our need for and use of memory. This final section explores these and other issues using a number of the historical themes discussed earlier: biographical, narrative, sociopolitical and institutional approaches to remembering in clinical practice.

Biographical

These approaches look across the life-span of individuals within the context of their families and social networks. They could inform parents, carers or clients about problems that occur commonly. Disabilities or mental health problems often result in dislocations from the events which serve to mark significant points in the life-course for non-disabled people; the timing of their own major transitions can result in unusual combinations of stressors for everybody involved.[20] Among people with learning disabilities first-person accounts co-constructed with academics, such as Bogdan and Taylor (1982), are useful but they rapidly become outdated, because accounts of what it was like to be admitted to an institution at an early age are relevant to fewer and fewer people.

Although rapid change in patterns of service make it difficult to create natural histories of the lives of people with a learning disability, the activity itself can also be questioned. Normalization suggests that such histories are unnecessary, since people ought to have lives like others in society, obviating the need for special studies; moreover, such studies support the separation of people with learning disabilities from society rather than their integration. On the other hand, as clinicians we work with current sources of distress as much as we work towards a better future, and dreams of such an ideal state have been expressed for a quarter of a century without it coming very much closer. Perhaps normalization's dogma should not continue to inhibit the investigation of common events and stall efforts to manage them better: after all, the idea of the 'career' has proved useful in studying a range of lifestyles from workers in the sex industry to women executives. The following brief sketches outline two types of difficulty which are common for people who have learning disabilities.

Jane Smith is an adult with a severe learning disability who started preparing to leave home as her father became terminally ill, and so she confronted multiple losses at one of the most challenging points of separation in her life. This is made more complicated by her 68-year-old mother, who has high blood pressure and is fully occupied nursing her husband; nevertheless Mrs Smith feels ambivalent about this separation. She has become dependent on her daughter's company, socially isolated by years of physical care and an excluding community. In addition, Jane's move out of their home requires Mrs Smith to trust a public service on which she has had to depend, but which has met few of her expectations.

Adam Jones is a young man with Asperger's syndrome who left college to face a jobless future just after his father retired from work through ill-health. The family were quite unprepared for the anger generated by both men competing for the mother/wife's time and attention, and their physical competition for the dominant position in the house – the chair beside the fire and opposite the TV.

Biographical research summarizing such mixed feelings and conflicts could help people to understand and prepare for the issues they may confront, just as research has helped modern families to prepare more effectively for adolescence. It need not be used to stereotype; it merely offers alternative ways to understand experience on which people can draw.

Attachment theory is much derided as a deterministic approach rooted in linear assumptions about the continuity of development: Slife dismisses it in a brief paragraph which refers mainly to 20-year-old research. This is unfortunate because authors such as Griffin and Bartholomew (1994) have accepted and moved beyond previous criticisms, making attachment one of the liveliest theories exploring continuity and discontinuity in psychological biography. It has also produced one of the few instruments to explore psychological events outside linear time, the Adult Attachment Interview (AAI). This identifies and focuses on discontinuities in personal history, fulfilling one of Slife's criteria for a non-Newtonian conceptualization of people's psychological past. In summary, it asks for adjectives that describe the relationship with each parent, memories that illustrate them, and a description of which parent they felt closest to during childhood. The interviewee is asked about painful childhood experiences that commmonly occur, such as illness, rejection, separation, emotional distress; and then about abusive or traumatic events that may have occurred. Finally, the person is asked to describe how much they think their parents knew of their feelings, how much their childhood influences them now as adults, and whether their relationship with their parent has changed.

Steele and Steele (1994) summarize their own extensive attachment research with adults using this instrument, amplified by research from others as relevant. The AAI is scored by trained raters: it categorizes people according to the coherence or conflict between their generalized evaluations and the specific incidents and experiences they give to illustrate them. It also looks for discursive coherence within the narrative, and for unexplained gaps and inconsistencies that reflect a childhood which itself felt unpredictable and fragmented. There is good predictive reliability between attachment ratings during childhood, where they exist, and categorization on the AAI. Nevertheless, studies on the general population without childhood records find that out of the majority of adults who are classified as autonomous-secure, 30 to 40 per cent describe adverse experiences that they countered with the assistance of another stable and supportive caregiving figure, creating a sense of earned security in adulthood.

Reminiscence therapy is another biographical intervention, generally used with elderly people to draw their past lives into their present experience, with claimed therapeutic effects on their self-esteem and other indices. However, it is difficult to untangle the within-person effects of such discussions from their systemic influence. Some suggest that the benefits of reminiscence projects derive from empowerment, from repositioning the elderly persons as experts possessing knowledge the young staff do not have, rather than from any direct benefits to the individuals themselves.[21]

Reminiscence is not always welcome. Hazan (1980) recorded the way that elderly persons attending a Jewish day centre in London supported dislocation from their past. He found that erasure of their history facilitated pairing between lonely people from dissimilar backgrounds who had little other choice of companion. Their complaints about neglectful children were not always accurate: such complaints again serve the rhetorical function of dislocation, liberating attenders to form new relationships. When an outsider tried to start a reminiscence project, attenders objected and ran noisy events in competition with it. They also became angry when some visiting musicians evoked unwelcome and distressing memories by playing emotive old folk-songs. Apparently this refugee group had experienced such suffering that special sensitivity and negotiation were essential for reminiscence work to be useful or acceptable.

Some people find work on all of their life story too difficult. Cox (1992) gives an exciting account of a project to provide sensitive and imaginative prompts for controlled recall to such individuals. Actors from the Royal Shakespeare Company performed a number of tragedies in Broadmoor Hospital[22] to audiences of residents who had volunteered, and who could leave at any point during a performance. There were also workshops afterwards where actors and audiences could meet, and speak of 'carnal, bloody and unnatural acts'. Cox, Consultant Psychotherapist at Broadmoor, observes that the project had unimaginable power because Shakespeare enabled actors and audiences to 'go and meet danger there', without intruding on each other. The book contains a fascinating collection of observations about the experience from all perspectives. One comment from a resident provides a little understanding of its power:

> I'm still thinking about *Hamlet* five days after the performance. For me it was a journey of self-recognition through madness, and it was healthy for me to experience it. Several times I saw myself in the guise of those brilliant actors and actresses. True, parts were traumatic, but somehow it was a positive calling up of my own savage memories. They could be viewed rationally from a distance, like in a play. (1992: 141–2)

Narrative

Life-story work has developed in a number of ways with different client groups, elaborating the life-span perspective that human lives comprise a gestalt which has integrity. Slife notes that such work need not fall into the traps of Newtonian thinking, but in practice it usually does draw on the assumption of continuity. For people with learning disabilities who have had many moves, or for children who have been multiply fostered, therapy using life-stories focuses on making positive meaning from these disruptions. Here it is assumed that problem behaviours arise from difficulty in making sense of such unusual experiences, people judging themselves to be 'bad' or responsible. This assumption is supported by research into the conversations of boys with learning disabilities,[23] whose fabrications about the police taking boys away because of wrongdoing allow them to explore reasons why some but not all of them stay away from home for short periods in respite care facilities.

Life-story interventions have in common an interest in gathering information about people, places and events in the person's life, but that is where the similarity ends. Social workers tend to use the term 'life-story' to describe a slow and confidential process that enables the person to re-live key events, by preparing a scrapbook around planned visits to places of importance; when speech therapists use the idea they are referring to the construction of a book with key people and places from the person's past and current life, a book intended for clients with limited speech to show others as they try to communicate about their life and choices; while psychologists are starting to use such books at moments of transition to support and develop the identity of people with profound learning disabilities as they move into community settings (Hewitt, 1995). Life-story work as a clinical intervention seems to be a useful idea, growing in popularity amongst a number of professionals, but one in need of both theorizing and research.

Charmaz's study of how people cope with chronic illnesses describes the way that people locate themselves in different timescapes in response to different degrees of illness or different treatment regimes.[24] These timescapes do not cancel out other time-frames: one merely becomes the most salient for them, the place where their authentic self is to be found. As

Einstein described, these are blocks of time that do not flow. They may be associated with physical, social or treatment circumstances: envisaging life after treatment finishes is a common way that people get through courses of chemotherapy. People who locate themselves primarily in past events use three different approaches.

One group see the past as a tangled web, are preoccupied by trying to make sense of their experience: Was the illness my fault? The doctor's? What would have happened if I had done this or that? The second group counterpoint a familiar past with an inexplicable present: their past life was pleasant and safe, their present unacceptable. The third reconstruct and idealize their past lives, feeding their sense of disconnection from everyday activities. This third way copes effectively with a pain-filled present and a grim future: however, when used by less sick people who are isolated or who have suffered emotional loss it is less functional, inhibiting actions that could confirm a new and more currently located self.

The timescape employed by chronically ill people may be an appropriate focus for intervention if it is creating problems rather than providing solutions. Charmaz found that differences between the chronically ill person's timescape and their partner's was a common source of conflict: usually that the partner focuses optimistically on a healthy future which the ill person cannot conceive. She also describes the usefulness of reconstruction: people rewriting their personal past to achieve a measure of transcendence from their illness. Slife makes passing reference to a 1930s study suggesting that people with brain injury or mental health problems cannot engage with a future timescape, limited conceptual abilities confining them to past or present perspectives. This opens interesting avenues for research into different clinical groups, the timescapes they employ and whether they can adopt others, given support. Boscolo and Bertrando exhort systemic therapists working with families or consulting with staff groups to be alert to the presence of past, present and future within conversation, and to keep a close watch on the different time-frames being used:

> Our basic assumption is that subjective time frames have to be softened and made to change, and that this change should involve all those participating in the session. Similarly the time frame of therapist and clients should develop in harmony within the therapeutic process itself. If this does not happen, the risk is that an impasse may develop. (1992: 123)

Hacking (1995) argues that recent focus on the word has brought too much prominence to narrative approaches; he questions the centrality of time's flow to human experience, as did Einstein.[25] Hacking suggests that many if not most memories are scenic, visions displayed in blocks which may be dominated by a particular time-frame in the person's life and associated with strong feelings. Thus he argues that flashbacks reported in post-traumatic stress disorder (PTSD) are no more than the scenes which commonly come to mind. They are more vivid and accompanied by strong negative emotions, but there is no reason to view them differently from other types of memory. They become transformed into narratives during the process of recalling them with another person.

While visual images themselves cannot be the totality of the complex process which is memory, Gibson's ecological approach to perception can facilitate the production of a narrative of recall during therapy.[26] When a psychologically important event is raised by somebody who cannot recall or comprehend it, the interviewer should focus on perceptual-level detail. This may involve the following:

1 specific enquiry into the physical/temporal event boundaries, i.e. when the personally important episode began and ended;
2 establishing the order of any mentioned sub-events;
3 establishing how descriptive words used in therapy map onto directly perceived but possibly low-level event information, or to later interpretations of the event;
4 identifying any important neighbouring events that might be influencing the way that the client interprets this event;
5 developing concrete narrative descriptions of the physical and subjective presences in relatively small temporal units;
6 connecting material presented in this narrative to current interpersonal relationships and situations.

The authors provide case material to illustrate their approach, emphasizing that the reason for selecting a particular event for this type of exploration should be theoretically driven.

Techniques to prompt or support narratives of remembering are particularly important for people whose intellectual limitations interact with lack of confidence, producing accounts which lack coherence. Although attachment researchers have found classifications of adult attachment status to be independent of verbal skills, age, occupation and intelligence (Steele and Steele, 1994) this applies only to samples of non-disabled adults: clearly, if every narrative a person gives has gaps and inconsistencies, the significance attachment theorists place on disjunctions cannot apply so easily. Kernan and Sabsay (1989) describe the problems of trying to follow extended narratives given by people who have mild and moderate learning disabilities, describing the listener's task as akin to that of assembling a jigsaw. Usually there is a central point or purpose, but it gets lost among diversions, repetitions and quotations from others.

Wood has explored the development of narrative skills among young deaf children, by showing them a story on video and then asking them to describe what they have seen to a camera.[27] He found that the most effective intervention was merely practice and feedback: the children knew that this was a regular component of the school curriculum and that they would see how they performed as soon as they had finished. This was suficient in itself to yield significant improvements in narrative coherence and flow, even after cohort effects due to increasing maturity were controlled. Turner described a similar project.[28] He carried a portable tape-recorder and started to interview people with mild learning disabilities whom he knew quite well, proffering the microphone and asking 'Who are you?' Initially all were flummoxed by the question, but after a while they started to think of ways to respond to him and a few became excited communicators, coming up to demand he ask 'that question' again. Both of these approaches offer fruitful ways to help people develop their narrative skills, and have great potential for enabling service providers to hear the voice of users whose communication skills are poor.

Sociopolitical

The past cannot be regarded as a fixed background against which the truth-value of memories can be assessed, nor should we think of memory as a videocamera. The debate about whether recovered histories of sexual abuse are false or not highlights the politics of memory,[29] since there is evidence that such memories are a joint production. Therapists to whom clients are more likely to report abuse are those who in the last two years have worked with more than 20 abused people; who use hypnotic regression techniques (more common in the USA than in Britain); and whose therapy focuses on early experience rather than on cognitive-behavioural strategies to manage current experience.

Hacking (1995) uses a historical analysis of multiple personality disorder (MPD) in North America to illustrate how 'memoro-politics' influences knowledge-creation. The interpretation of personal histories is important because the acts being remembered and recalled are indeterminate events, not fixed episodes. Actions spring from a variety of intentions and our judgement about that intention plays a vital role in determining the way events are assessed. Hacking's illustration is informative: he considers the father who showers with his nine-year-old daughter. In the light of current concerns about sexual abuse of children this could be considered abusive, since the standing child must confront his genitals and touch is probable in such a confined space. But how should this be viewed when discussed by a 39-year-old woman retrospectively? Her father might have been part of the 1960s counter-culture, hoping that shared showers will help her to avoid the inhibitions about nakedness his parents had imposed on him. As Hacking observes: 'The retrospective redescription and reexperiencing of human actions is the most difficult of topics' (1995: 241).

He tracks the development of multiple personality disorder, a concern that first arose in 1876, two years after the formation of the first society to halt child abuse. He argues that the two have always been closely linked, regardless of whether the focus of abuse is physical or sexual in nature. MPD is defined as a dissociative disorder where the person experiences more than two distinct personalities; MPD allegedly arises from prolonged sexual abuse in childhood. Ignored by most psychiatrists, it is promulgated by many alternative therapists in the USA and by some feminists. The number of people diagnosed as having MPD has increased exponentially in the USA since its psychiatric classification in 1982. In 1992 a group of parents in the USA formed the False Memory Syndrome Association, arguing that unprofessional therapists were planting false ideas in their offspring's minds; a similar group developed in Britain soon afterwards.

Hacking argues that people are being enlisted to shoddy causes on both sides; that the argument is not about memory but about religion versus secular society, and about constructions of the family and its role in society. Social science research cannot resolve the problem, any more than research alone can referee the Facilitated Communication dispute, because their origin lies in cultural differences. He criticizes utilitarian arguments too, which imply that sexual abuse is bad because it causes harm, citing research with non-clinical populations to suggest that poverty does much more long-term harm to more people. Criticizing social science research, however, does not mean that we cannot take a position: in Hacking's view the opposition needs to come from ethical argument. For him this is that sexual abuse is bad because it is an abuse of power, it is unethical behaviour that diminishes society irrespective of its immediate consequences. In similar vein he argues that therapies supporting the multiple personalities which supposedly result from sexual abuse are also bad, because such MPD therapies result in a thoroughly crafted person with many 'alters', but not a person who serves the ends for which we are persons.

Barham (1995) questions therapy altogether as appropriate for traumatized people. Focusing on the Holocaust he observes that many people do not wish to work through or get over their experiences: he cites Friedlander's conception that such events are perceived as an open wound in the landscape of the present and that people wish to keep vigil over its meaning. The urge for encounter, for people who witness rather than resolve, is also expressed by seriously ill people critical of interventions by health psychologists (Frank, 1992). Barham notes that historians and film-makers have been instrumental in creating a conception of living historically, that is of requiring all in society to be changed by the knowledge that we live in a world of which the Holocaust is a part. For him memoropolitics needs to be as much concerned with audiences as with individuals. He criticizes the psychologization of trauma because clinicians release the community from any responsibility to witness and alter shared meanings. On the other hand such narratives themselves can be criticized for making the victim role seem glamorous. This debate is a good illustration of the need for clinicians to be alert to sociopolitical aspects of memory when they intervene or discuss past events.

Institutional

Engeström et al. (1990) treat institutions as organic wholes capable of learning, remembering and forgetting. They contrast their activity-theory account against classical ethnographic approaches which are typically oriented to space rather than time; and to discursive approaches whose narratives are based on very small slices of time. They propose a three-dimensional model of organizational remembering.

The first axis is social, exploring knowledge such as 'the way we used to do things'. Such information can act powerfully and be difficult to change because it acquires mythical status: often none of the people who were present at the time being recalled are now on the staff. Engeström et al. conceptualize organizational remembering as a recursive process emerging from movement between the poles of this axis, which concern socially communicated knowledge such as myths versus external records describing past practice. It also interacts with information held in activities and actions rather than in words: this is their second axis: 'how we do things here'.

Memories on this second axis are prompted by procedures arising from local conventions such as the way this set of staff record information in files. If new staff make different records which do not connect with the understanding held by their colleagues, the information cannot be remembered: by failing to connect with the collective past the information has no meaning within that organization. Accompanying structural changes would be necessary to enable staff to recognize and understand the relevance of historical information. Furthermore, failure to relate one's activities to those of one's colleagues creates the 'breeding ground for an exclusive preoccupation with biography as an individual career or trajectory. Time becomes a chain of individual actions and accomplishments, disconnected from their collective meaning and activity context' (1990: 143).

The third axis looks at power. Some memories can be recalled by all because there is equal access, while the social relations operating in other institutions may limit access to archive material which could prompt more elaborate memories. Examples include access to medical records, which allow some people to 'remember' aspects of the client's past but not others, an issue which can cause considerable irritation to professionals who lose this access when they transfer from the public to the private sector.

From this perspective, institutional memory and history lie outside any individual head: they are constructed through active and ongoing processes. Forgetting is conceptualized as ruptures in the information which moves between these axes; learning requires a constant flow of information between them. It contrasts with sociological literature that focuses on forgetting: Goffman (1961) documented the erasure of personal histories as easing the client's acceptance of their new condition and reducing interpersonal demands on staff. Valuing a fresh start and avoiding historical context is supported by many psychologists in learning disabilities who cite labelling theory to justify ignoring medical case notes.[30]

Hazan's research with elderly people cautions against transmission of past histories as a wholly unwelcome breach of confidentiality. Yet positive reasons for improving institutional memory are clear and can be ethical when services are offered to people who have few channels of communication. They cannot hold their own history nor share it with the oft-changing staff who care for them, and once relatives lose contact a substantial amount of their personal information is lost. Medical notes become the only source of history, a function they were never designed to serve and which they do badly. Yet staff struggling to relate to people with little communication describe the background information they get from families as central to their development of an appreciation of the client.[31]

> *Polly is an adult with profound learning disabilities and impaired vision whom staff found 'unfathomable'. They noted her pleasure in rubbing pieces of material behind her neck, the origin of which her sister recalled. When their now-deceased father returned from work he went through a ritual with Polly, undoing his tie and leaning over her in greeting. She would slide it from his neck, put it over her head and laughingly rub it across the back of her neck before he retrieved it.*

If institutions could value personal histories more, such information would play a part in carers' developing ability to see clients as individuals with a character of their own, and in humanizing the care setting. Equally important, it would give carers something to talk about in a situation where the common ground of everyday conversation has little meaning. Such change would also enhance the value of past interventions with clients, which would avoid the current situation where people are commonly taught road-crossing or head-control skills on many occasions. They learn them but for a variety of reasons do not maintain these skills independently: some remain dangerously distracted when seeing a friend and forget road safety; for others head-control is effortful and only displayed when they are comfortable with someone and there is something to look at.[32] The enthusiastic if ahistorical professional is rewarded for their intervention by the person apparently learning the skill – again – while the client must feel they are endlessly treading water.

Two current axioms of psychological practice are that low expectations held by staff are more limiting than any disability the client possesses, and that studying past records labels the client and clouds original thinking. Generated by appallingly low resources, when few constructive activities were offered to people, such axioms are overdue for re-evaluation. Elaborating the historical contexts that created them would assist such re-evaluation enormously.

A grounded theory study of staff conceptions of the appropriate management of bereavement in a learning disability service (Clegg et al., forthcoming) shows how services work to co-construct an understanding of this event with the client. This was in part determined by what is known about the client's history, a concept which itself had two main properties. Firstly, the access staff had to NHS information was highly variable, because different qualifications determined levels of access and the degree of detail available. They also heard from members of the client's family, where a single narrator's version of events – for example, whether the client had understood or benefited from attending a previous funeral – tended to be regarded as truth, often because staff had no other sources to draw on and little time to explore further.

The second property was the person's attitude towards personal history in informing care and planning responses to bereavement. A minority of staff felt that history was vitally important because it constitutes personhood; they were frustrated by the fragments of information they had to work with. However, the majority described past experience as something to be escaped or transcended. One issue determining these views was whether the professional carer was able to integrate, from chaotic files and perhaps contradictory information from relatives, a coherent account of the person's life which they could draw on in practice. If they could not then they avoided reading information which seemed of no practical use to them or the client. From this research it is clear that incorporating historical perspectives into clinical practice throughout services will require major change: not only does information need to be stored differently, but staff also need new frameworks to enable them to integrate histories into their understanding and practice.

Conclusions

This chapter draws on different schools of thought to consider how clinicians can usefully recast past experience within current intellectual frameworks. That poor understanding of history results in self-referential accounts can be seen both in historical sketches by clinical psychologists and in staff descriptions of client change. To draw on history we must incorporate aspects of its method. More important, however, is to appreciate the way that ideas we now regard as muddle-headed could have held sway for so long, so that we gain some purchase on the concepts dominant in current understanding. No subject can allow its ideology to remain free from scrutiny: history is not the only way it can be examined but it is a very powerful one.

A historical perspective on narrative allows us to see how useless it is to treat any account as *the* account. Important as it is to hear from clients about their perspective on services to redress the balance, such voices cannot be viewed as incorrigible in quite the way they often become. Accounts need to be laid side by side, not to discredit one but to see where they articulate against one another to create a new perspective. In particular the values of therapies which aim to resolve past traumas are being questioned and placed alongside other values which bear witness; people may be seeking ways to accommodate and live with their experiences rather than wishing to have them neutralized.

Nevertheless, we cannot be swamped by information about past ideas. In advocating a reappraisal of the role of historical knowledge in practice, I do not follow Blackman in believing that all practices should be historically situated. I am advocating attention to genuine historical studies, and that many more should be carried out, to help current clinicians to identify key issues and to ensure that useful ideas from the past inform our understanding of present problems.

Summary

The *contemporary issues* discussed in this chapter derive from concern to reverse the current relationship between psychology and time where the tail is wagging the dog. It follows from the last chapter insofar as the insertion of time is an important defence against the worst effects of postmodern fragmentation. The conceptual changes proposed by Slife are far-reaching but quite difficult to grasp because ideas about time are taken for granted. He urges us to recognize and question assumptions that there are laws about human experience that apply across times and cultures; acknowledging that the experience of memory and recall have changed during this century is a useful counter to any idea that we can accumulate 'facts' about an unchanging phenomenon that adds up to knowledge. He also questions reductionist ideas that complex phenomena can be understood by studying their components, without concern for effects that may emerge between those elements; the assumption that time is uniform and all events occur as continuous processes, rendering discontinuities and simultaneity of no interest. Finally, Slife questions the idea that time is a linear process that always flows from past to present to future, preferring the Heideggerian perspective that each timescape is present to some degree in all human experience.

Histories of the present, however, need a method: organizing a set of ideas into chronological order will not suffice. Different approaches to the construction of a history, both classical and Foucauldian, were discussed and exemplified. Consideration was also given to the way history is communicated using complex structures that hold the attention and enhance the meanings of the text, approaches not normally considered to be legitimate components of psychological accounts. A history of the present that remains to be carried out is a study of the shifting time perspective adopted by clinical services: from past-focused clinical reviews and histories of institutions to individual programme plans and new forms of care, such as group homes and other patterns of community care, where neither staff nor residents have any history to draw on. Recording the effect of those changes on the patterns of life experienced by residents would provide useful lessons for future reorganizations.

Histories are shaped by the relationship between teller and audience, whether in person like the Adult Attachment Interview or imagined, as are readers of written histories. In considering these sources of *intersubjective meaning* it is clear that memoro-politics will play its part. Histories may also shape and be shaped by subjective engagement between researcher and final account, creating an important means whereby past information and experience can be incorporated into, and valued by, contemporary clinicians.

Clinical histories enhance our *critical thinking* about contemporary issues: summaries of Hacking's historical account of multiple personality disorder and Boyle's history of clinical approaches to women's sexuality exemplify their utility. They help us to see when 'evidence' may be unable to resolve a dispute which has its roots in cultural differences or ideology. Yet this does not make social science research nor clinical intervention impotent. Biographical life-story interventions have their place, although they remain in need of theoretical scrutiny; helping people to develop their own narratives can let others know what they may experience and prepare for, can help clinicians to see how adopting different timescapes can be both helpful and problematic, can enable people with little communication skill to affect their circumstances; and noticing how sociopolitical factors influence the way people recall past events is an essential critical skill for practitioners.

The *reflective researcher-practitioner* has had little mention in this chapter, although the temptation to write *my* history of service change and present it as *the* history of service change was noted. I have started to question the idea of psychology as a young science, still adolescent, with an eye on future power and little interest in past ideas or interventions. Understanding that past events are always played on a new stage enabled me to see that history is a vibrant and relevant activity.

Being able to see how memory can stand outside of any individual and act at an organizational level is the main aspect of *human systems* discussed here. This important perspective will surely save many clinicians from frustrated attempts to change the way histories are recorded and used.

Notes

1 Commentary on considerations of time in the projected millennium dome, by M. Woollacott, the *Guardian* 20 September 1997.

2 Most practising behaviourists dispute this statement, emphasizing the role of reinforcement histories in understanding current behaviour. However, this is an article of faith rather than something examined during functional analysis, which only includes people present during observations; or analogue analysis (Iwata et al., 1982) which uses experimental conditions to test the person's current response to a range of strange social circumstances. Another example comes from a review of behavioural interventions with people who have learning disabilities, where Tennant and Cullen (1987) make no suggestion that psychologists should seek or incorporate any information about the client's past experiences or relationships.

3 For a review of the project and its current renewal, see three 1994 papers in *American Psychologist*, 49: 120–32.

4 Described in Blatt (1981).

5 Jay (1979).

6 Reviewed by Trent (1994).

7 Dickens (1994).

8 A good example of the latter was Grant's (1993) preliminary report of an investigation into care management in Wales. One year into its implementation most of the staff had been given no training in this radically new professional role, and they were unable to purchase many services because the costs had not yet been calculated.

9 Hutton, 1995 provides a useful and readable introduction to economic influences on social policy.

10 See also Berrios (1995b).

11 This participatory way to think about research is being discussed by researchers in both arts and science subjects. Following the work of Latour and Woolgar (1979) and subsequent studies in the sociology of scientific knowledge, even 'hard' scientists have come to recognize the effect of measurement on both the measurer and the natural world. As well as checking the foetus, amniocentesis marginally increases the risk of abortion. As well as studying the world, researchers may be affected by doing so: discovering that social and technological change during the Renaissance was associated with a rapid increase in the torching of Jews and women might make a researcher review modern events, and rewrite their account of the history to reflect that concern.

12 For example, many horror stories are told of oppressive universities threatening staff who fail to produce four significant publications per year. I started to ask for details of how this message was communicated: when asked, most people backed down and said it had not actually happened to them, but they felt threatened because it had happened to someone they knew. Thus are government goals achieved, not by direct threat but by creating environments where we oppress ourselves by the repetition of myths.

13 For example, Rose (1996).

14 This is in contrast to the genealogical approach, which has been more commonly used in social science applications of Foucault's ideas. This also has three domains or axes, which have a starting point in how problems evolve rather than the way they are solved: all three were represented in *Madness and Civilization.* The domains are an ontology of ourselves as subjects of knowledge, which Foucault explored in *The Order of Things*; the power through which we act on others (*Discipline and Punish*); and the ethics we refer to in construing ourselves as moral agents (*The History of Sexuality*). For further information see *The Foucault Reader* (Rabinow, 1984).

15 Previously discussed in Chapter 1.

16 Romney, in the *Guardian* 14 November 1997.

17 See review by Bowers (1991).

18 Everett, 1957; cited by Gribbin (1984).

19 Bruner (1990) describes how the cognitive revolution which he and others proposed in the 1950s was hijacked to a positivist cause. Setting out to chart the interaction of cultural and individual factors in the creation of meaning, he found the emphasis in psychology soon shifted away from the construction of meaning to the processing of information.

20 Goldberg et al. (1995) provide a useful family therapy perspective on problems associated with transitions amongst families with a learning disabled member.

21 Middleton and Buchanan (1993).

22 A secure provision for the violent or disturbed offenders with associated psychiatric disorders.

23 Cromby (1995).

24 Charmaz (1991). This comprehensive grounded theory study followed some participants for over 10 years as they lived with chronic rheumatoid arthritis and other illnesses which flare up and settle down. Discussion of the experiences which encouraged people to respond by living in a present or future-focused timescape is discussed in Chapter 5.

25 This was disputed by the philosopher Bergson in 1934 (described by Slife, 1993), who countered that the human experience of time does have duration and is not the same as physicists' time.

26 See Trierweiler and Donovan, 1994. This paper has some fascinating and clinically useful insights, wrapped up in something of a conceptual *mélange* which includes a long section of logic. It is perhaps typical of some of the creative work which is coming into clinical psychology. The main disadvantage of this account is the dependence on a concept of real or proper time.

27 Personal communication concerning work in progress: contact D. Wood, Department of Psychology, University of Nottingham.

28 Turner spent one afternoon a week for 10 years with people who have a learning disability attending a sheltered workshop in Los Angeles, exploring many different issues and publishing much of the output (e.g. Turner and Graffam, 1987; Zetlin and Turner, 1984); the narrative work was not published.

29 Andrews et al. (1995).

30 For example St Claire (1989) describes how the label of mental retardation has three major components. She suggests that failure in only one of the components results in all areas of difficulty being ascribed to the person – for example, people with a bodily disability such as cerebral palsy are often presumed to have cognitive deficits as well.

31 Clegg et al. (1996).

32 Gleason (1993).

5 Culture, Community and Psychology

This territory has been fought over many times; it contains more hidden tensions and confusions than any other significant group of ideas affecting clinical practice. Yet greater clarity is vital because terms denoting social location, such as 'community', have such a dominant role in shaping our purposes. Drawing on the geographers' world makes it easier to see that many different kinds of maps of location can be produced – social, political, physical – and that while all have substantial validity none can claim to be the definitive account. It also helps us to see when incommensurate ideas are combined on a single map to muddle our thinking.

This chapter teases apart some contemporary strands of thought. While acknowledging that past unities were achieved through abuses of power, where one narrative was imposed to silence other voices, it nevertheless advocates going beyond current celebration of difference to move the horizon of clinical practice towards a greater degree of unity. An initial exploration of community care in Britain, which evolved first in the learning disability service, is followed by an unravelling of two key terms: culture and community. This leads into the final section which explores ways that clinicians may work towards unity with different groups of people whose connections may be social, political or related to their physical neighbourhood.

Clinical Perspectives on Community

The 1969 report of abuses at Ely hospital initiated a decade of enquiries into neglect in British hospitals for people with learning disabilities. They documented brutalizing conditions experienced by staff and residents alike, conditions which also existed in a number of other countries. People were devalued and the response was to expose the lamentable societal values which supported such conditions. Goals of the new community services were expressed in the Jay Report (1979) and in two King's Fund publications, *An Ordinary Life* (1980) and *People First* (1982); these ideas about care outside hospital were later adopted for all aspects of health services.[1] The difference in opportunity and location is illustrated by the lives of two women with learning disabilities.

Siobhan was 35 years old in 1975. She had lived in the hospital since she was seven years old, receiving no schooling because she was classified 'ineducable'. A lifetime passed toe-walking resulted in permanently shortened Achilles tendons for which she wears built-up boots: the hospital had no physiotherapy service. Siobhan lived with 29 ambulant women who could not speak; they had two main living spaces, a dormitory and a day room. Staff described them as 'low grades' and as children, irrespective of their age. One qualified nurse was generally in charge of the villa with three nursing assistants who engaged in an endless round of washing, dressing and feeding. Staff got relief from the noise and smell generated by 30 bored and incontinent women by organizing 'bundles' in the linen room, pre-selecting a day's set of clothes to speed the process of dressing the next. Residents got relief from their noisome setting during brief visits to the main block for medical treatments or psychological interventions.

Institutional memory is so short that it is important to document the conditions which failed Siobhan on every level, lest the shortcomings of current services encourage people to romanticize past patterns of care. Her life was literally given very little value: even the food she ate was cheaper and poorer than that given to other types of hospital resident. Similarly, staff were expected to deliver humane services while themselves working in inhumane conditions. There are many contrasts between Siobhan's life in 1975 and Bella's life 20 years later.

Bella was 35 in 1995. From the age of 14 she lived in a large Victorian hospital moving at 30 to her current home, three interlinked houses for a total of 12 residents supported by three care staff. Bella is an accepted customer of the adjacent bingo hall cafe, although brief greetings and partings have not developed into personal relationships. She is assertive, able and mercurial: people find it difficult to predict when Bella will refuse to do something. Her dissatisfaction with various day centres, but inability to keep a job, creates many tensions in a project with insufficient staff to cover days. Bella's family were unable to visit when she lived in the distant hospital but are in intermittent contact now. She craves their care. Her mother copes with mental and physical health problems of her own. Promising to visit on particular days she often does not come; occasionally she arrives unscheduled and under the influence of alcohol when staff believe that she asks Bella for money. Hurt and anger certainly follow such visits. On one occasion Bella shouted, screamed and threw objects down the stairs for over two hours. Clearly affected by a painful past history, she has been offered counselling and therapy by three different professionals, each time refusing to attend after the first few sessions.

Bella's lifestyle is in every way more humane than was Siobhan's, and her greatest concern after outbursts is that she will have to leave her new home. Nevertheless, research confirms that staff and family remain almost the only significant figures in the lives of people with learning disabilities like Bella who live in community settings;[2] and while she wants family contact, sometimes it prompts such disruptive behaviour that her place in the community home is in jeopardy. Community policies have changed the location of care but not the social relations experienced by its target group.

The intellectual motor of the change in services between 1975 and 1995 has been 'normalization', an ideal based on positively valuing the norms and patterns of mainstream society. Originating in Scandinavia, it was popularized in the USA and Britain by Wolfensberger (1972). During the 1980s the agenda moved away from advocating normative lifestyles to focus on the creation of valued social roles, along with an attempted name change – social role valorization – which never really stuck. This thinking was encapsulated by O'Brien's (1987) five accomplishments, simple propositions which constitute the putative goals of British services a decade later: they are choice, competence, respect, participation and community presence. In the USA these have evolved into a goal to create 'inclusive communities', projects based on the idea of zero exclusion, and the development of mutual dependencies between people at all levels of a community or institution. Wolfensberger himself pours scorn on such projects:

> It is really imperative to quit emitting the absurd, contrived, phony, deceptive and saccharine messages of optimism that are still normative in the population. . . . It is precisely because modernism gives people decadent weakness and lies instead of inner strength that they feel driven to an opium of phony optimisim. (1994: 32)

He concludes that only the commitment of unpaid volunteers can produce genuine relationships with people who have learning disabilities, and such volunteers will always be few in number. People will have to depend on statutory services while being aware that these are inevitably flawed at the human relationship level.

Often described as a philosophy, normalization is no more than a set of principles which lack heuristic power, that is, they lack the power to develop and to connect with other ideas. Taylor (1989) argues that affirmation of ordinary good living – the basis of normalization – was an important ethic developed by Enlightenment thinkers to challenge the power of kings and priests, but one which has remained troublesome through the ages. Other principles can be elaborated by describing people whose actions are widely agreed to be exemplary: it is much more difficult to achieve consensus over ways to depict or recognize good ordinariness. Nor should the affirmation of ordinary life be given hegemony over other sources of good which can be identified; this ethic should be held in balance with others. Concern to provide culturally sensitive services provides a further challenge to normalization's set of values: some communities value obedience over choice, domestic and religious life over presence in public places, shared activities over individual competence. Although these and other criticisms of normalization are recognized by professionals specializing in mental health or rehabilitation, attempts to call them into question in learning disability services meet substantial resistance.[3]

Calvez (1993) analysed the problems of integration for people with learning disabilities who leave institutions in France. He suggests that these people obtain a position in social space relative to each community and relative to their own personal development. The experience of integration at a personal level has three stages, although that experience is significantly affected by interaction with others. People need to separate from their previous group, then enter (and tolerate) a threshold or liminal status where marks identifying them with their previous group are obliterated. Only when that has been achieved can they attain a new status Calvez calls aggregation, where interactions with the group create a new identity. He notes that liminality is an ambiguous position: if maintained too long it can be transformed into a threat because by their presence the people may introduce disorder to a previously ordered community. Using Douglas's cultural theory, Calvez identified four different social structures which affect the experience of newcomers: individualist, hierarchical, egalitarian and subordinate societies. He concludes that each type of society shows little compassion for people who have learning disabilities, often leaving them to inhabit a liminal status very close to complete isolation. This is Shotter's concern, that members of marginal comunities have no sense of belonging:

> To live within a community which one senses as being one's own, as 'mine' as well as 'yours', as 'ours' rather than 'theirs', a community for which one feels able to be answerable, one must be more than just a routine producer of it; one must also in a real sense play a part in its creative reproduction and sustenance. (1993: 16)

Community services have made little progress in helping people with learning disabilities or mental health problems to gain a sense of belonging, despite a decade and a half of deinstitutionalization. This will not be promoted by continuing to emit saccharine messages of optimism, to reiterate Wolfensberger; practitioners need to abandon the hope that artificially created relationships developed within 'befriending' schemes are going to provide the solution. Moreover, feedback from consumer groups shows that services promise much but deliver little; this is feedback we should heed.

Community policies have achieved much change for people with disabilities and mental health problems, transforming their physical living conditions: there are many hurdles yet to be confronted concerning their social experience. Understanding the origin of words we use to describe shared social experience may allow practitioners to reconceptualize the problem more successfully.

Culture

> Culture – the medium of social action. Culture – local meanings. Nationality. Ethnicity. Class. Gender. Sexual orientation. Age. Disability. High versus popular culture. Cultural studies. Cultural psychology. Sociocultural psychology. Multiculturalism.

A small sample of what Raymond Williams – the originator of cultural studies – described in 1983 as one of the three most complex words in our language. Most usages of it derive from two classes, which might be given the shorthand dichotomy passive–active. The passive meaning of culture as agar jelly or a well-manured garden is the oldest; it feeds the implicit assumption that some growth media are better than others. Thus:

> culture as the medium through which the drama of human action is performed. (Jahoda, 1992: 194)

> culture as a medium constituted of historically cumulated artifacts which are organized to accomplish human growth. (Cole, 1995: 35)

These passive meanings use 'culture' as a noun; it then describes the works of intellectuals, especially artists. From this perspective the 'high' culture of arts and classical education should grow superior humans than does low or folk culture. Such modernist assumptions came under challenge this century when it became clear that these cultured people could not prevent the carnage of two world wars. Their distance from the bulk of the population made them and their ideas easy to marginalize through death or oppression, while the esoteric culture they had created was irrelevant because most people could not understand it.

Anthropologists introduced a more active sense of culture. For them it is the system of meanings created and used by any group of people, or their system of activities with its own settings, rules and roles. This has been merged with the previous ideas by philosophers, who suggest the following definition:

> Culture may be thought of as a causal agent that affects the evolutionary process by uniquely human means. For it permits the self-conscious evaluation of human possibilities in the light of a system of values that reflect prevailing ideals about what human life ought to be. Culture is thus an indispensable device for increasing human control over the direction in which our species changes. (Honderich, 1995: 172)

This perspective implies that it is important to express and discuss our culture so that it can be understood and changed. Then we will be able to cease being an administrative science (the accusation Danziger levels at psychology) and create a discipline which genuinely assists people to live their lives in ways which serve them better.

For clinicians, culture has recently come to the fore, influenced by literature from the USA and concerns about low uptake of health services in areas where there are significant numbers of people from ethnic minority groups. This low uptake is attributed to service systems that are incompatible with the wide range of cultural belief systems held across the population, or to services that are positively racist in delivery. However, attempts to describe the customs and meanings of different groups of people have often focused on the structuralist concerns of early anthropologists: thus texts informing clinicians about bereavement now include sections on death rituals amongst different groups (Dickenson and Johnson, 1993). This implies that learning about the way different cultures perform key activities with which we are familiar is sufficient. Of course this is a traditionally colonialist stance which employs a discourse of similarity rather than of difference.

Crude efforts to translate one culture into the logic of another more dominant culture were criticized by Clifford Geertz in 1983. He emphasizes that the challenge is to grasp another culture's common sense, in its own terms, before making the hazardous attempt to communicate it using our language and frame of understanding. Similarly, members of ethnic groups argue that mainstream culture's concern to become 'more sensitive' to their needs misses the point: they have materially different ways of understanding the world, and these should be valued and used in knowledge-creation. The argument here is that exploration of different cultures should strive to be as open to difference as possible. Starting from the premiss that marriage and the family and death are important in our society, and so there must be equivalent structures and processes in all others, closes too many avenues and imposes too many of our assumptions. Researchers cannot escape their subjectivity, but should try to avoid its effects by – for example – making their own cultural assumptions explicit, using anthropological techniques such as recursively immersing and then standing outside the community under study, or working with a team accustomed to critical debate rather than doing studies alone.

Thus, rather than focusing on the equivalence of cultures as the first issue, Stansfield (1994) discusses the strategies which members of oral cultures use to understand the world. This provides ideas that could inform research into the experience of people who are unable to read, as a result of disability or accident, or to understand the language of the country they are living in. However, Stansfield dilutes the power of his argument by asserting that oral cultures are just as valuable as literate ones, confusing the issue of respect with the issue of comparison, an issue to which I return.

Instead of exploring structural issues such as the boundary between life and death, or childhood and adulthood, another approach to multicultural thinking in clinical practice focuses on process. Perelberg (1992) proposes a three-stage process: finding out about patterns of interaction between family members, deriving family maps of the ideas which guide behaviour in everyday life, and linking these into social organizations, structures and culture. She then incorporates structuralist concerns by offering only two possible models of family maps, hierarchical and symmetrical. Perelberg's evidence about family types, their social networks and spousal relationships depends on two studies published in the 1950s.

Perelberg's model highlights one of the problems of multicultural practice: it requires clinicians to draw on myriad sources of information, which makes keeping up to date very difficult. Lynch's (1992) guidelines for practitioners avoid that problem by providing 67 questions to ask the family before starting any intervention. These concern major topics such as family composition, childrearing practices, perception of help-seeking, and interaction styles. They are supported by more checklists for working at different stages of the intervention, and another checklist for evaluators. However, they lack conceptual coherence. Without an intellectual focus it becomes difficult to exclude anything: in current form the checklists propose that clinicians carry out lengthy initial interrogations that will do little to enhance the therapeutic relationship. An open-minded, questioning approach may be useful but this application offers the novice no map of the territory.

It seems that practitioners who try to develop a multicultural service have few reliable signposts to follow. Moreover, what was radical and exciting has become overwhelming as burgeoning numbers of cultures acquire an advocate. Whether collating fragmented knowledge will create the desired cultural change is now being called into question by a number of thinkers such as Eagleton (1994) and Said (1994). Said describes contemporary culture as one containing a formidable onslaught of perspectives, observing that hand-wringing impotence is not the answer:

> Now everyone comes forward with new and often violently opposed views of the world: one hears endless talk about Judeo-Christian values, Afrocentric values, Muslim truths, Eastern truths, Western truths, each providing a complete programme for excluding all the others. There is now more intolerance and strident assertiveness abroad everywhere than any one system can handle.
>
> The result is an almost complete absence of universals. . . . One of the shabbiest of all intellectual gambits is to pontificate about abuses in someone else's culture and to excuse exactly the same practices in one's own. (1994: 67–8)

From another position, Shotter also exhorts psychologists to stop collecting fragmented pieces of information and develop an interpretive, sense-making approach instead. Cultural psychologists are addressing the problem of how to create unity within diversity, proposing a psychological research agenda which can inform our understanding of human experience in multicultural settings. Eschewing cross-cultural psychology as colonialist in its assumptions about human experience, cultural psychologists are attempting to find common processes underlying emotion, memory, health perception and so on: 'Psychic unity is what makes us imaginable to one another, not what makes us the same' (Schweder and Sullivan, 1993: 517).

The main question which emerges for me from this initial consideration of culture is: *How can we stop 'tooling ourselves up' with dislocated pieces of information and work out what really needs to change in the knowledge that influences practice and in practice itself?* But ideas of culture and multiculturalism exist on one plane or map: they interact with another set of ideas revolving around the term 'community'.

Community

> Community – locale. Community – social network. Inclusive communities. Community politics. Community psychology. Communitarianism. Conceived communities. Community as site of belonging. Community care. Community as not-hospital.

Williams (1983) dates the word 'community' from the fourteenth century, when it was used to distinguish the common people from people of rank. This developed the meaning of a group of people distinct from the state, significant when one recalls that the majority of British people had no right to vote until early in the twentieth century.[4] 'Community' began to describe people in a small geographical district four centuries later, the description of actual social groups remaining a common feature.

In parallel to the idea of community as a group of people in an area, another distinct set of meanings evolved. These described social relations between certain people, a community of interests where the members felt a sense of common identity. It differs from the first meaning because in this sense people may belong to more than one community, or to none at all.

Lefebvre distinguishes these two meanings as concrete place and abstract (social) space.[5] In these terms, the particularities of everyday life occur in place: space is the range of both proximal and distal interdependencies, and so here it includes both the global network and relationships with people who are absent. Confusion has led some people to rename the idea of place as locale, locality or neighbourhood. Mainstream philosophers certainly regard the second meaning of community as dominant:

> Any collection of persons who, usually because of some common condition or parallel experience, share a perspective. . . . The significance of this kind of community is that having a common perspective makes communication possible. (B. Singer, 1993: 97)

> A group of people living a common life through reciprocal relations. (Honderich, 1995: 143)

Since both meanings of community, as place and as a set of social interdependencies, are represented in publications for practitioners, their confusion continues to create difficulties. One important problem is that it increases the distance between intellectuals and clinicians, because most publicly funded community services are organized on place while most academics focus on social relationships. Clinical services which do focus on social relationships were more common during the 1950s and 1960s, when hopes for the potential effects of closed communities in the mental health service ran high. These are dubbed 'conceived societies' because they follow a blueprint concerning ideal social relationships, one usually developed by a founder.

Politically the prescriptiveness of closed communities associates them with Fascism and extreme enactments of communism; in clinical settings, behavioural token economies of the past are a good example.[6] However, conceived societies also take more radical positions, creating different ways of co-existence in communes and therapeutic communities. They have the potential to introduce new forms of communication. This can meet the needs of particular groups – signing amongst people with hearing impairments is an obvious example – and so they often occur amongst clinical populations. Parents of people with disabilities are reassured by their direction and purpose, which contrasts sharply with their experience of public services:

> Parents like me cannot afford to ignore them [special projects, specifically the Peto Institute in Budapest], even to permit Dr Oliver to find a totally ideologically sound approach to alleviating disability . . . we have had direct experience of the unfocused and frequently inept workings of rehabilitation professionals in this country. . . . For most practical purposes society has already written our children off. (Beardsmore, 1993: 167)

Yet therapeutic communities often founder. Problems stem from having to introduce the community's culture to each new person entering the place; from their dependence on the originators' vision and charisma; and from members finding that they are ill-equipped for life beyond that place's reach. Maintaining different forms of interaction tends to insulate them from contemporary society, leading to ossified values and practices. Also, some users find the close-knit relationships intrusive and want greater privacy, while problems of confidentiality and loyalties split between the community and outside carers and families can also arise.[7]

In the USA some social scientists and politicians have united under the banner of communitarianism, which expands the social interdependency aspect of community. Like therapeutic communities, this movement contains both right- and left-wing politics. By focusing on altruism, trust and honesty, communitarians are associated with humanist liberal individualism; by discussing solidarity, they ally with Marxism. However it is their prescriptiveness which provokes the greatest criticism: their contention that human life is better in communities such as the family and that this should be supported and strengthened. It is only a small step from here to the belief that societal ills originate in single mothers and thus that benefits should be cut and divorce made more difficult: some communitarians have taken that step.

Honderich (1995) argues that communitarian thinking has not been systematized at a philosophical level: although communitarians identify philosophers such as Taylor and MacIntyre as members of their camp, both repeatedly dispute this classification. Lasch (1994) criticizes communitarianism for being an imposition, a mirage rooted in no particular group nor in any way of making a living: it has a nostalgic view of progress. He asserts that if elites wish to exercise leadership of this sort, they need to be much more securely rooted in the communities they would lead.

Moscovici views all attempts to solve social problems by remaking society as misguided. He argues that conceived societies create a sterile space where personality is subjugated, a world which is constantly refashioned like a workshop where nothing is ever finished:

> Society continues to scintillate in all its brilliance. The idea of it burst forth during the last century like a volcanic island after an eruption on the sea bed. . . . It doubtless corresponds to some reality, but it is as some all-powerful, transcendent being that it imposes itself upon everybody. Society comprises the solution to all the problems of existence and becomes a way to salvation for each of its members . . . [yet] Society is no longer the locus that bestows a direction upon our lives . . . only the framework of routine remains, one from which all passion has flown like bees from a dead hive. (1993: 345–6)

Moscovici challenges our wish to believe that coherent communities exist which can combine the place and space senses of the word. In the past communities had power through continuity while individual lives were brief: now people experience as much change in a decade as used to occur in a century, and it is the adaptable individual rather than the group which has longevity. Shotter (1993) describes in similar terms how fast-changing societies make life an improvisatory art, suggesting that adjusting to discontinuity is the emerging problem of our time. Because the materials making this world change and relationships are always in the process of being forged, Moscovici questions how we can hope to anchor individuals into such environments: he suggests that community policies as currently formulated are unrealistic. Gregory (1994) makes the similar argument that when communities do seem to exist they are inevitably temporary and probably phantasmagoric.

Some localities are described as communities because they share a common physical space, although residents have no shared meanings at all. This was illustrated clearly by Campbell's (1993) study of the places in Britain where riots flared in 1991. Various cultural tensions contributed to the problems. Some white people disliked and resented black shopkeepers; racism and sexism existed within the police force and were expressed in their decision-making; and there were many tensions between men and women living in these communities. However, Campbell argues, it was the culture of the white male youths that was decisive and explosive. Their disengagement from social institutions started with high rates of truancy and school exclusion and continued into early adulthood when unemployment rates gave them little chance of a job. When anger started to flare there was little shared meaning or acceptance of leadership amongst the young white men, and so they had no means to communicate their grievances or address them with anything but violence. Campbell's conclusion is that the riots were not an assertion of will but its defeat: that most people wanted to stop them but had no means of doing so. There were too many people without a voice, and no structures that could enforce inter-group planning about ways to live together.

These views make a serious dent in the hopes practitioners hold for community care. Accepted unquestioningly a decade ago as a model that moved away from medical hegemony and hospital provision, community care is an approach to service provision based on physical place rather than social space and thus it fails to address the social relationships which are the primary concern of many client groups. Often there are few existing patterns of relationships into which people with disabilities or mental health problems could integrate. Moreover, community care is a policy which has been constantly re-fashioned in exactly the way that Moscovici (1993) predicts for all conceived societies.

Unity in Diversity

> A major intellectual problem facing the Western liberal democracies in the contemporary world is to develop an appropriate understanding of cultural diversity. . . . Public policy debates are likely to hinge on the answer one gives to the problem of diversity.
>
> (Schweder and Sullivan, 1993: 504)

Said (1994) and Campbell (1993) warn that reasserting cohesive societal values prevents the necessary redistribution of power, stifles dissent and increases the homogenization of society. Not only do cohesive societies inhibit change, but their members frequently fight dissent with extreme intolerance. Moscovici (1993) observes that the worst human fanaticisms emerge out of intense relations with people. Voluntary marginalization is a route many people choose when they want to increase their power and create change. For example a disabled theatre group has recently rejected the goal of enlightening the non-disabled population, using their missing limbs and provocative acts instead to create solidarity and meaning amongst their own community.[8] There is no effort towards unity here.

Researchers from ethnographic, phenomenological and hermeneutic traditions also regard the search for universals as misguided, as colonialist in nature. They fear being brought within the ambit of mainstream thinking, their unique contribution neutralized. Writers from these traditions castigate social scientists for being far more conservative in their approach to cultural diversity than academics from the liberal arts. Fowers and Richardson (1996) identify four main rationales for changing psychology in the light of multiculturalism: inattention to cultural factors represents a tacit statement of universality that has become untenable; the colour-blind approach to discrimination fails to recognize authentic differences that are defining features of identity; psychology should use its resources to fight political oppression and injustice across the world; and the nurturance of diversity will enrich us all. These add up to a compelling moral force.

On the other hand, critics of the over-assertion of difference believe that its emphasis supports stereotyping which prevents people from defining and redefining themselves. University departments of cultural studies may have had a progressive effect in changing the balance of academic interest and helping us to extend our intersubjectivity towards more cultures. Yet commentators such as Eagleton (1994) castigate them for doing little more than vie for student loyalty. He also accuses them of intellectually dishonest practices because they select from past events to feed a progressivist history, and edit out less positive episodes of their development. A number of commentators complain that describing other cultures tends to stereotype and homogenize; for example Hollinger (1995) argues that it is not biological purity but mongrelism that is the social norm, and so individual perceptions of ethnicity can only be personal and private. Like religious faith, such identities may be affiliations people are brought up with and stay within, but they may also be wholly or partially discarded and aspects of different ones adopted at any point.

Shotter (1993) values the tension between mainstream and marginal groups, even though in general he advocates working at its margins, because dialogue between these positions generates positive change in all societies. There is certainly historical evidence that the four European countries where religious tolerance permitted Catholics and Protestants to co-exist and clash (Poland-Lithuania, Scotland and England, Switzerland, the Netherlands) were the places where Enlightenment rationalism started and flourished. The Netherlands was the place where intellectual refugees like Descartes and Spinoza went (Davies, 1996). Nevertheless, cultural debates may be exciting and creative but they are also disruptive: history suggests that when transformation in social meanings is both too rapid and too fundamental, social anxiety occurs on a mass scale.[9]

Unity within Diversity in Practice

All community policies entail bringing different groups within society closer together in one way or another. Such policies, and the context in which they occur, affect clinicians as much as service users. This section considers three related topics: acknowledging structural limitations on the service, holding dialogue with diversity, and developing bridging skills.

Acknowledge Structural Limitations It has become almost commonplace to compare the supposed aims governments hold for clinical services against the actual effects of their policies. Rosen (1992) explores the strategies for people with mental health problems in Britain, Australia and New Zealand. Each country exhorts professionals to provide integrated services while making what Rosen describes as 'nonsensical' moves: separating health from social care, separating providers from purchasers, and empowering those inexperienced purchasers to further inhibit dialogue by commissioning some services from the private sector. Rose (1996) uses moral panic about care in the community for mentally ill people to make a similar point:

> Thus, speaking in August 1994 in the light of a report into homicides committed by discharged psychiatric patients, the UK Junior Minister of Health declared: 'The aim of our policy is to ensure a seamless chain of care around the discharged psychiatric patient in the community.' But the response of his government was to seek not to reinvent the coordinated machinery of welfare psychiatry, but to develop procedures, targets, standards, audits, evaluations and the like. . . . In this new psychiatric order, both subject and object are to be regarded as responsible, playing their part in the strategy of reducing risk and minimizing harm under threat of sanction and within the disciplines imposed by a plethora of practices of blame. (1996: 18)

These tensions inevitably impact on professionals in community teams.[10] Constantly exhorted to work collaboratively, not least by committees of enquiry into abuse or manslaughter, community teams operate within an implicit model that communication will lead to co-operation and thence to co-ordination in the delivery of good care. Research commissioned to identify barriers to collaboration suggests three main scapegoats:

- lack of guidance about the actions required;
- role-blurring across professionals in teams;
- cultural differences, for example between the communication styles deployed by health versus social services staff.

Rarely is the problem placed in its wider social context of wholesale fragmentation, disaggregation and individualization occurring at all levels of society, even though community teams are bound to reflect these trends. Little research has been commissioned to ask more open questions about the way community care functions.

Trevillion's (1996) study is an exception. He looked at the interaction patterns of members of two social work teams specializing in HIV and in mental health respectively. For eight weeks they recorded their interactions and their feelings about them. Results showed that people had multiple professional identities and team affiliations. These were relatively short-term and participants took an instrumental view of their professional relationships, making little or no emotional investment in any of them. The social workers had rare contacts with either team members or their parent organization, the characteristic working pattern being a personal network which was short-term, individualistic and defensive. They were conscious of organizational nihilism and of the dissonance between the views they received about collaborative teamwork and their day-to-day experience: participants had no rationales with which they could make sense of their work. Perhaps most important, there was no evidence to support the contention that failure of co-operation originated in any of the scapegoats previously identified.

Although they considered very different groups of people, Trevillion's conclusion is consistent with Campbell's analysis of British riots during the 1990s: that there were no social spaces where dialogue could take place. Trevillion found that not only were there no structures or systems that could facilitate collaborative relationships across the team, there were no plans to set them up. Short-term contracting will only exacerbate these trends, developing a pattern of work which, he argues, is quite unsuited to the putative goal of an open-ended, user-driven system of care. Despite these gloomy findings, the research did identify people who were networking and collaborating against the oddds. However, people who try to create providential spaces within clinical services need to acknowledge the structural difficulties they confront, and set their expectations accordingly.

Dialogue with Diversity In research about people who riot on council estates, about community staff struggling to live up to an agenda which is subverted by organizational policies, and about people leaving learning disability hospitals, the message is the same: not only are people failing to co-operate, they are failing even to connect. A new approach is needed to confront the experience of rejection and social isolation. Although policies to heighten awareness of the oppression of women or members of ethnic minority groups encourage tolerance they also increase fragmentation, and bypass the disenfranchised young white men whose actions were at the core of the problems which Campbell (1993) described. It is necessary to go one step further, to use particular knowledge to create new connections between people, and to cease thinking that the issue of cultural diversity in clinical practice is only about ethnicity.

Gregory (1994) sees the evocation of different people, places and landscapes as a necessary first step towards tolerance and understanding, but argues that in itself this is ineffective. Further analysis and interpretation are necessary to create dialogue between this group of people and others. He urges social scientists to reach beyond parochialism, to enlarge their own and others' sympathies by developing the skill of adopting the perspectives of more groups of people. Setting up new services for any single group may seem to redress the balance of social justice but their effect is to fragment society further. The development of dialogue between cultural groups should become a universal and pre-eminent ethic guiding all service development.

An example of analysis that supports dialogue comes from Parker (1993) who describes four major protagonists in disability services. Firstly, younger people with mild levels of learning or physical disabilities who assertively demand not care but resources: they aim to remove socially constructed aspects of disability (poor transport, access to buildings and so on) and to increase control over their own world. These self-advocates are in conflict with organizations of informal carers, normally parents but also the spouses or siblings of older people with disabilities. Such informal carers do not seek change, they seek recognition of their work and support to maintain the status quo. In turn, feminists criticize informal carers for failing to object that the burden of care usually falls on women: they argue that community care is a myth, the reality being family care shouldered by women. Finally, there is a small but powerful lobby from parents who feel that only paternalistic village communities can provide the situation they feel their son or daughter needs: unconditional regard and protection from an uncaring society.

Parker elaborates the apparently irreconcilable positions she identifies amongst users of disability services, in order to create some common ground. The groups do not acknowledge that they are talking about different types of disability which in turn are affected by age and level of frailty. Informal carers give little value to the call for reduction of environmental barriers encountered by disabled people, although this position does not conflict with their perspective. Feminists and other political radicals do not respond to the accusation that it is unreasonable to expect the most vulnerable members of society to occupy the vanguard of social change. Parker identifies topics different groups could support on behalf of one another while leaving their own position unaffected; she also identifies key points of difference that require dialogue. She urges people to avoid establishing mutually incompatible groups which oppose each other, since this defuses the power of their response to government policies and does a disservice to the people they intend to help.

The language of 'rights' has been another major component of normalization, of multiculturalism and of community services; some statements have emerged from the United Nations, such as the right of all people to take their place in the community. However, while the legal tradition regards rights as the legitimate claims individuals can demand from society, B. Singer (1993) argues that rights are intrinsically relational. That is, by asserting my right to freedom from bullying I am asserting this as a right for myself *and for everybody in my group* because rights are mutual, they are statements of value honoured throughout a community. Thus the assertion of a right is simultaneously an entitlement and an obligation: it can only occur in a community of what Singer calls 'dialogic reciprocity'.

Singer concludes that the way to establish minority groups within communities is to develop shared perspectives, and worry about the assertion of rights and conflicts of interest after common ground has been established. Agenda-setters can foster this: she cites the memorable suggestion that one approach to the conflict in Bosnia could be to offer both sides financially advantageous membership of the European Community, on condition that hostilities cease. Similar attempts to move beyond cultural and professional fragmentation can be seen in rules governing access to EC research funds, which often require the co-operation of researchers from three different nations; and in the NHS, where audit and R&D funds again often require joint submissions by people from different professions.

Moscovici (1993) and Shotter (1993) criticize attempts to create ideal societies by the assertion of rights or the pursuit of blueprints, because such causes become self-sustaining and prevent people from entering into dialogue with others. Dialogue occurs when both parties are trying to approach truth by having the discussion: therefore a precondition of genuine dialogue is that the participants come to the table willing to change their minds. Weak liberalism militates against dialogue by implying that comparison is necessarily competitive or carried out in the service of subjugation. This view may be caricatured as refusing debate and believing that all positions can be given equal power. Rorty argues that attempting to take a tolerant stance towards all other groups has made us into wet liberals who have lost the capacity for moral indignation or contempt: 'We have become so open-minded that our brains have fallen out' (1991: 203).

An example of weak liberalism is Stansfield's (1994) statement that oral cultures are merely a different way of life, neither better nor worse than literate ones. Taylor (1989) suggests that different lifestyles can and should be compared to allow us to distinguish desirable from less desirable states, offering methods to facilitate such comparison. One example is judging whether the transition from culture X to culture Y occurs through a process that is error-reducing and ethical. Another method considers what groups X and Y can understand. If Ys can understand everything Xs can but not the reverse, this means that members of group X only understand their own comunications but not those of group Y and so the lifestyle of group Y is preferable, because it has access to a wider range of knowledge. It follows from this type of comparison that literate cultures are preferable to oral ones despite Stansfield's claim, because they provide access to more knowledge; the proposition is supported by Ong's (1982) evidence that once members of oral cultures are aware of literacy they see its power and want to acquire it. Closer to home, Taylor's method shows that the command of culture and access to work afforded by being fluent in two or three different languages gives members of many Western European cultures an advantage over most British monolinguists.

Such comparisons are not crass efforts to claim that the lifestyle of one nation is in any overall sense better than that of another. They simply allow us to see difference and reflect on its implications, to use culture as an indispensable human device which allows reflection on values and identifies new directions. Becoming better equipped to examine and compare values is a vital component of the quest to go beyond diversity, to enable people to gain control over their own destiny and work towards solidarity with others.

Yet dialogue with diversity is far from straightforward. Fowers and Richardson (1996) note that multiculturalism has compelling force for Euro-American civilization just because we value democracy, egalitarianism, tolerance. They argue that exponents of multiculturalism fail to acknowledge their intellectual roots in that Western culture; nor do they address the 'ultimate irony of multiculturalism – the imposition of our ideals of tolerance and respect on other groups who hold ethnocentric or racist views' (1996: 615). Fowers and Richardson celebrate the success of the debate so far in moving psychology beyond self-satisfied overvaluing of Euro-American civilization, but argue that the debate now needs to evolve further to take inevitable moral clashes between cultures seriously. It is likely that many of us will find some beliefs and practices unacceptable and be unwilling to enter into dialogue with them. With other groups, Fowers and Richardson argue, we can evolve by being willing to fuse our moral horizons and be changed in the process: it is that evolution in the values of multiculturalism that they are advocating, for psychology to be grounded afresh.

Clinically, the ethics of holding dialogue with people whose belief systems clash with the therapist is discussed with impressive lucidity by Goldner et al. (1990). They confront squarely the problem of how to work ethically with couples where violence occurs, by arguing that one level of explanation does not exclude another. Thus to develop a psychological explanation of violence is not to explain it away: to say that there are psychological components of violence, subordination and victimization does not mean they are not also material, moral or legal. They describe feeling considerable freedom of movement by switching their focus between levels, sustaining a balance between constructionist ideas of language and belief and an observer-independent world-out-there which has no simple view of truth but acknowledges pain and fear. At an ethical level they hold the batterer responsible for the violence and intimidation, and the woman responsible for protecting herself as far as she is able. They aim to keep their therapy separate from social control but acknowledge that this is not always possible, agreeing that violence is a criminal act for which legal sanctions are appropriate.

This allows a dialogue with difference that many family therapists avoid for fear of 'blaming the victim'. Goldner et al.'s work enables us to understand that rigid gender roles and fear of blurring them is the setting for violence; that the woman often needs to establish or re-establish her own sense of agency and the man to abandon his fear of seeming female before they can move beyond violence. It has helped them to stay outside judgement and understand the violent moment, when many voices from the past overwhelm the man like explosive flak around a plane. It helps them understand what makes the woman stay, get involved in arguments and even cast the first stone: that in arguing she feels she is asserting herself effectively though dangerously, while staying is what gender pride and self-respect demand because she feels she does not count unless she tends to the needs of others. Once the therapist can understand, the people caught in these traps can also understand and start to find their way out of violence.

Developing Bridging Skills Working with significant cultural difference is a topic influenced by North American practice and literature, although the degree to which Britain maps onto these communities is rarely considered. While it is important to develop flexibility and confidence in working with people from many different cultural groups, it is also useful to know the size of the populations since we cannot assume services are inequitable without that information.

For the first time in 1991 the British census asked how people define their ethnicity. Owen (1996) analysed and discussed these figures. They describe 3.015 million, or 5.5 per cent of the population of England, Scotland and Wales as coming from an ethnic minority group; people from South Asia comprise half of this population. The vast majority (44.8 per cent) of people from all ethnic minority backgrounds live in Greater London, with another 14 per cent living in the West Midlands region. It is difficult to generalize about the distribution of the population beyond these figures, because members of different ethnic groups tend to gather in particular major cities.

Given these figures it is not surprising that the majority of British clinicians who write about multicultural practice work in London. The implications of these ideas for practitioners working elsewhere are less clear. Rees and Phillips (1995) observe that the maps of seven of the 10 ethnic minority groups are dominated by Greater London: they break census data down into local maps and provide lists of local authority districts where significant groups of people from particular ethnic minority populations live. These should be used to inform debate about cultural sensitivities in most districts, since there is such enormous variation. Peach and Rossiter (1995) summarize the distribution of people from ethnic minority cultures as follows:

> Unlike the USA, there are no towns or cities in which minority ethnic groups constitute a majority, and at district level this is also true. (116)
>
> The proportions that individual minority groups form, of the population of even quite small areas like wards, is nowhere as high as that formed almost uniformly by the African American population in the United States. (117)
>
> A high proportion of minority ethnic groups live in areas where they constitute a small proportion of the total population, or of the White population. (118)

It seems that there are many differences between the British and the American positions. The age distribution is also important because that affects demand for clinical services. Owens (1996) notes that children form a third of the total ethnic minority population, while only 3 per cent of this population were over 65 in 1990 (this contrasts with 16 per cent for the whole British population). The age and dependency pattern reflects the recent history of significant amounts of immigration, which occurred primarily among young men and (more recently) women who came seeking work. This may mean that British services are more likely to encounter the psychological effects of rapid cultural change across the generations than is the case among established and indigenous minority populations in the USA. Overall, the figures suggest there is a clear need for culturally appropriate services to be developed in many districts of London, and for cities with significant ethnic populations such as Leicester (28.5 per cent of the population) and Bradford (10 per cent of the population). The issues are less clear for clinicians working outside metropolitan areas, who need to consider realistic ways to shape services for groups of people who represent less than 1 per cent of their local population.

Having highlighted the differences between Britain and the USA, it is nevertheless useful to learn from the USA's experience of working transculturally. Lynch and Hanson (1992) describe the anxieties which make us so cautious and restrained that we are literally unable to 'be ourselves'. McGoldrick puts it eloquently: 'Worse than our ignorance, which could be overcome by learning, is our inability to acknowledge our ignorance' (1994: 148).

Sue and Sue (1990) provide a stage model of racial/cultural identity which discusses both the experience of people from minority cultures, and changes in self-identity which members of white majority cultures can move through in order to be able to think flexibly about the role of culture. The ideas seem to have been informed by conceptual frameworks current when they started this work in the USA during the 1970s, and the authors acknowledge the artificiality and limitations of stage theories in general. Despite that, their work is rich in thoughtful observations and knowledge about transcultural practice. They provide a useful description of different styles of understanding that therapists and their clients may be drawing on, styles which could influence the content of therapy and disempower an intervention. There are four stages:

- **Conformity** – to the values and norms of the dominant culture.
- **Dissonance** – developing awareness of cultural tensions.
- **Resistance and immersion** – at this point people react against the dominant culture: feminists will want a woman therapist, members of minority groups someone from a similar background. There is considerable anger. Some people will believe that their difficulties originate in oppression, or may be confused by their distress over an unrelated event such as the death of a parent or child. Group work may be more helpful than individual therapies: clients will be testing.

- **Introspection** – a reflective and accommodative position. More flexible, more valuing of the accomplishments of individuals rather than groups of people, with a positive stance towards own identity.

These stages are discussed as they affect members of dominant cultures who develop insight into their own cultural assumptions, but for them the main events in the model are slightly displaced. Conformity includes denying any responsibility for perpetuating a racist/sexist culture. Resistance/immersion involves associated guilt and a tendency to see oppression by one's own family and colleagues everywhere: dangers include an over-identification with oppressed minorities that is inappropriately paternalistic, and meets rejection. This can lead back into dissonance rather than forward into introspection.

Sue and Sue conclude by describing the culturally skilled counsellor as one who is sensitive to their own cultural heritage, who values and respects and is comfortable with difference. This counsellor has some knowledge of their own biases, is aware of some of the effects these could have on clients, and actively engages with the issue of culture within their practice as an ongoing process.

Various writers consider the problem of working with families through a translator. Lynch (1992) recommends that professionals avoid using a child to interpret between parents and professionals if at all possible: this is likely to trangress family values about when it is appropriate for children to speak, and the child may be unwilling to translate comments they consider inappropriate for outsiders' ears. Professional interpreters are always preferable, and she gives useful advice about how to work with them.

Guidelines for Working with an Interpreter

- Interact throughout with the client(s) not the interpreter.
- In systemic work, assume the interpreter is part of the client system not the professional system.
- Check the interpreter's knowledge of the therapy/intervention you are using, preferably in advance of the session.
- Explain the roles of everybody in the room and how you suggest the session should unfold.
- Aim to restrict remarks/questions to two or three sentences.
- Check client(s)' understanding periodically by asking them to paraphrase their view of the session so far.
- Reinforce words with actions and visual aids.
- Allow extra time; do not oversimplify important explanations.

These guidelines are as useful for working with somebody signing to a deaf person as for an interpreter translating into a different language. They may also be helpful if the session involves working with people immersed in a faith community unfamiliar to the therapist, who may prefer to have a priest or religious leader present. Religious differences can be aspects of culture that are of central importance during therapy, but until recently these remained very separate. Frosh (1997) describes his position as both a family therapist and a member of an orthodox Jewish community, complaining that outsiders construct a homogeneity to his Jewishness that masks the divergent nature of beliefs within it. He criticizes multiculturalism for accepting simplistic definitions of religious groups; he also criticizes the politics of both anti-racism and anti-fundamentalism as being more concerned with the boundaries between communities than with the tensions within them. If he were to receive therapy from a non-Jewish worker he makes the following points:

1 Therapists should recognize the misleading nature of many assumptions held about religious groups.
2 Therapists need to respect religious beliefs and practices but assume there are important internal dynamics about the relationship between this person and their faith that they do need to understand.
3 However, they should also assume that people may neither wish to explain everything about their religious practice, nor always be able to do so.
4 People from minority religious communities do not all want to act as representatives of their culture.

Frosh concludes that he would like to be able to declare himself as belonging 'to a diverse, conflictful and creative cultural-religious tradition' and for people to understand him. This could be a useful way to approach people from a variety of unfamiliar backgrounds, whose difference from ourselves can at times feel overwhelming. Woodcock (1995) describes therapeutic work with people in exile, at the London Medical Foundation for Care of Victims of Torture. Often working on many issues at once such as PTSD, bereavement, cultural dislocation and downward shifts in status, they view all sources of distress as episodes in a life which has other qualities and components. They may employ a variety of strategies to help somebody to control flashbacks, either through guided recall or by successfully 'burying' the memory as some people prefer, but they do so within a holistic plan focused on the creation of new understanding. Connecting with their culture of origin is the major source of meaning, out of which healing rituals may be developed. Their new homeland is connected to their place of exile through discussions which act as bridges: talk of different rituals surrounding particular events, about weather and climate and the rhythms of the seasons.

Krause (1995) argues for the value of contemporary anthropological research in transcultural family therapy. Distinguishing between personhood as socially constructed and expressed through a variety of social roles, and selfhood as the mental and physical awareness people have of their individuality, she explores the balance between them. This varies from culture to culture but is not always accessible to individuals. In addition, cultural difference between therapist and client(s) may be so great that commenting or being curious about it may inhibit rather than facilitate the relationship. In both cases consulting the anthropological literature may be productive, although she warns against its mechanical or dogmatic application. It should stimulate the therapist's imagination and intuition by expanding their knowledge of the great range in behaviour, thought and feeling expressed by people from different cultures. Clearly, this is consistent with the earlier recommendation to strive for greater psychic unity within diversity.

Conclusions

Maps of psychological location suggest that people are suspended within a number of different cultural forces. As societies get more complex and people attain higher levels of education the number of communities people belong to tends to grow, and so the forces multiply. This increases the number of ethical dilemmas people face, because they often originate in value-conflicts between the different communities to which they belong.

Sociologists suggest that communities are dwindling or undergoing such rapid change that the concept of 'community' is no longer a reliable one; there are fewer places into which clinical populations leaving hospitals can be 'integrated'. One response is to create communities that provide an illusory security. These look attractive to relatives dissatisfied with fragmented services, but such conceived communities encounter a number of difficulties and rarely last beyond the working life of their charismatic leader. Since most of us lack the force or drive to make such projects work, it is a poor model of service: 'Pity the land that needs heroes.' Another failed response is to draw blueprints of human relationships and pursue them inflexibly: the way that normalization is construed in many learning disability services is an example. New ways to evolve dialogues and services that meet more of the emotional needs of families and their relatives do need to be developed.

Superimposed upon these problems in the 1990s has been the centripetal force of multiculturalism, where difference is celebrated and unity viewed with suspicion. It brings many benefits: increasing social justice through inclusion, enlarging our sympathies and knowledge, and helping members of mainstream cultures to see their implicit assumptions. Interest in cultural difference has stretched beyond ethnicity to include many different aspects of human experience, including religion. However, multiculturalism carries tolerance to impossible extremes that bring ethical problems. One solution is to take a clear perspective about what types of difference we are willing to engage with and to do so with a wholehearted willingness to merge our moral horizons with the other. This carries the possibility that we may refuse to work with people whose stances we consider outside our ethical understanding, but facilitates genuine dialogue with the majority. I have followed others in arguing that such dialogue is our best chance of moving beyond diversity towards greater unity, an important goal since fragmentation weakens protest: divide and rule is a familiar axiom. In a political climate where a Labour government can consider taxing the benefits provided to disabled people, anybody concerned for disadvantaged members of society must respect difference but strive to construct consensus.

Summary

The *contemporary issues* were meanings of culture and community, where the geographer's perspective was used to show how these two concepts affect clinical services. With regard to community, conflict was identified between services designed on physical space and those concerned to promote connections in social space: shared interests rather than shared location. Services have to be designed on space to ensure they are available to all, but they work more effectively when designed to enhance communities of interest. Multiculturalism and its implications for practice were discussed extensively, alongside the vexations and achievements of community care.

Histories of the present played little part in this chapter, which prioritized social and physical space rather than time. Nevertheless, intellectual histories illustrating the fertility of debates between mainstream and opposing views help to create confidence that debates between marginal and mainstream communities can be productive for both, if conditions for genuine dialogue can be created. Brief background histories about patterns of migration into Britain also help us to see how the experiences of people from ethnic minority groups in this country differ from those in the USA. This enables us to interpret with caution literature about multiculturalism written in the USA, while the age profile demonstrates why transcultural issues are more familiar to clinicians working in children's services than to people working with the elderly. It also invites each clinician to become interrogative, to discover the patterns of ethnicity in their district because they are so variable that relatively few generalizations can be made about culturally appropriate services in Britain.

Intersubjective meanings were implicit in the concern to evolve unity from diversity. Achieving this requires understanding and respect for differences, accompanied by a willingness to adopt aspects of neighbouring projects which do not conflict with our own. The absence of providential spaces where commonalities, mutual interest and co-operation can evolve is a major barrier to the development of intersubjective meanings. Their creation is more important than the pursuit of service blueprints.

Critical thinking: off-the-shelf approaches to service, such as a quarter of a century of normalization and the shifting goals of community care, were reviewed critically and their conceptual basis found wanting. The achievements and limitations of multiculturalism were also reviewed. The ideas have moved societies a little closer to social justice and have enriched people by expanding options for living, but they also support the wet liberalism that is unwilling to evaluate different ways of living and unable to object to abuse.

Considering research about racial/cultural identity can give the *reflective researcher-practitioner* a personal connection to ideas they may have ignored hitherto, providing some equipment to explore the meaning of cultural differences between ourselves and our clients. Ideas of culture have expanded to include many styles of living: black people have suggested that secular white professionals will not understand them as long as they remain uncomfortable with religion, and differences in belief and faith are starting to be discussed in psychotherapeutic and family therapy journals. This has been accompanied by a warning not to assume that other cultures are homogeneous. Therapists have to tread the delicate path of exploring how this person engages with their ethnic, religious or other community, while avoiding a lengthy interrogation about matters irrelevant to their concerns.

Human systems: cultural differences may be so great that interpreters are necessary. These radically change the intervention system and their contribution needs to be managed carefully. The wider systems in which we work were also touched upon in a discussion which urged government to reverse the fragmentation which current policies impose; in the absence of such a rethink, practitioners need to set realistic goals about how much concord they can achieve when service structures pit welfare systems against each other.

The argument was made that coalitions among different interest groups are vastly preferable to internecine war, which favours the status quo. This has the corollary that clinicians should challenge single-service developments in favour of those that grow at the interface between different groups and facilitate dialogue. In the preface to this book I posed the problem of whether it is appropriate to support a demand for a single-sex respite care service for Asian women. One answer to the issue is that it depends where the demand is made, since the population distribution suggests it is more likely to be viable in Leicester than in Aberdeen. However, even though an argument for equity can be made, addressing injustice by creating more fragmentation is no solution. Negotiation would identify what are core features of an acceptable service to those who request it; provision would not need to be exclusive to them. Perhaps a women-only respite care service for people from all cultures and faiths would be viable; if so that would open the possibility of new forms of dialogue about gender between different cultural groups, out of which new understandings could emerge.

Notes

1 Community care was established in the UK by the Griffiths Report (1988).

2 All of this work is detailed in Clegg (1993).

3 An example concerns a 1995 discussion document on community services which was issued for comment by the Department of Health, citing O'Brien's five accomplishments as the shared values on which all future services should be developed. I responded that this initial statement would inhibit the committee's thinking and prevent them from developing a new perspective on any of the problems practitioners now face. A young woman telephoned me in response, not to hear why I made such a heretical suggestion but to 'reassure' me that they were not closing down any avenues, they just thought it important to make an initial statement of values. Her tone suggested that these were incorrigible, as indeed I fear they have become.

4 In 1910, 8 million voters participated, while in the next election (following the armistice) 22 milllion people had the vote, including women over 30 (Baker, 1995).

5 As described by Gregory (1994).

6 I visited a token economy ward in 1978 which contained three recalcitrant people: their overdraft of points meant that each had to behave perfectly for the next year to break even! Values underlying their points system were clearly one of the problems: hitting another patient lost you 50 points, but hitting a nurse 150.

7 For a contemporary review of therapeutic communities in clinical practice, see Millard and Oakley (1994).

8 In Britain the most well known theatre group is Graeae, a title taken from a Greek myth about three old women who were abhorred by men and gods alike. The myth says that they lived far away in a land without sunlight, where the women shared their only assets, one eye and one tooth, which they used by turns.

9 Lotman (1991) analyses events during the Renaissance, a period which many regard as progressive but which caused huge discontinuities in the lives of the 'masses'. Lotman describes everyday life as coming apart at the moorings, causing fear of anyone who spoke or dressed or prayed differently. That fear resulted in witch hunts and immolations, so extensive in some areas that some German towns were left with no women in them at all. The period ended when social and political stabilization occurred, fear dissipated, and the 'awakening' characteristic of the Enlightenment was felt by all. Loss of a psychological bond with the immediate past led to attempts to break the chronological bond as well, cultural myths of the Enlightenment relegating these events to the remote Middle Ages. Lotman argues that periods of cultural anxiety creating common cause across communities can be traced at many points in history, but that these only result in destructive social movements when the entire system of sociocultural semiotics changes.

10 This section is informed by a paper given by Steve Trevillion, Lecturer in Social Policy at Brunel University. He has other publications on collaborative teamworking: *Caring in the Community*. Harlow: Longman, 1996; also P. Beresford and S. Trevillion, *Developing Skills for Community Care: A Collaborative Approach*. Aldershot: Arena, 1995.

6 Meaning, Discursive Psychology and Narrative

Holding a small flame of attention under David's hesitant and whispered words, I strain to understand through articulation blurred by Down's syndrome. It is our first meeting late in the afternoon, in a strange building: a knock at the door to announce the next client breaks the moment. Disappointed for us both at the lost effort, I wind down. After David leaves, I remain conscious that Penny and her social worker are waiting in a corridor for me. The normal reread of a file in preparation for another first interview seems overcautious and I head down to meet them.

Penny's eyes are bright and edgy. She is 21, tall and athletic, referred following a recent disclosure of long-term sexual abuse by her father. Two weeks ago she moved out of the family home to live in a hostel which she dislikes. In the corridor the social worker explains that Penny has just visited home for the first time: this is against their advice and she admonishes Penny jokingly.

In the room Penny speaks very fast, in short sentences. She uses her eyes to demand that I keep up as she mentions her brothers, people in the hostel, social workers, police, trivial and important events. The day my accelerator cable froze comes to mind, a problem I recognized with horror as the car got faster despite my easing off the throttle at the top of a hill. Penny goads me, implicitly demanding that I make something of the session even though she blocks every effort. Her hostility is palpable. I aim to stay with the conversation long enough for Penny to have some basis for deciding whether or not she wants us to meet again next week. Out of the blue she claims I have just asked something she has already mentioned, triumphant in her proof that nobody cares enough to listen to her properly. We end after an exhausting 20 minutes.

I berate myself for seeing two new clients one after the other, late in the day and at the end of a demanding week. Appalled at how slow I was to adjust from the painstaking speech of the first person to the steamtrain talk of the second, I wonder whether I should have started a session which looked so unpropitious. Yet Penny came the following week, to a different and better location, and on many other occasions. She was never again so testing or hostile. The meanings we struggled to create in that fiery conversation were sufficient for a relationship to be born: it saw her through the challenges associated with a thrice-deferred court case, a failed hostel placement and a slow settling into sheltered accommodation.

This chapter considers what practitioners are doing when they work with clients to create alternative meanings.[1] Naturally, I assume meaning to be neither discovered nor uncovered, but made; much if not most of clinical practice entails the co-creation of new meaning. This practice occurs within a context: Taylor (1989) describes the meaning of life as the most problematic aspect of twentieth-century ethics and thus the most important. Meaning is often quested for without being attained, such seekers switching focus or belief systems frequently through their lives; when achieved, meaning can be experienced without words, but words and narratives are generally necessary to communicate that experience.

Slife (1995) suggests there are two distinct approaches to contemporary meaning-making: social constructionist and hermeneutic. Both approaches assume meaning to be multifaceted, comprised of aspects of the therapist's experience and the client(s) problem; social constructionists go beyond that to consider interaction with the myriad social influences which engender human distress and constitute clinical practice as its remedy. This approach is sometimes dubbed 'discursive psychology' because it emphasizes the essentially dialogical nature of knowledge and experience. With an approximate genealogy stretching from Nietzsche, Foucault and Derrida on the continent to Potter, Parkinson and Kitzinger in the UK, discursive psychology is said to occupy the 'revolutionary' wing of social constructionism (Honderich, 1995). Feminists, and more recently disability activists, have exhorted discursive psychology to move beyond talking heads to encompass the disputed territory of bodies, work that Howard (1997) argues it has incorporated effectively.

Hermeneutics is the alternative strand of constructionist thought: it has more in common with activity theorists such as Vygotsky and Valsiner and theorists on the other wing of social constructionism such as Bruner, who are described as 'reformist'. Like discursive psychology, hermeneutics is explicitly concerned to avoid mind–body dualism, but does so by adding the dimension of time instead of layers of context. For the hermeneutic psychologist the person does not change moment to moment; they engage over time with their own past experience and future beliefs and with other persons and objects. I will argue that hermeneutics provides a more effective conceptual framework for narrative therapy and clinical practice than does discursive psychology.

Discursive and narrative psychologies are often combined, but Howard (1997) distinguishes them. He describes discursive psychology as concerned with all the linguistic utterances made by people, whom he imagines to be adrift on a rudderless ship, moved and occasionally engulfed by shifting seas. By contrast Howard paints narrative psychology as assuming that people have more agency in their lives. These sailors wait out tides and tack into the wind to assert their own direction, one of many possible options. However, he thinks that narrative psychology has generally limited its horizon to talk and needs to theorize the role of embodied experience more effectively.

Whether we consider meanings to be created more by contexts than by activity over time, both approaches go beyond the client to theorize the clinician's contribution. Although psychology maintains a general interest in technique and content rather than process, process research in psychotherapy is an honourable exception, as is Bischoff and Sprenkle's (1993) demonstration that the number of hours a practitioner has spent doing family therapy predicts client satisfaction. As will become clear, psychologists from the discursive and narrative traditions take very different approaches to understanding the therapist's contribution to meaning.

This chapter briefly introduces discursive psychology, as it is primarily a research position and is covered in the next chapter too. It then explores in some detail ideas of interpretation within a hermeneutic framework because these ideas provide a useful basis for clinical meaning-making; because they connect to a moral position on meaning that is touched upon here and developed further in the chapter on ethics; and because hermeneutics can be shown to connect with other philosophies discussed in this book. This leads into the main practical section, which explores narrative therapies and the creation of meaning in a variety of clinical settings.

Discursive Psychology[2]

The contexts of practice that contribute to meaning in clinical settings are explored less often than the ideas held by the people involved, but are regarded as extremely relevant by these practitioners. For example, there are some clients who prefer to attend appointments in a large university hospital: it seems to give value to their difficulty and persuades them they are getting the best treatment in town. Others are confused about where they should go, feel the building is intimidating, and prefer to have appointments on more familiar and local premises. Deciding upon the location of a clinic is therefore an explicitly political act, defining the types of clients it is provided for. Similarly the therapist has to balance ideal therapeutic conditions, which include an adequate waiting room, against the less ideal but local when constructing a therapeutic contact, so the location influences content as well as clients. Legal constraints on the content of case notes and the need to think about personal safety are further influences on the contexts of meaning that envelop therapy; they interact in turn with broader social influences like client poverty and service cuts. Attention to such contextual detail is the mainstay of discursive approaches to psychology.

Some clinicians claim to draw on Foucauldian constructionism within therapy (Epston and White, 1989), but those claims have been disputed widely and White no longer presents his therapy as constructionism in action. Even one of White's protagonists, Madigan (1992), had to admit that this therapy is open to criticism from discursive psychologists: 'This turning of real lives into writing is viewed by Foucault as yet another mechanism of social control' (1992: 268). Luepnitz points out the contradiction in claiming to use a Foucauldian approach to therapy when Foucault's entire project was to challenge the role of experts; to criticize and deconstruct, not to advance solutions. She offers three hypothetical projects to illustrate a Foucauldian agenda for family therapy (1992: 283), projects that would be more archival than empirical and are intentionally works of criticism:

1 Research the ways in which the writings and methods of nineteenth-century social workers and community activists were subjugated in order to generate family therapy's current creation myth, according to which the field was conceived by brave white male psychiatrists in the 1950s.
2 How could his analysis inform a critique of the one-way mirror in family therapy?
3 Show how this (technologies of the self that create 'docile bodies' willing to submit to experts) applies to the practice of informed consent in family therapy.

Harper's critical research deconstructs the process of making a diagnosis of paranoia, but in more recent work (1996) he develops his thinking to show how a constructionist perspective can bridge the pathological/normal divide and so work towards the positive incorporation of diverse voices into practice. He discusses the importance of remaining open to diverse accounts, challenging assumptions that only one version of events can be 'right'. He cites his own and others' research in arguing for diverse voices in mental health practice: for placing the accounts of service users alongside biological and psychiatric accounts, and for challenging the psychiatric notion that it is only the form of ideas that counts, not their content. He suggests that practitioners explore the degree to which abnormal beliefs may function to (for example) maintain self-esteem, confer special status, provide comfort, or remove responsibility for negatively judged behaviour. But he also argues for the development of a concept which can encompass both form and content in working to help distressed people who hold abnormal beliefs.

St Claire's (1989) analysis of different facets of a socially constructed model of learning disability also calls into question the process by which people become classified: she shows how people with one role failure tend to be categorized as learning disabled on the assumption that they also have characteristic organic impairments, and vice versa. Unlike mental health, learning disability suffers from having different accounts of the experience that continue to compete; it has yet to encompass the co-existence of multiple meanings in this multiply determined and constructed condition. Accounts of experiences such as epilepsy or cerebral palsy certainly need to contain physical, personal and social aspects to be comprehensive. Yet in many quarters discussions of corporeal aspects of experience meet accusations of essentialism,[3] or the medicalization of human experience. Remaining blind to bodily experiences derives from Descartes's separation of mind and body: summarized by the term 'dualism', this separation still pervades the thinking of many social researchers and practitioners.

Sampson (1996) suggests that there are three different approaches to embodiment in psychology, but that none gives a real foothold on the theoretical problem. He begins with traditional psychological topics such as cognition, memory, personality and so on, disembodied work where only a few studies explore the brain–mind interface within the individual. Second comes the idea of embodied individuation. From this perspective most people experience body as the ground of their experience, but it becomes the figure – or subject – of experience when pain, disability or other unusual experiences bring it to the fore. Eastern religious practices conceptualize enhanced intellectual insight as an experience achieved through the body and bodily disciplines such as meditation, rather than by ignoring it. The revival of Pentecostal religions in the USA and, to a lesser degree, in the UK also focuses on 'the embodied nature of human religious endeavour' (1996: 614).

Other social researchers also discuss meditation. Blackmore (1995) reported that when she took up meditation she understood experientially how her thinking is intrinsically connected to her body, and her body to others in the human and non-human world. Similarly, Claxton (1994) describes the mindfulness of Zen Buddhism as a state which prevents him from being carried away from the here and now on a stream of thinking: it provides a vantage-point from which to see better, enabling him to be open and curious rather than striving to be in charge. However, rather than accepting constructionist and Buddhist arguments against the concept of self, Claxton argues that the 'Self System' is an accretion of culturally acquired beliefs which themselves change the way that the mind–brain system functions and thus the way the world appears. He draws widely on consciousness research to show how well-used systems of thought develop fast connections within the brain, giving a physiological basis to automatic thoughts and perceptions. He emphasizes that these can be switched off and others acquired.

Sampson notes that there is a huge leap from these perspectives to a third approach to embodiment, taken by social constructionists. Here the body is not inhabited but inscribed, by cultural practices such as teaching young men to walk with the commanding gravitas of a lion.[4] There are multiplying conceptualizations of the body, influenced by culture and history, but they are mediated almost entirely through language, with no contribution from the interior nor from the body.

Grosz (1993) argues that mind has been accorded the higher status and masculinized, while bodies became women's business and had been ignored. She uses a twofold approach to theorizing the body: examining sociopolitical factors such as gender, race or disability which are *inscribed* on the body and the way that those experiences are *lived* within the body.

In learning disability, the body certainly is the place where social forces are inscribed as well as the place where disability is experienced. This often creates great distress:

> *Yasmin experiences extreme but infrequent stomach pain for which no physical cause has been identified, despite extensive tests; she can also sleep and be unrousable for days on end when away from home. At school she was called names, at college people threaten to beat her up as well. She yearns to be like her sister, who drives a car and is married; like her friend, who is having a baby. She knows she is different, that people in night clubs do not want to dance with her, but she cannot see why. In common with many of her peers she attends an endless series of further education courses, the implicit message being 'you are not good enough, but might become so if you learn more skills'. Community staff create new experiences away from her family, but then the stomach pains develop.*
>
> *Yasmin's body has truly become the arena for experience: of her disability, of social inscriptions concerning that disability, and of the emotional conflicts which result.*

Deployed in isolation the scientific language of organic impairment or the so-called 'medical model' removes the person from their position in time and relation to others. It privileges the present as the most important timescape, making it difficult to understand how that person exists within their social world. It also further separates clinical populations from society. People such as Yasmin and Penny exist on the margins of an out group, and welcome any process that questions the label they despise.

There is another side, however, where criticisms grow of verbal sleights of hand that constructionists use to argue that neither death nor furniture exist. Such redefinitions give politicians licence to dismantle specialist health and welfare systems under the guise of inclusivity and increased 'freedom' for clients, without transferring the funds that would enable mainstream services to cope: this process is predicted to continue (Rowitz, 1992). Whether integrating children with learning difficulties into mainstream schools is progressive policy or a cost-cutting measure varies from area to area, but it is far from being clearly advantageous. Discursive psychology helps to show how dialogue constructs people and lives and can be altered to construct more amenable social spaces, but it needs to stand alongside rather than deny embodied experiences such as voice-hearing, confusion, bullying or disability.

In conclusion, discursive psychology is very good at creating critical accounts that help us to see complex social experiences anew; it is a point where academic psychology provides ideas that are of central utility to clinicians. One problem it poses to therapists is the way it handles subjectivity: this seems largely to depend upon declarations of one's biases so that others can avoid people whose positions they do not like, and on publication of large amounts of original interview material so that readers can dismiss or dispute the interviewer's thesis if they see fit. If one pushes further at that door, prominent constructionists such as Potter generally question what function these questions serve within these particular circumstances. By analysing the rhetoric of such discussions and ignoring their content, they sidestep the therapist's problem of what skills, understandings and stances are most likely to help clients and least likely to damage them.

The idea that social constructionism can be compatible with therapy was promoted by an influential text edited by McNamee and Gergen (1992), although like the term 'postmodernism' the meaning of social constructionism has undergone many changes in the succeeding six years. Two chapters from that book come from individual therapists, but the majority draw on or discuss family and systemic therapy. I will argue that most of the therapeutic work described in that text actually relates more closely to, and benefits conceptually from, a hermeneutic model of constructionism.

Interpretation and Meaning

Hermeneutics was briefly introduced in Chapter 2, with Valentine's description of it as one type of explanation used in psychology. It underpins German *Verstehen* psychology, which developed an approach based on empathic understanding rather than the psychophysiological studies which developed elsewhere. However, it originates in theology and means 'the art of interpretation': the sense in which I use it here derives from Heidegger whose hermeneutic phenomenology gives an understanding of self, social and physical environment over time. It concerns a way of seeing people and events that includes the possibilities inherent in these things. Hermeneutic interpretation for Heidegger goes beyond the discourse analysis of Derrida, where words of the text are all there is; for Heidegger words show something beyond themselves, being intimately connected with both what is being interpreted and the person doing the interpreting. His heirs are Gadamer, and Ricoeur, the latter taking issue with Derrida and other post-structuralists (who include discourse analysts) for 'what he sees as their relentlessly negative stance with regard to questions of meaning, subjectivity and truth' (Honderich, 1995: 774).

Heidegger[5] employed subjectivity to understand *Dasein*, literally 'being there', the-person-in-the-world:[6] *Dasein* was his unit of analysis rather than the isolated, reflective individual. He is credited with having driven through the horns of the dilemma facing modern people, both the subject–object dichotomy and the meaning of life. Heidegger did this by challenging the subject–object metaphor of consciousness as a black box with walls that separate the self from the social and physical world. By conceptualizing the human and physical world as standing outside any position in time or space, our experience is rendered unintelligible in a world which *is* temporal and *does* have location. He intended to loosen up traditional subject–object thinking and provide a clearing where *Dasein*, being-in-the-world, could be understood. Human beings are already in the world, they are not a box walled off from it: to know is to be involved with something or someone. Nothing stands outside of a context: the world is certainly 'there' but it is unintelligible without its temporality, it exists only in dialogue with us. For Heidegger, knowledge is created through and out of practical, everyday life.

Faulconer and Williams (1990) provide a cogent history of the concepts 'objective' and 'subjective', ideas rooted in metaphysical assumptions about the relation between humankind and knowledge. For the ancient Greeks, people did not come to know the world by grasping it and putting it into the container of the mind as we now conceptualize understanding – encapsulated by the exclamation 'I've got it!' Instead, Aristotle described understanding as coming awake or learning to look. It involves expanding consciousness of the world.

This is not so abstruse as it may seem. I recently saw a videotape of a family therapy session which I first saw 18 months ago. On the first occasion I watched while wondering whether to commit myself to family therapy training, concerned to make a simple judgement: either this can be useful to families with a disabled member, or it is not worth my time. I knew little of the strategies and techniques and so noticed little about them. The second time I had been steeped in family therapy theory, practice and technique for over a year; that made it possible for me to discern subtleties I simply could not see at the first watching. From an Aristotelian and Heideggerian stance, education involves acquiring and engaging critically with a new set of ways to look at the world; becoming better equipped to enjoy its multiplicity. Heidegger follows this to argue that people who live less excellently live more illusory lives, lives not fully informed by experience.

The Greek and medieval idea that understanding derives from right looking and harmony with the world is consistent with the Zen Buddhist conception of knowing as a way of being, a moral way. During the Enlightenment, philosophers separated knowledge from morality and started to focus on individual knowing. Knowing was no longer attunement with a divinely created world, it became power over an objectified one; chaos is fundamental and the ordering power of the human mind should control it. Faulconer and Williams argue that the question was no longer how we can be brought to comprehend the world, but how to ensure that our perception of it is certain rather than capricious. While Enlightenment science has allowed many nations to avoid the worst consequences of the *natural* world's disasters and to make great strides technologically, many continental philosophers and psychologists influenced by them believe that Enlightenment science results in misinterpretation of the *social* world.

Polkinghorne (1990) describes the Enlightenment as being founded on four assumptions: that the real is unchanging, that ordinary knowing is flawed, that truth is only revealed by specific methods, and that humans can access a set of natural laws on which truth claims can be based. These assumptions soon lost any degree of tentativeness in their restatement. In the middle of this Enlightenment world was the self-defining individual, to whom all others were related. If there is a God then its reality must be proved to these selves, for individuals are the centre and origin of all knowledge: 'In Aristotle, the ultimate reality is in charge; in Bacon, the individual self is' (Polkinghorne, 1990: 29).

This self-defining individual occurred when Renaissance thinkers decentred the divine; the individual moved into the centre of this system of knowledge, where meaning resides in the rational individual who exists in a world of objects. Polkinghorne asserts that from Kant onwards modern philosophers describe the relation between self and the objective world, but not that between the self and other persons; Kant made it explicit that his philosophy is only a metaphysics of objects.[7] Subsequent philosophers, including twentieth-century thinkers such as Hare (1989), use logic to treat humans as if they are objects because this conceptual system provides no other way of knowing them. By making the self-defining individual central to metaphysics, the self is *by definition* rendered contentless. The conditions were set whereby people would inevitably experience a crisis in the meaning of their lives.

Two ways to overcome the dilemmas created by dividing the world into subjects and objects have emerged. One is to establish objects which transcend self and world and can act as bridges: this is the most common solution. Culture, technological progress, or political organizations such as the socialist or Fascist parties have all been raised to this transcendent position. The problem is that humanity is made the subject of these objects and so becomes enslaved by them, creating various dilemmas: does spending hours at a computer screen inhibit a child's development, or provide her with a fast track to success in a technological world? How can pacifists persuade poor, disadvantaged and undereducated young men to abandon the sharp sense of purpose which war gives them: what else would provide such a vibrant sense of meaning?

The second attempted solution focuses even more attention on the self: this produces the worst excesses of the human potential movement, which Faulconer and Williams believe results in nihilism when taken to its limits (an issue which Taylor also discusses: see Chapter 8, p. 182). The nihilism at its centre may explain why many of its exponents engage in endless quests; each approach fails to provide the meaning sought because the goal of expanding one's consciousness or experience *for its own sake* has no meaning. These two failed solutions to the subject–object dichotomy can be seen in adherence to scientific empiricism, which includes research into the laws of human behaviour; and in the self psychologies that stretch from Gestalt to Rogers, leftovers from the modern age with little connection to postmodern culture.

By contrast, with *Dasein* as the starting-point the problem of meaning retreats, because it is assumed that human beings already live in meaningful worlds, worlds full of practical activities and relationships of mutual concern. Knowledge of humanity is not the exclusive province of trained experts but available to all people who engage honestly in-the-world. Here, knowing makes sense in terms of already-being-involved-in. This way of knowing is not 'relativist'. It emerges from a way of being-in-the-world that creates truths and not falsity, truths that are and can only be temporal and relational. Thus while there are truths, there is no final truth. Truth is how things are: temporal and textual, not static and otherworldly, and these created truths in turn make up our world. Yet to engage with the world honestly, truthfully and so on as Heidegger discusses presupposes a clear position on ethics or morality, a huge topic in its own right that is elaborated in Chapter 8.

Reder and Duncan's (1995) exploration of the meanings some children have for parents is an important example of hermeneutic thinking in action. They studied 35 fatal child abuse cases to ask why certain children in a family are abused more severely than others. They conclude that all children have psychological meaning for their parents, meanings that derive from unresolved conflicts or losses and make the child the carrier of certain expectations of role or behaviour. These meanings become particularly distorted in cases of abuse, where the child becomes 'an actor in someone else's play'. Their illustrations include the killing of Maria Colwell.

> *Maria was a child imbued with special meaning by her mother, Pauline, because she was the last of five fathered by Raymond Colwell: he left one month after Maria was born and he died three months after that. All the children were taken into care because of neglect, but Maria was the only one that Pauline insisted be brought up as a Catholic like herself: also she asked for Maria to be returned continually. When Pauline was settled within a stable relationship where she had another four children, Maria was returned to Pauline and William Kepple aged six years: she died from William's violence a year later. Reder and Duncan's conjecture is that Maria represented Pauline's lost relationship with Raymond Colwell; they had too little information on William Kepple to suggest his perspective. Pauline's concern to be reunited with Maria may have been an attempt to deal with feelings of loss which went wrong, probably because Maria could not play Raymond's role and because this distressed child rejected her new caretakers.*

Reder and Duncan recommend that assessors in child abuse cases consider the possible contribution of cultural beliefs; patterns in the family's history in particular unmourned deaths or losses close to the birth of this child; parents' unresolved conflicts; current interactional patterns; the child's personal history and characteristics such as gender, easy or difficult delivery, or disability. They end with an example of how such assessments can result in explanatory links which, if accepted by the abusing parent, can form the basis of therapeutic change.

The main criticism of hermeneutic explanation is that if researchers interpret the world entirely from their existing knowledge, the approach cannot explain where new ideas come from: its explanations are circular.

Yet circularity is central to hermeneutic philosophy; perhaps the translation into English of the original German idea is unfortunate in conjuring a process of going nowhere, of chasing one's tail. Exponents of hermeneutic methods argue that interpreters must move recursively between a literal and a psychological perspective, and between the whole and its constituent parts, changing perspective in a way that cannot be stipulated by rules to create the new. This goes to the heart of meaning-making: that without any effort towards open-minded curiosity and the adoption of different perspectives, researchers and clinicians risk merely recreating their own prejudices when studying the social world.

Heidegger was trained in phenomenology though he rejected it later. He learned to attend to the essence of a matter, to shift his attention beyond a particular instance to see the totality and its connections with other essential things through intuition. 'Bracketing' the objective world is the first step to achieving such a phenomenological reduction. This involves learning how to look at things unclouded by personal prejudice or theoretical presupposition about its nature: to see the thing itself. Describing the essence of something is the first step towards being able to interpret it. Heidegger rejected this 'objective' approach as distant, uninvolved, atemporal, and striving towards a transcendental truth which cannot be identified. Nevertheless, when moving from subjective immersion to distant appraisal, it is possible that he would have used some of those phenomenological skills.

So circularity is not a negative description of a fruitless search, but a process of changing perspectives that is generative. Freeman (1993) provides another argument for using hermeneutic interpretation in psychology. He uses biographies to show that although the self cannot be the sovereign origin of meaning, since the tools it employs inevitably draw on ideas and words used by others, nevertheless the 'I' does do something unique with the words it internalizes. In doing so it enlarges the scope of self and, sometimes, of the world – it does not merely reorder and regurgitate the ideas we already have, as Valentine (1992: 199–200) suggests. Freeman focuses on moments of transcendence exemplified by St Augustine, by Helen Keller, by the story-teller in Sartre's *Nausea*, by Philip Roth in his autobiography, by Sylvia Fraser's memoir of incest, and by Jill Ker Conway's decision to leave her cultural homeland in the Australian bush to live a different narrative. In doing so he identifies moments when the object-self that is prey to cultural forces also becomes a wilful-self who can act to change the world. His study links hermeneutic philosophy and narrative psychology.

Narratives and Clinical Practice

Social science interest in narrative occurs during a time of crisis for the modern novel. Books are marketed more on the author's credentials than on their context: at Christmas 1997 the media were filled with tales of a 96-year-old woman having published her first book. Yet hoaxes and deceits are performed on a credulous public who want to believe that accomplished first novels can be written by an Aboriginal woman with no education, rather than valuing her life for its own integrity – and who discard such 'bestsellers' as having no value once their authors are revealed to be middle-aged men with fertile imaginations.[8] This is a curious context for social science, unused to working within such explicit cultural forces; yet narratives are a powerful way in which we communicate and understand ourselves and should not be hived off as the preserve of elite specialists.

Nash (1990) suggests that a first flush of ecstatic theorizing about the way narrative helps us understand culture is being followed by a second, more pragmatic wave that explores narrative as a technique for gaining coherence. Narrative is certainly set to become one of the dominant ideas of the late 1990s. Mentioned by Harvey as one of his cracks in the mirror of postmodernism, narratives challenge the worst excesses of postmodern image-making because they unfold over time.

There is currently enormous variation in the meanings that philosophers, human scientists and therapists place on the term 'narrative'. Some see all human experience as a nest of stories-within-stories; others restrict narrative to special kinds of human exchange which are employed to serve particular purposes. I follow Reissman (1993) in using narrative in this second, more bounded sense. She suggests that people narrativize particular experiences, often those where there has been a breach between ideal and real, or self and society.[9] Her 70-page booklet is a gem of clarity and brevity, rooted in academic sociology but aimed precisely at the research–practice interface. Many of her doctoral students and colleagues have been clinical psychologists weighed down by 300-page transcripts, puzzled by incredibly rich information they have no idea how to handle. Analysis of a narrative sequence focuses on how the story was put together to make sense of actions and lives; what linguistic and cultural sources it draws on; and how it persuades the listener. This section explores four different approaches to clinical practice that incorporate narrative.

Four Types of Clinical Application

Narratives about the meanings people create in their lives move readily into intervention and clinical practice, because stories can change, and with those changes the options which lie before people multiply. Becoming alert to the narratives we employ to make sense of clinical issues can 'unstick' situations by helping practitioners to generate new approaches. Similarly, recognizing how people construct past events into a story-line which makes sense to them and their audience, you, can also give a new perspective on clinical conversations. Whether two parents report that their daughter with a learning disability is better or worse depends on a combination of meanings: selective memory – recalling how she behaved a year ago must necessarily be selective – mixes with other meanings such as that they have had to accept that children with learning disabilities cannot be cured, so perhaps they do not change at all (see Clegg and King, 1998).

The first approach concerns narrative approaches to therapy with adults and families, although it is a conceptualization which applies to any client group. White and Epston's *Narrative Means to Therapeutic Ends* (1990) introduces many of these ideas. Often referred to as the leading text in narrative re-authoring as an approach to therapy, they argue that therapy is a political act if it challenges unhelpful cultural constructions. Based on the idea that disempowered people are more likely to internalize social values about what manner of person they 'should' be, externalizing the problem by separating it from any defining feature of 'self' is therefore seen to be an important solution.

Exciting and fertile as these ideas have been, subtle interpretive work has to be done to construct an appropriate problem on which to work. People often arrive for therapy defeated by the problem as they see it, with accounts of lives that are saturated by it; this is not a promising start and meanings need to be shifted before progress can be made. The therapist tries to avoid imposing an alternative reframe but does co-construct a different sort of definition through discussion, asking questions that are clearly aimed towards a problem definition he or she can work with. White (1989) describes moving the problem of a young girl failing to go to sleep alone to one of a more general problem of insecurity; when another family complained about tantrums, this changed to a more fluid description of the role that guilt plays in the way they relate together; when people brought the expert definition that Jim has schizophrenia a more personal definition evolved, that the habits and experiences of schizophrenia were creating a problem between them all that Jim was becoming a passenger in his own life. This interpretive work carries its own ethic: White (1989) warns against externalizing problems like violence and abuse, because it would be wrong to redefine or enable people to disown them. It also requires good timing to prevent digging the family further into their problem-saturated discourse: initial work may need to focus on aspects of their selves and lives that remain outside the problem's power. White does not go on to locate that process of interpretation within a hermeneutic framework; I believe that doing so will open up an aspect of his therapy that remains mysterious to many.

In my view one of the most important contributions made by White and Epston's (1990) narrative therapy is their focus on recruiting and changing audiences. The general thrust is not only the constructionist one that new meanings can be co-created to expand the range of options people have available; they also use the written word in a multiplicity of ways to support change beyond the clinic. They send letters expressing regret over a missed appointment, explaining what topics they had planned to discuss and hoping that the person will feel able to join the discussion at the next session. They give childen certificates for defeating their tantrums. They give a number of copies of a letter to people who are trying to change, which they can pass on to friends to explain what is happening. This moves to change the social network's expectations, to minimize unhelpful reactions that disempower the person's efforts at re-creation. It is another way of thinking about the idea of providential spaces: people who want to change need to create space to do so. Whom they feel able to give the letters to remains entirely within the individual's control.

Sometimes these letters are about children trying to give up difficult behaviours for which they have a well-earned reputation. They come in the form of a reference from the therapist: it notes that Freddy has long been a mischief-maker who lied, bullied and stole, but that he is trying to become more sensitive to others and to defeat the urge to lie and cheat. The therapist cannot guarantee that he will defeat his urges all at once: that is up to Freddy. However, he has made good progress and is going to deliver this letter to important people in his life, so that the new Freddy does not take them by surprise and they can think of different ways to treat this non-mischief-maker.

Another letter was written for a woman recovering from a traumatic rape, to give to friends who might make the mistake of thinking she was unchanged. It explained some of the terror and nightmares she lives with each day, but that what she needs most is not to be advised or forced against her will: she is not strong enough to tell them that directly, so is giving them this letter to solicit their support rather than their coercion. The letter concludes that the responses which other people make to victims of violence and rape is known to be an important factor in their recovery.

A final example from many different and useful written narratives concerns an adolescent who was distraught by the deaths of his two elder brothers in a car accident. Following individual discussions the therapist wrote a letter to the dead brothers on the client's behalf, which he could read out at a memorial service he was dreading. This documented the ways that the client was keeping their memories alive by following their talent at cricket; ways he was growing up and having girlfriends while remembering their advice not to behave hurtfully; it ended by saying how sorely he missed their company. The boy said later how helpful this had been, how relieved he was when the memorial service was over, and that he did not need other people to calm him down any more because the feelings were no longer too strong for him to manage.

In working therapeutically on meaning it is important to attend to the pragmatics of communication. Just as institutions are unable to recall information if it is presented in ways which make no connection with their collective memory,[10] so people receive suggestions and observations most easily when they are couched in familiar terms. Bateson's famous dictum that the therapist needs to introduce just enough difference to make a difference is relevant here: too much and the meaning is missed. In the same way that one member of an observing team in family therapy attends exclusively to words and phrases which a family use, all meaning-makers should use an understanding of clients' communicative styles to shape their interventions.

Another way to use narrative with clients is to consider the timing and manner of disclosures they wish to make to others. It is not uncommon for a woman who was sexually abused by her father to want to confront her mother with the news. Weingarten and Cobb (1995) discuss this within a narrative framework, to maximize the probability of disclosure being believed rather than dismissed. They suggest that the client write it as a letter which is read aloud during therapy, itself celebrating the move from silence to voice. The following sessions explore its narrative coherence, to help the client to see – for example – gaps and inconsistencies which would allow her mother to introduce a counter-narrative; to see where she assigns blame to her mother in a way that will create defensiveness, not support; and to identify the points where her account challenges the family's cultural beliefs, since these are most vulnerable to being re-authored by others. The wish to disclose is then re-examined: it is an opportunity to vent anger, but if there is no hope of being believed and supported the person may feel painfully disempowered. Should she wish to go ahead, one option is to help her to change the disclosure story (not her own account) to one that she feels her mother will be able to hear and support.

Hermans and Hermans-Jansen (1995) provide a hermeneutic focus on self-narratives that draw simultaneously on people and events in the client's past, present and future. They describe how to set the scene to develop a self-narrative which arises from commitment, co-operation and shared responsibility. The process is prompted by a set of questions based on significant meanings ascribed to events or persons or relationships in each time dimension. Through discussion these meanings are reduced to a set of about 15 self-evaluations with which the person describes their current perspective. These are overtly concerned with self and are specific: the general 'hill-walking is wonderful' becomes transformed through conversation into 'I love walking high on the hills, especially on a crisp winter morning' and is then checked against other descriptions of enjoyment to see whether this or another is more important. There is a scoring procedure which is explained to the client; each evaluation is ascribed to one of four main affect terms:

- Self-enhancement – esteem, confidence, strength, pride;
- Other-contact – caring, love, tenderness, intimacy;
- Positive affect – joy, happiness, enjoyment, inner calm;
- Negative affect – unhappiness, despondency, disappointment, worry.

This allows the client to see how evaluations that arise from quite different situations, perhaps a past remark from a teacher and a present one from a workmate, may be associated with similar affective patterns. Discussion of the interaction between these apparently different evaluations with the client, and an inspection of their evaluations in the light of this approach to scoring, allows the person to identify imbalances or hindrances which they may wish to address. It can also serve as the basis for a comparative re-evaluation of their self-narratives six months or a year later.

The second set of applications comes from story-telling as education. This is used by psychologists in paediatric hospital settings to prepare children for potentially frightening procedures, and can be a useful way to share experiences and research findings with clients. MacInlay (personal communication) suggests that the stories for children coping with hospital procedures should meet the following criteria:

- interest the child;
- provide information that is meaningful to both the child and their parent(s);
- provide milestones throughout the procedure, particularly marking the half-way point;
- emphasize that crying is not a catastrophe;
- raise enough anxiety to be able to inoculate effectively, without raising it too much;
- engage the staff in the child's experience and fears;
- provide coping strategies for both children and parent to practise.

An example written by Collier and MacInlay is *Darren has a very important test* which describes a boy with a bladder infection who has to have a micturating cistourethrogram.[11] This can be very distressing, as it involves passing a catheter up his penis and requires that the boy pass urine onto a bed while being watched. The story gives concrete descriptions of the people he met, and what the room and procedure look and feel like; it explains his mixed feelings, torn between exciting new machines and anxiety about what will happpen. Frequent comparisons are made, between how much the catheter hurts, which (for a child who is not afraid) is less painful than the stinging feeling he had during his bladder infection. These are interspersed with normalizing descriptions of his home, his schoolmates, hugs from his mum and praise from the nurses. Parents are encouraged to read the story to their child a week before the procedure, again the night before and again the next morning: Phillips et al. (forthcoming) give a detailed evaluation of such preparation which shows good overall effects.

Stories can also be used to alter a child's social environment, by ameliorating responses to deformity rather than behaviour. An example is a story about being born with a cleft lip and palate, which describes the operation and explains how this creates a few problems in learning to speak clearly. This story helped one girl to make the change from nursery to primary school. It was read to her peers, who were told that they might not understand what she says at first but that it is all right to ask her to say things again: they were also given permission to be curious about her appearance.

Story-telling is one way that people can share their experience with others. It has been used to describe living with voices or becoming a survivor of sexual abuse. This sort of project is undertaken by self-advocacy or empowerment groups but the potential for facilitators to impose their perspective on inarticulate members is high. An example comes from a document about people with long-term mental health problems. The third part was apparently written by four service users, Brigitte, Sue, Mem and Veronika:

> All of us have been recipients of mainstream psychiatric services for varying lengths of time. . . . The people who have treated us have mostly settled on the diagnosis of schizophrenia. . . . We get together as a group once per month and invite Michael White to join us to keep a special record of our conversation and to ask questions that assist us to express our thoughts on various issues. After each of these meetings he puts together our ideas in a document which serves as a record of our evolving knowledges. . . .
>
> **Changing our relationship with the voices**
>
> . . . In developing an exposé of the purposes and operations of these voices and visions, we become clearer about the extent to which what they want for our lives is not in our interests, and we become increasingly knowledgeable about the strategies they use to achieve their purposes. (Dulwich Centre *Newsletter*, 1 (1997): 26–7)

Anybody familiar with White's work since 1989 will recognize the last paragraph as quintessentially his ideas written in his style. The project sounds useful for the clients, but one has to question what contribution this particular set of users made to this text. Perhaps more than one middle-aged antipodean man considers it useful to present his ideas as if they were written by disadvantaged women. The difficulties presented by articulate professionals trying to help people with emotional and intellectual problems to express their experience must not be underestimated. I am not arguing that professionals should abandon the attempt, but that all final written accounts of such projects should be handled with extreme caution.

Perhaps a safer way to use narrative is to stick to the oral tradition, to use story-telling to share research ideas with people who may not understand its conventions or who do not read. One example might be debating comments adults with a learning disability made about their identity (e.g. Davies and Jenkins, 1997; Todd and Shearn, 1997). These authors suggest that the avoidance of labelling and refusal to discuss the nature of learning disability leaves people in a vacuum with no way of understanding why they cannot achieve normal markers of adulthood such as learning to drive, getting married and having children, or getting a job. Saying that a small minority do achieve these marker events merely ducks the issue: in Nottingham 97 per cent of adults with a learning disability have no contact with any form of paid work, even on a part-time basis. Avoiding talk about the condition while having the experience has long been criticized as unhelpful for people who are terminally ill, yet it continues to be regarded as progressive in learning disabilities. It runs the risk that 'learning disability is not so much rendered socially invisible but it is hidden from the people themselves. That is, many people with learning disabilities may be invisible to themselves' (Todd and Shearn, 1997: 363). Nothing can change as long as the experience has no voice.

The third way in which narrative is applied helps children to overcome psychological difficulties, from insomnia and bedwetting to trauma associated with sexual abuse. It could be dubbed story-telling as therapy. Here it is assumed that the child is either too young or too vulnerable to be able to address their problem directly, and that they may be able to use the experiences of somebody similar to them instead. This approach was pioneered by Bettelheim and has developed in two distinct ways.[12] Gardner's (1971) mutual story-telling technique uses it essentially as a projective test. The child is invited to tell a story which should have the following characteristics: be an adventure; not be about television characters or actual experiences the child has had; should have a beginning, middle and end, and a moral point. The therapist may help the child to get going by introducing a story-line but leaving many pauses which the child is invited to fill. The stories are tape-recorded and analysed later for psychodynamic meaning. Therapy involves working with the child to reflect on the story and alter it: using the same characters and setting, it is transformed into a psychologically healthy account. Friedberg's (1994) adaptation of this approach is informed by cognitive rather than psychodynamic theory.

I stumbled into this work when unsure how to help Clyde, an extremely agitated young man who had a mild learning disability and long-standing anxiety problems. The referral was prompted by his distress over the accidental drowning of his aunt, which had amplified his agitation enormously. His difficulties included wanting to check where the rest of his family were by phoning them, which led to embarrassing situations in shops as his elaborate explanations of why he really did need to use *that* phone *this* instant became increasingly urgent.

> *As we started to know one another, it became clear that even though Clyde would open discussions about his emotional world or communications at home, the affect accompanying these was painfully overwhelming. A less direct approach was required. What was striking about him was the press of words which introduced the stories he would employ to describe his week, a perspective which clearly had little in common with the perceptions of people around him. I decided to attend to these.*
>
> *The stories usually started by describing Clyde driving a truck which broke down, but which he managed to mend; later he returned it to the garage, finding it difficult to reverse into a tight space but just managing. As the weeks went on these stories of whether he would fit in or have a place – common amongst people with disabilities who are exploring personal identity - led onto different tales*

around the theme of water. Often he described seeing someone drowning, casting himself as both the observer who called the alarm and the person in the air-sea rescue team who was winched down. There was much acting as he described straining to pull the person out of the water and managing to do so.

Initially it was difficult to see what meaning these stories could contain, because they were filled by less obviously relevant material. His working through the accident and his wish to have been the rescuer became topics which we co-created and explored: he started to discuss the issues directly after about six months. Gradually he became able to limit the stories and his agitation subdued. Although stories continue to play an important role in his communicative life Clyde also began to talk directly about the aunt who drowned, naming her and exploring some of the feelings he had about the accident.

Price-Williams (1989) describes a similar approach with clients who have a lively fantasy world, but he uses guided imagery as one way to help people externalize some of their thoughts and feelings. This involves providing a basic story structure which invites projection. For example, 'You climb a long way up a mountain to visit a wise man who will give you three things to help you. Imagine greeting him and sitting down in front of him. Has he told you his name? Tell me the first thing he gives you.' Price-Williams gives brief case studies to illustrate how guided imagery allows clinicians to understand and work with people with mild learning disabilities whose experience of psychological distress is difficult to discuss directly.

The other way that story-telling as therapy is used with distressed children builds on fairy tales. Here, the therapist provides stories that address psychologically pertinent matters. These are intended to help the child indirectly: provoking intellectual and emotional development by stimulating her imagination, helping her to confront anxieties through an acknowledgement of the difficulties these inspire, and promoting confidence in self and future by suggesting solutions to problems. Described by Levine (1980), the therapist creates a story relevant to each child. This should address their stresses or conflicts, while incorporating favourite foods, animals, colours, activities. Fantasy figures interact with the child in the story, and these should be the same age and sex as the client child; the stories end by suggesting relaxation or comfort.

The use of fairy tales as therapy has been elaborated by Davis (1990) into a pack of skeleton stories for children and adults of different ages and genders, confronting different types of problem. While this provides interesting examples of stories she has found useful in the USA, there seems little doubt that this approach needs to be culturally sensitive. Davis's slightly anodyne tales with rather upbeat endings are in a different tradition from the darker tales of the European tradition. They may be particularly irrelevant to members of minority cultures whose narratives enter another dimension of difference in both structure and content.

Narratives that give witness and meaning to illness form the fourth application. Charmaz (1991) explores the way that people with chronic illnesses create narratives of meaning: these centre on the number, pacing and quality of events. Some live in a Filled Present, where speed and activity anchor the self in a crammed time which leaves no room for emotion. Often these individuals were doing more than their healthy counterparts: for some it seemed to be a fear-controlling strategy, for others an energetic response to a foreshortened life. Living in the Slowed-Down Present was another possibility. Here time is a space to fill between periods of sleep: depression, dysfunction and medication all contribute to this limbo state which tends to dominate the existence of many institutionalized people, broken only by visitors. Before they can move on from this state, where anger and blame flare easily, people need to change their views of themselves, their illness, and their criteria of self-worth. Both of these timescapes are contrasted with living in the Intense Present, a state which feels vivid and passionate. The intensity seems to follow temporary or longer-term physical recovery, or spring from a period of re-evaluation of their life, or from having faced and accepted death.

Charmaz observes that most people respond to chronic illness by moving between loss and partial transcendence. Loss is associated with loss of a key component of the self-concept, for example that one is autonomous. A measure of transcendence over the master-narrative of the illness is achieved by finding ways to overcome the loss and retrieve their sense of self. They prevent the illness from flooding their consciousness even though it floods their body, by re-evaluating their value system to allow renewal. In order to achieve this people need the following:

- the time and ability to reflect;
- some tools to ameliorate their situation;
- the identification of essential and positive aspects of self distinct from their body;
- the support of key members of their social network in redefining self.

People often need to abandon goals valued by society in order to maintain their self-esteem; the key struggle is for control over defining images of self, their body and – where necessary – their death. People who achieve partial transcendence often reconstruct their past, moving it from a chronicle of loss to an account of their creation of a more aware and different self. However, when there are many losses Charmaz argues that the boundary of the self-concept becomes vulnerable to demeaning images offered by others. Transcendence is not achieved by all and is fragile, plummeting with each new loss or diagnosis of an additional illness. She strongly advises health services to take a more responsible approach to working with the social network of chronically ill people to ameliorate the worst effects of such additional losses.

Frank (1992) criticizes psychological therapy for people who have physical illness for being literally meaningless. Professional texts objectify major assaults on body image, such as having testicles or breasts removed, or a colostomy. Frank argues that although these require huge change in the meaning systems people use, the only recommendation to health care providers is that they should use standardized tests to assess each patient's needs. Key words are adjusting, adapting, accepting: Frank criticizes psychological work ancillary to physical medicine as exploring the patient's fears merely to secure compliance with treatment. He is critical of psychological efforts to help people 'get over' their feelings. Every first-person narrative on illness he could find emphasizes that people want the space and time to suffer, and to have the experience affirmed: deep anger is felt towards professionals who give out sleeping pills or coping strategies rather than join and bear witness.

What is lacking is social engagement, recognition of the losses people have experienced such as feeling they are left with half a body or that they are de-sexed. He argues for a hermeneutic stance: the psychologist should encounter ill people with the intention of sharing something meaningful, aiming to help them find some way that they may continue to live while acknowledging that suffering. That meaning should also involve important others in the person's life. He notes that psychology is having a hard time moving to the systems perspective which he feels is essential, since some aspects of an ill or newly disabled person's life will be affected by the disease fundamentally, others contingently, others not at all; such effects will also change from time to time.

Frank advocates what he terms narrative ethics, an approach which puzzles over how to encounter suffering; this is contrasted with the interest in competing rights which dominates decisional ethics (should we tell this depressed, chronically disabled man that he also has cancer?). Frank believes that the research encounter, which explores and listens and bears witness, is far more useful to ill people than most clinical interventions – another argument in favour of clinicians being active researchers. He further believes that social science should return to the idea of exploring and teaching. Helping people to know their own experience and to share it with others is useful because it extends society's capacity to reflect on itself, and expands its circle of care.

Frank conjures a dystopia where technology reshapes or replaces parts of our bodies which we call our selves, where the pretend body has no boundary with the not-me; where virtual reality makes the idea of false consciousness no longer a reasonable question since there is no 'real' experience against which to judge experience. Yet in his view resistance to this takeover of technology is possible. Like many postmodern thinkers, he depends upon spirituality, ending with reference to a Confucian thinker. His conclusion echoes Sampson (1996) in advocating the blending of meaning and narrative within an ethical stance:

> The best work does not simply do research on the body; it is embodied research. I read the point of that embodiment as ethical. To write about the body is not to theorize abstractly; it is to join fates with other bodies. The work is not only

'research'. It is the construction of a common autobiography of shared humanity, and the assertion of a responsibility for the future of that autobiography. (Frank, 1996: 757)

To summarize, these four different forms of verbal and textual narrative focus on the therapeutic quality and witness that words carry. They do not exhaust all of the options. Life-story work is another growing area of activity, which was discussed in Chapter 4. It is used by social workers therapeutically to help children and adults to make sense of their personal histories; speech and language therapists use life-book records of experiences of people who cannot speak to give them and people around them a communication tool; a PhD has been completed on the use of life-books to construct identities for people with profound learning disabilities who move home. However, this work is currently untheorized and unfocused.

All narrative approaches stand in contrast to the rather brutal language employed in some other interventions. Some programmes for people with learning disabilities ask staff to make apparently simple statements: hands down, say after me, well done, pick up the spoon. These are usually specified by the person who writes the programme, in the belief that the same 'commands' must be given by everybody if the client is to learn what they mean. No consideration is given to what sort of atmosphere is created by using consistent, commanding language. Yet a constructionist view of language must ask what are the consequences of narrowing down the range of possible worlds staff can employ, and what are the constitutive effects of requiring people to use abrupt rather than expanded forms of language.

The power of speech content became clear when I watched some videotaped interaction sessions between teachers and children who had severe hearing impairments.[13] *The project explored the effects of different styles of interaction, and so each teacher was asked to adopt on successive days a different discursive approach with the same child. The approaches varied the amount of social control exerted. The most pressurizing was the correctional 'say after me' to a child who spoke indistinctly; then the conversation was to be dominated by closed questions (who, what, when, why). The other strategies involved asking mainly open questions; avoiding questions and instead making personal contributions to the discussion, that is, statements which invite a reply but do not demand one; and initiating nothing, instead responding to all child utterances with encouragers like 'mhm' or 'really!'*

As we watched the same teachers using these different strategies with the same children, one of the most striking aspects was the huge change in their manner at each change of discursive strategy. This behaviour change had been neither discussed nor requested by the researchers. When the teachers used less controlling language they also used a gentler tone of voice, a different pace and quieter body language. It was a strong reminder that when words are put into people's mouths, an interactional style may also be put in place.

Words may be vehicles for meaning, but just as often they are imbued with meanings and implications of their own: we are created by those meanings when we use them.

Conclusions

Who are we to co-create meaning? Blatt (1981) was concerned about the destructive quality of stories which describe people with learning disabilities, and proposed a set of what could be termed narrative ethics. These include accepting that we have a duty to avoid trivializing, to provide instead grand and optimistic stories which people can live up to. Clinicians inevitably join debate about the meaning of life through their contact with clients, and need to be alert to the implications of such actions. There is a need for checks and balances in its creation. The main check on undue influence being imposed upon clients in the co-creation of experience lies in enlarged discussion of ethical practice.

When considering meaning-making through narrative, it is helpful to return to Shotter's (1993) question: who should live in whose reality? We are on safest ground when meaning-creation emerges from dialogue not monologue. Clinicians have become interested in narratives because narratives have power, which of course means that they have the potential to be abused. Interventions that provide new stories for distressed people cry out for ethical consideration, because they are closest to monologue. Exponents report that if they tell a story that fails to resonate, the child merely ignores it. Yet we need to debate the rights and wrongs of interventions designed to affect somebody's assumptive world when they cannot give permission. It is an entirely different matter to work with people on their own stories, and to debate stories told by others, than it is to provide people with stories we believe to be good for them. We need to know how to recognize when story-providing interventions are intrusive, to know what limits should be placed on this approach.

Discursive psychology's strength lies in its focus on contexts of meaning, on the way that human experience is shaped by large forces over which we have little control. It also maintains a tradition of debate and conflict whose radicalism keeps it ahead of other forms of psychology: in theorizing experience and the body as well as talk and the mind, and in helping us to see how these can co-exist. Nevertheless, narrative psychology's assumption that people can be agents in their lives and not hapless victims of circumstance is a more useful and fertile starting-point for clinical practice.

Summary

Contemporary issues discussed in this chapter concern a distinction between the revolutionary and reformist wings of social constructionism; it seems to map onto a distinction Slife makes between meaning-making as it is performed by social constructionists and by hermeneutic psychologists. I argued that narrative therapies and interventions draw more on an interpretive (that is, hermeneutic) approach to social constructionism that occurs over time; discursive psychology (expressed in 'revolutionary' social constructionism) is more concerned with context, underpinning effective criticism but rarely building anything new.

A history of the present was provided by mapping the origin of the subject–object dichotomy to clarify the elegance of Heidegger's solution to it: by making the active person-in-the-world his basic unit of analysis, rather than the static and isolated individual, Heidegger causes the subject–object dichotomy to vanish. Hermeneutic interpretation of both people and objects occurs by immersion in the person/object over time, exchanged recursively with more distant consideration; similarly by moving between literal and metaphorical understanding.

Sources of intersubjective meaning are the main focus of the chapter. Frank urges us to witness the loss and suffering of people in hospitals, moving beyond concern to make them cope to puzzling about how to encounter and share their experience. Freeman uses biographical research to identify moments when people change from being object-selves prey to cultural forces and start also to become wilful-selves who take on and shape those forces. Clinical interventions in this area include narrative family therapy, where the therapist needs to stay attuned to the client's meanings while reconstructing their difficulty into a problem about which they can think anew; and stories that inform a child about a hospital procedure while also enabling parents and nurses to engage with their fears.

Discursive psychologists have done much of the *critical thinking* discussed in this chapter: questioning the social position that patients, clients or users are put in by therapists and therapies, asking in whose interests problems are defined and treated, and observing ways that service cultures blame and control staff. Discursive psychology has also encouraged exponents of talking therapies to incorporate the embodied experiences so often ignored by mainstream clinical psychology, and supports multiple and parallel models of the experience of mental illness.

However, the greatest dangers in discursive and narrative work are not really being discussed: that the *reflective researcher-practitioner* needs to be alert to the ethical implications of creating new meanings with clients. White and Epston argue against using narrative approaches to externalize problems like violence and abuse that need to be acknowledged. Written accounts of experience purporting to come from service users need to cease blurring the goals, perspectives and contributions of professional facilitators and be more concerned to show how all voices that contribute to advocacy projects can be recognized. Finally, therapists using these approaches must accept that all stories arise from and contribute to a moral position, which makes reflecting on the therapist's moral starting-point crucial.

Notes

1 Since I wrote this chapter an edited collection of perspectives has been published by Power and Brewin (1997) which explores how individual psychotherapies consider changed meaning. Influenced by cognitive psychology, it excludes the development of new or altered meanings in family and systemic therapy.

2 A number of the ideas expressed in this section were first developed in a paper 'Embodiment, variability and agency' I gave with John Cromby to the psychology conference Understanding the Social World in Huddersfield, in 1995.

3 To criticize a position as essentialist is to consign it to a school of thought entirely rejected by postmodern theorists because it derives from Enlightenment rationalism. It is the insistence that each particular has a property that only it could possibly have, a property that gives it its 'thisness'. Feminists have been concerned that femaleness not be seen to be such an essential property that it overwhelms other forms of identity which could originate in profession, ethnicity or whatever; disability activists have similar objections. Essentialism belongs to the philosophy of necessity, rather than of possibility, a point elaborated in Chapter 7.

4 He cites an early attempt to teach such manly deportment as having been written in the second century BC; not much seems to have changed in societal expectations of embodied gender roles since then.

5 This section arises from the following sources: Kearney and Rainwater (1996), Macann (1996) and Faulconer and Williams (1990), being most heavily influenced by the last of these.

6 The cumbersome English phrases that describe Heidegger's ideas, employing many hyphens to signify the interconnectedness of people and things, is a widely used convention.

7 Quoted in Faulconer and Williams (1990).

8 'Space prohibits anything like a comprehensive Who isn't Actually Who of contemporary Australian letters, even supposing that all the skeletons are out of the cupboard. . . . Earlier this year, a 47-year-old white male, Leon Carmen, confessed that he was Wanda Koolmatrie, the aboriginal woman whose "autobiographical" *My Own Sweet Time* (1995) had won the Dobbie award for a first novel by a woman. . . . In 1996, Paul Radley – the winner, 16 years earlier, of the first ever Vogel award for an unpublished manuscript by a writer under thirty-something, and subsequently voted Australian of the Year – admitted that he wasn't in fact the author of anything, that it was his uncle Jack who had written the prize-winning novel and the three successful novels that followed it, having calculated that there was a better market for books by young authors than by old. . . . Helen Demidenko, whose tit-for-tat holocaust novel, *The Hand that Signed the Paper* (1994) had won just about everything that a novel can win in Australia was revealed to be Helen Darville, not of Ukrainian descent as she claimed, not the child of a family brutalized by Jewish Bolsheviks. . . . *It is difficult to imagine any of [these hoaxes] playing as well as they did in a culture less susceptible to mischief*' (Howard Jacobson, *Times Literary Supplement*, 3 October 1997, emphasis added).

9 Details of the process of narrative identification and analysis in research are given in the next chapter.

10 These ideas were reviewed in Chapter 4.

11 Booklets available from PALS, Paediatric Renal Unit, City Hospital, Hucknall Road, Nottingham NG5 1PB, UK.

12 Bruno Bettelheim, *The Uses of Enchantment*, New York: Vintage, 1975. Cited by Friedberg (1994) and by Levine (1980) whose papers inform this brief summary. I am grateful to Dr Chrissie Hart for introducing me to these ideas.

13 David Wood showed these as part of a presentation of his research into teacher–pupil interactional styles, reported in Wood and Wood (1984).

7 Research as Practice

Research was a contribution that early clinical psychologists made to health services as the profession became established, one that was and remains highly valued by other professions; it is still a major source of service development and an effective way to share knowledge. Research is probably the most important way that small professions like clinical psychology can make their contribution to a service visible.[1] Yet most clinicians continue to avoid it: they have little contact with researcher-practitioners while training, they lack supportive colleagues struggling with similar issues, are sure neither where to start nor whether the time devoted to research can be justified.

Yet clinicians need curious intellects to stop their work solidifying into a set of practices which neither adapt to different client needs, nor allow different conceptualizations of human experience to stop them short from time to time. Regularly struggling to create new concepts and approaches during research helps clinicians to remember that familiar techniques may have some grounding in research but that does not make them truths: they always remain open to revision. It also helps us to remember that the first approach we generate to intervene in somebody's distress is unlikely to be the only possible answer, nor necessarily the best one. The tension that researcher-practitioners have to contain is staying open to that knowledge while preventing it from paralysing action.

Another reason to consider research within practice is that it will soon be the main way that renewal occurs in health services. Teaching other professions will become less and less necessary as all health professionals learn how databases can update them – although the need for consultancy about ways to use those ideas will remain important and may grow. People who would continue the role of intellectual innovator need to be creators, researcher-practitioners who go beyond reflection and therapy to ensure that research informs practice and that practical concerns shape research agendas. However, this chapter also identifies situations where the research process itself creates sufficient change to be a helpful and change-promoting intervention.

Exploratory research can enlarge the sympathies of staff more effectively than teaching programmes, as long as it is part of a sustained programme. A seminal exploratory study was carried out by Tizard (1964) with children who have learning disabilities. The Brooklands project was radical because it shifted away from the previous focus on individual characteristics to explore the effects of environment on play, relationships and development. The results became accepted practice in residential provision very rapidly. Tizard then pursued the theme of intervention through environmental change, not with a new building or type of service but by studying the effects of different patterns of residential care provided by staff (King et al., 1971).

Tizard told administrators at what was then the Department of Health and Social Services that the research he and his colleagues produced affected practice for two reasons. It was carried out within a theoretical framework that shaped understanding, and it had continuity of both purpose and personnel. He believed that short-term project research generally creates only short-term effects: 'The major impact of most research, including ours, is not upon the Department or central government, but at a local level and on the climate of opinion' (1983: 250).

Contemporary researchers such as Frank (1992) describe the way that the research encounter, which generates knowledge about an experience and shares it with a wider public, can be more effective at helping physically ill people than a problem-solving clinical intervention. However, it is not necessary to divide research from practice: some contemporary clinicians succeed in combining them. McGaw works with people who struggle to parent their children successfully, in part because of learning disability or borderline intellectual skill. Her reviews of the research literature and her establishment of an assessment and support project which encompasses evaluative research, provide an excellent model of the researcher-practitioner developing a new area of service (McGaw and Sturmey, 1993). Beail and Warden (1996) have done the same for psychodynamic psychotherapy in learning disabilities. Similarly Brown et al.'s (1992) research into community support services for adults with learning disabilities in Canada led them to develop a new model of service which they evaluated, because existing community services focused on skills and activities produced no significant change in the clients over three years. By contrast, Brown et al.'s service, which places a counselling relationship with clients at its core, produced significant results in directions relevant to both clients and their carers.

Negotiating research knowledge with clients, rather than using it to treat them, is another way that research may constitute practice. Working in psychiatric rehabilitation services and in community psychology, Shepherd (1995) exemplifies this 'psychoeducational' model with adults who have long-term mental health problems. He argues that most psychological ill-health in this group consists of long-term, low-grade, largely untreatable but nevertheless manageable symptomatology. Yet professionals are reluctant to accept this. Believing that most interventions either have not been applied or were not done properly, professionals serially impose irrelevant treatments on clients whose main problem is that a key supporter has moved away or died, or some other adversity has knocked them sideways. Shepherd argues that interventions should focus on helping people to understand and manage their disabilities rather than hoping they can be cured:

> A different approach to the sharing of information may be the single most important vehicle we have for changing the relationship between professionals and service users. . . . Good teachers aim to share their knowledge and skills. (1995: 7)

Perhaps it is this psychoeducational effect that gives good research projects their power, particularly with cohorts of people who meet researcher-practitioners over a number of years. Participants join research projects because they address issues that are important to them, but also because through their participation they receive regular updates about this condition or learn about conundrums the research community is currently exploring. This may be a valuable way to use research about the experiences of carers: it seems unethical to draw on the ideas without debating them with the people they describe. For example, Todd and Shearn's biographical research on carers and clients with a learning disability as they enter adulthood suggests that identity is a major issue: families face the dilemma of hurting their child by discussing the limitations imposed by their learning disability, or entering into various silences and secrets to protect them from such a stigmatizing identity. They reach a powerful conclusion:

> The data presented here suggest that 'learning disability' is not so much rendered socially invisible but that it is hidden from people themselves. That is, many people with learning disabilities may be invisible to themselves. (1997: 363)

It seems to me that such information can only be drawn into clinical practice ethically by debating it with the people it describes and with their carers. Trying to discuss identity with clients without their carers merely places the client in an untenable position of divided loyalty.

If the idea that research should comprise clinical practice is accepted, we need to identify situations where research would be useful. Examples are when the knowledge base of a condition or experience or issue is low, and when significant gaps in the resources available to clients have been identified. A research approach should also be used when the validation of experience, and expanding the circles of concern that sustain people, are more relevant goals than creating change in individuals. Other situations that make a research perspective useful are when there is difficulty transferring research ideas into practical knowledge; and when services are stuck in dichotomous discourses (normalization versus institutional paternalism) and there is a need to create new ideas and find new directions.

Finally, if research is a component part of practice and not an esoteric sideline, what sort of research should be done? The first section in this chapter considers the idea of synergy, of aiming to make research and practice complement one another instead of fighting for limited resources and energy. It explores the thorny problem of how to develop relevant research questions, and how clinicians can work at the interface between research and clinical audit. Research methods are outlined in the second section. There is a number of very competent books describing quantitative methods in clinical settings;[2] qualitative approaches consistent with post-modern and constructionist psychologies are explored here. Assumptions underlying research studies open the section: ideas are elaborated in brief outlines of five qualitative methods used by clinicians. This is not an exposition of approaches which are easy – quite the contrary, their newness makes them fraught with uncertainty – but of methods that both use and develop the abstract thinking skills many clinicians already possess. The third section considers the ethics of research relationships; while the final section challenges writing as reportage, reframing it as a creative component of the research process itself.

Seeking Synergy

Identifying Research Questions

The most terrible question inexperienced researchers hear is 'yes, but what is the question?' when they are discussing an area of interest. Sometimes a good question emerges from reading and talking, but perhaps not as often as one would hope; when it fails to appear the result is the sort of unfocused project most clinicians have struggled to complete at some time. While starting with a topic that is interesting and reading about it are important, additional strategies do make it easier to come up with questions which are answerable, focused and pertinent.

Clarkson (1995) suggests that insights can develop from clinicians' practical experience into research which in turn helps them to reflect on and change their practice. Comprehensive questing after understanding and conceptualization should be valued as research in itself: case studies giving fine detail about one or a few people are as valuable as broader projects that pursue generalization. Theoretically, case studies refine theory, establish limits on its generalizability, and suggest complexities for further evaluation. Stake (1994) provides six criteria of the good case study:

- The 'case' is bounded so that it conceptualizes the object of study.
- Phenomena/themes/issues are selected for emphasis.
- Patterns within the data are identified which develop these issues.
- Key observations and interpretations are triangulated.

- Alternative interpretations are generated and one selected.
- Assertions or generalizations about the case are developed.

Clarkson (1995) argues that it is easier to identify relevant research questions when clinicians use a research method that is coherent with the theory they espouse. Thus trainees on her psychotherapy courses are encouraged to conceptualize what psychotherapy is, what creates change, what strategies or techniques they use to facilitate that change. They explore the epistemological assumptions contained in those beliefs – for example does their theory of practice assume that present problems always originate in past traumas. This leads to questions about clinical and research evidence that supports this position, helping the person to see gaps and contradictions. In this way trainees are assisted to create their own coherence as clinicians, and to identify related research questions. Experienced clinicians may find it equally useful to pose this set of questions to themselves.

Another fertile source of research questions arises out of the desire to adapt interventions used with other client groups or in other cultures. For example, Davis's (1990) stories for traumatized children in the USA discussed in Chapter 6 contain material that needs both cultural translation and evaluation with different clients. If one wanted to use such stories with adults who have a learning disability, that immediately leads into questions about what types of stories they employ now. Answering that question would enable both the form and the content of therapeutic stories to be adapted for this audience. If the speculation about narrative forms in oral and chirographic cultures is correct, the form would follow a different and probably episodic logic and not the sequential style of literary tales. However, such research would have important effects beyond the adaptation of Davis's stories for therapeutic purposes. Knowledge of the narrative forms used by this client group would have many other applications; the participants who worked with the researchers would also have been taken very seriously, a validating experience generally absent from problem-solving interventions which focus on future change.

People who have read around a topic but remain stuck could take a month to record each time they made a clinical decision based on too little information. Each event on its own may be insubstantial, but some ideas will cluster around a topic that is significant and on which no research exists. However, naive note-taking will not suffice: the adage 'fortune favours the prepared mind' was coined from experience, and scholarship is an essential component of research. Assiduous reading is necessary, even though it adds new complications. Some people suffer from having too many ideas swirling around their minds and can find no good reason to settle on any of them. Becker's (1986) solution is that they should fill four sheets of paper with all these titles: he says that most people start to repeat the topic that interests them within the first 25 lines.

Becker also identifies the 'writing on a sphere' problem. This hurdle inhibits many social science researchers as they start to report their project, because they know that human experiences interconnect and cannot work out where to begin. Becker suggests that it does not matter, that the issue will emerge regardless of where we start: getting going is the key. I believe this problem is encountered not only during report-writing, but in research design as well, and that Becker's proposed solution applies equally well to both.

Organizational Considerations

Action research was introduced by Lewin in the 1940s to encourage social investigation that both addresses pressing problems and also advances understanding, within a 'mutually acceptable ethical framework'.[3] Action research is not a single method but a collection of approaches which serve those aims, conceptualized as a cycle of activities with feedback loops to create organizational change. Action research focuses on people rather than structures: people who generate, implement or are willing to adopt the proposed changes. It assumes that change is difficult and requires multi-faceted interventions, a position encapsulated by the phrase 'light many fires'. Strong during the 1970s, the development of action research approaches seems to have slowed recently.

From the opposite direction, the organizational literature discusses the need to balance the development of new ideas against the need to turn existing ideas into locally usable knowledge. Vicari et al. (1996) distinguish these two types of research, emphasizing that discovery research has the biggest payoffs for organizations but it also carries the biggest risk of failure, because there are fewer practical spin-offs for the organization when the project is inconclusive. They also emphasize that research adapting new ideas for local conditions needs to take an organizational perspective; successful projects invariably recognize the needs and assets of the organization within which they are carried out.

Vicari et al. (1996) assume that practical knowledge develops within organizations in response to 'perturbations' of various kinds; thus it is only possible to develop such knowledge in organizations that can encompass the disturbance it entails. It follows that all research efforts need managing from an organizational perspective as well as from an intellectual perspective, if their net effect is to be beneficial to the organization. Considering research from the organizational perspective assumes that benefit to the organization is the same as bringing benefit to the clients it serves, a rather debatable position! Nevertheless, an organizational perspective is essential to the argument that research itself benefits clients. Without it, potentially exciting projects make people in unstable situations feel defensive, and useful work is wasted.

Vicari et al. identify three organizational states between order and disorder: inertia, extension and dissolution. Inertia is described as a state in which stability is valued above creativity or change. This can arise from an emphasis on survival, although paradoxically a rigid rejection of new ideas and exploration may contribute to a failing organization's downfall. Such organizations are unable to participate in creative projects which go beyond existing understanding. Sometimes they can tolerate the lower levels of perturbation that arise from research that adapts an approach developed elsewhere.

Organizations in a state of extension can contain contradictory forces. These contain groups of people who can explore competing ideas by finding ways in which they do not compete but can co-exist: moving from either/or to both/and is not as easy for people in states of dissolution. Organizations in a state of extension have few constraints on rules or policies, and many examples of self-organization and creative thinking within small groups. Management priority here is growth: many projects will be seeded and fail, but those which root and flourish are worth the resources devoted to development. These organizations thrive on debate: taken-for-granted knowledge is challenged and new ideas are generated internally. Organizations in a state of extension can cope well with the perturbations created by discovery research. However, staff may refuse to co-operate with proposed research if it neither contributes to, nor is consistent with, their beliefs. Therefore local creativity should be recognized and built on by researchers wherever possible, as it draws on practical knowledge and reduces the risk of research being rejected or sabotaged.

The final possibility for organizations is that they are in a state of dissolution. Such an organization welcomes research and the perturbations it brings but is unable to contain the disruption. The warm reception given to all new ideas tempts the unwary. Yet there is insufficient order for the organization to be able to adopt change and use new ideas: staff are bewildered. Outsiders can find it difficult to identify organizations in a state of dissolution. Doing so needs discussion with senior managers responsible for services as well as with the people who deliver them. With hindsight many of us can recall carrying out studies in organizations whose staff were bewildered, but who welcomed and even initiated research. In such circumstances the most well designed project helps neither them nor their clients, because exploration and questions create more uncertainty than these environments can contain. The research may make things worse, as the manifest failure of the staff team to grow with the project as they hoped fuels their despair.

Five management responsibilities for promoting knowledge within organizations are proposed by Vicari et al. (1996). First is the assessment of states within various parts of the organization, identifying groups which are changing from one state to another and supporting change in a positive direction. Stimulating research and providing a framework within which it can be carried out is the second responsibility. Third is balancing different types of research, where the lower risk of adapting ideas from elsewhere is weighed against the greater risk but also greater gains derived from discovery research.

Ensuring that knowledge which results from research is shared and retained within the organization is the fourth responsibility, one which is being enacted in Britain by the development of clinical audit and R&D initiatives within NHS services but which continues to be given insufficient priority. We need to go well beyond the obligatory presentation of research results to a smattering of staff two years after the project finishes, to the active promotion of ideas developed by research. This may include challenging the hegemony of written accounts by aiming to embody the knowledge in stories and conversations which contribute to the culture of the organization. There are always accounts of research that will engage audiences but are too detailed to go into research reports. Giving the development of one's thinking various names, or describing ideas through key characterizations, or giving phases of the research memorable names, can be useful vehicles that get the ideas widely understood across a clinical setting. Fifth and finally, decisions need to be taken about when and how to bring research to a close: this can be particularly relevant to discovery research, which will always generate ideas but despite what seems a reasonable time may prove unable to make them meaningful to the organization.

Clinicians supervising or directing research should consider these responsibilities or debate them with a relevant manager. Such discussions threaten to encroach on academic freedom: they are open to managerial influence that will diminish professional control of research if we are unwary. Clearly, research designed by administrators usually precludes any useful result because the questions are inappropriately framed. Trevillion (1996) illustrated this by questioning government-commissioned research into community team functioning aimed at understanding how role-blurring or the incommensurate cultures of different staff leads to miscommunication. As he observes, research grounded in a powerful set of assumptions like that tends to confirm those assumptions; he was concerned to avoid 'how' questions in favour of what or why, to ask what types of communication each commmunity team member had over two months and why they act as they do. He found that communication problems originate in staff responding defensively, making little investment in professional relationships because they change with every new policy; role-blurring was not an issue. Moreover, job demands left staff almost no time to spend with the professionals with whom they were meant to form a 'team', a further blow to the concept of role-blurring. He concludes that the first priority in overcoming poor communication is to create social spaces in which staff can meet, and to provide reasons for them to do so.

This example shows why researchers need to retain the initiative when entering negotiations about the content of research. Nevertheless, by claiming that research itself can comprise practice I am asserting that research can contribute to the organization's goal of increasing the well-being of clients. If that is the case then clinical research cannot place itself beyond the purview of the organization. Projects that have significant effects need the support of others, and must be framed and run in ways that elicit such support. That will include developing negotiation skills, and grasping some of the tasks facing managers as well as knowing the issues facing research.

Audit/Research Interface

In Britain, audit was introduced by government in 1989 with the intention of making reflectiveness and self-scrutiny central components of professional practice.[4] It was based on a number of fundamental principles, including that it must be professionally led, confidential at the level of the patient or professional, and involve users. The whole enterprise should be conceived as an educational process that leads to changes in routine clinical practice. Initially structured as medical audit alone, it supported national scrutiny of issues such as death during operations, and of suicide. Audit was reconceptualized in 1993 to involve all health service professions and renamed clinical audit:[5] from October 1995 clinical audit became a required activity.[6] Purchasing authorities are allocated significant funds to support clinical audit which they disburse to committees of professionals within Trusts. By sending finance through professional clinicians and working outside the usual managerial paths, clinical audit is clearly controlled and led by clinicians and is not the inspectorate imposed by managers that wary professionals sometimes believe.

At its simplest, audit is described as a cycle. It involves determining a relevant topic, preferably in conjunction with users; establishing standards of good practice from research reviews or from existing national guidelines; and measuring local performance. So far this mimics most service evaluations and action research, but continuing around the cycle reveals the distinction. What 'closes the audit loop' is the development of a plan to improve aspects of the service which fall short of audit standards, and re-auditing later. Closing the loop may involve in-service or further training, distributing information packages to clients or service staff, or establishing confidential reviews of case management by peers. The re-audit shows whether the initiatives have resulted in change: this seems the boring part of audit projects, but creating significant change in practice is far from easy in such enormous organizations and re-audits commonly fail to demonstrate change.

Not all topics are amenable to this analysis, but the basic distinction between research and audit is that audit includes creating and measuring changes in practice. This does not mean that audit can do without research skills, and some Trusts take the view that the two should support each other very closely. Without some understanding of research design and the problems inherent in comparing anything, audit can become an over-simplistic tool for making crude comparisons between services. The national audit of peri-operative deaths could be portrayed to show that one hospital was bottom if total number of deaths were counted, in the middle if corrected for age of population, and near the top of the league table if severity of condition was also partialled out (Devlin, 1996). Clearly it is essential that professionals with research qualifications remain in touch with initiatives that are open to both positive and negative interpretations. Ignoring clinical audit makes it more probable that inappropriate measures will be imposed upon human services and analysed with little understanding of the issues involved.

There is widespread confusion about the interface between audit and quality initiatives. Both were introduced to British health services around the same time, and use many similar terms such as 'clinical effectiveness' and 'user involvement'. Users in turn find it difficult to evaluate the content of treatments and tend to focus on quality concerns. Many services overcome the problem by combining audit and quality under one umbrella, apparently to save time and duplication. Others see this as an error.

Quality initiatives derive from Total Quality Management ideas that primarily focus on the way that a service is delivered. Administrative responsibility for quality usually lies with the Director of Nursing Services and is carried out through line management systems with a hierarchical method of reporting. Such management control of quality immediately makes other professionals wary. Structures that frame audit need to be separate from the way quality is administered because of the professional autonomy of psychologists and psychiatrists, who are not answerable to a line management system for clinical judgements unless a legal issue or complaint arises to draw the Trust into debate. Such autonomy must be protected, without compromising the client's right to a competent service: audit provides a good way to achieve this.

Clinical audit can be contrasted with quality not just because of different management arrangements, but because it is concerned with the content of interventions. It evolves through professional self-scrutiny and peer review, is confidential, and depends upon staff staying abreast of current research literature to identify for themselves areas of practice which require audit. Vital though it is that telephones are answered promptly and waiting areas made less seamy, quality draws on different ideas from those of clinical audit and the two should remain separate.

Nevertheless, confusion is encouraged by the evolving nature of audit. A content analysis of British policy documents issued by the Department of Health found 62 different definitions of audit published during five years (Cooper, 1996). The National Centre for Clinical Audit (NCCA) (1996) provides the following definition:

> Clinical audit involves systematically looking at the procedures used for diagnosis, care and treatment, examining how associated resources are used and investigating the effect care has on the outcome and quality of life of the patient.

Their more detailed criteria are in five interconnecting areas (see Table 7.1).

TABLE 7.1 *Summary of NCCA criteria for clinical audit*

Area		Criteria	How (examples)
Design	1	Important areas of concern	High cost/risk; user demand; purchaser need
	2	Objectives agreed by audit group	All affected staff agree with plan
	3	Objectives measurable	Succinct, achievable
	4	Audit evidence-based	Draws on available research
Measurement			
	5	Standards established	Indicators include outcomes for clients, critical incidents, etc.
	6	Rigorous method	Adequate sampling and design
	7	Data collection piloted	Reliable, valid, ethical
Evaluation	8	Compare actual practice with ideal	e.g. formal review of cases not meeting standard and feedback
	9	Identify improvements needed	Consistent with good practice
Action	10	Plan developed	Addresses causes of problems found and assigns responsibility for action
Improvement	11	Implement plan	Give evidence of this
	12	Re-audit	Confirm implementation and sustained change

These criteria help to separate audit from any basic monitoring system, since self-scrutiny and local agreement are central activities. The emphasis on change in the service as a component also prevents audit resources from being hijacked for basic monitoring purposes.

The NCCA document reveals its background in the quantitative, scientific tradition of acute physical medicine. Nevertheless, there is substantial interest in many quarters in using audit to tighten up communication between different parts of the service, as interface issues are commonly identified as causing problems for users. There is also concern to go beyond the straightforward audits of drug administration which have dominated medical audit in mental health services. Firth-Cozens (1993) gives a helpful discussion of different approaches to audit, the degree of psychological threat they impose and the insight to be gained from them.

Audit depends on research evidence but it also has resources that can support small-scale research which develops good practice guidelines if they do not already exist. It can complement and extend basic research. For example, we recently carried out independent research into the way that learning disability services manage bereavement in their residents.[7] This concluded that the dominant counselling model needs to be extended into systemic considerations such as the relationship between staff and relatives and, where appropriate, into an elaboration of the range of responses to bereavement available to staff, based on debating and negotiating meanings of bereavement and connecting these to other losses such as those that occur when staff leave. We have been awarded audit funds to support the development of workshops that will discuss how research on the management of bereavement can be turned into locally usable practice: these will enable staff to develop responses to bereavement that are authentic, to develop systems of supervision and support for staff and relatives where appropriate, and to adapt record-keeping systems so that details of key relationships and bereavements are kept for clients who want to discuss their feelings years later. The audit funds will also allow us to establish a prospective database of bereavements, so that the way these new systems impact on their management can be evaluated and re-evaluated over the next three years.

It is easy to perceive audit as the latest managerial initiative to put pressure on health service professionals. Yet its objectives are laudable, as long as audit remains in professional hands and is not reduced to foolish and inappropriate checklists affecting decisions on the distribution of resources. It should be welcomed as an opportunity to bring research more squarely into clinical services.

Clinician-friendly Research Methods

Slife and Williams (1995) detail the assumptions different research traditions make about human experience, concluding that practitioners should stop hoping that criticism itself can create new possibilities. Instead we need to recognize that inevitably every theory has a limited range of application and cannot explain things we consider important. Despite that knowledge, they urge us to find the courage to espouse some theoretical position. In particular Slife and Williams argue against eclecticism, because it requires sophisticated theoretical skills: the eclectic not only has to master many different theories, but must also develop a metatheory which describes how each theory combines with the others. Some people manage this. Theoretical clinicians such as Bowlby and Bateson brought together a number of different ideas, altering them in such original ways that they went beyond a simple eclectic composite to state a new, coherent theory. However, such skills are rare. The authors suggest it is more common for eclectics to espouse a set of mutually conflicting ideas without recognizing their contradictions.

Slife and Williams organize the assumptions that researchers make within a simple dichotomy, theories based on philosophies of *necessity* versus those based on philosophies of *possibility*, giving a slightly different perspective on the distinction between reductionist and emergent theories discussed earlier. For Slife and Williams, theorists of necessity assume that there must be a relationship between a phenomenon and its cause. They draw on sets of assumptions used by many physical and behavioural scientists: phenomena must happen the way that they do, and can be described by universal laws. Such approaches reduce events and experiences to simple principles. Thus psychological time is often reduced from its three dimensions to only one, the past; or time is treated as inevitably linear and continuous without any other possibility being considered. Similarly, challenging behaviours are often assumed to depend entirely on histories of reinforcement or punishment.

For theorists of possibility, there is no 'must' involved. It is assumed that there is always the potential for events to occur differently. Postmodern theorists such as social constructionists and hermeneuticists are theorists of the possibility in human events. They explore parallel social worlds or multiple social selves and the way that these affect each other. Another form concerns the temporal holism described by Heidegger, where possibility derives from past and present experiences as well as future fears and hopes, and all are present to some degree in each experience. Protagonists of possibility eschew any idea that people can be single entities in thrall to necessary, causal laws.

Theoretical possibility is fundamental to the narrative therapies discussed in the last chapter. Therapy focuses on experiences and thoughts that disconfirm an unhelpful perspective on self and enable the client or family or group to develop new narratives on which they and others around them can draw. Similarly, research which affects practice often does so by creating new possibilities for services and people, and by communicating them in a variety of stories which of necessity extend beyond the written research papers to affect local conversations.

Qualitative Research

The debate about qualitative and quantitative research methods and their relationship to knowledge is relatively new to psychology and to many branches of medicine; however, the ground has been well prepared by anthropologists and sociologists.[8] Hamel et al. (1993) give a useful brief history. Sociology moved between domination by first qualitative and then quantitative method throughout the twentieth century. Hamel et al. note that one set of methods tends to flourish while criticisms of the alternative mount, but that neither delivers as certain a hold on social reality as it claims.

Concern about the representativeness of the people studied is one issue at the heart of debates about qualitative method; management or control of the researcher's subjectivity is another. Hamel et al. view good qualitative research as starting with description, but going beyond that to generate theories or abstract models which explain how this example informs wider issues. They evaluate research on the following criteria:

- successfully distinguishing the purpose of the study from the case(s) selected to illuminate it;
- the quality of the thinking or strategies used to select the case(s) at the centre of the study;

- the degree to which the researcher can externalize their subjectivity and therefore demonstrate a measure of control by accounting for it; and
- the methodological rigour displayed in describing the subject.

They record the elegance with which a French-Canadian researcher justified his selection of one town to act as the case in his study, because it was one where two problems of concern to Canadians in 1939 intersected. The small French-speaking town was undergoing the simultaneous enlivenment and disturbance of large industrial development, in projects entailing a degree of linguistic imperialism because they were started and managed by English-speaking incomers.

The problem of authority is another major debate in interpretive research: why should my interpretation have greater warrant than *Old Moore's Almanack*? Being less contentious, how do summaries of different accounts differ from the work any competent journalist would do? One response is to undermine the authority of 'objective' knowledge by showing that science constructs ideas as much as it discovers them.[9] Another is to argue that the success or otherwise of our theories is determined as much in the court of public opinion as by academic criteria (Deleuze and Guattari, 1994; Richards, 1996).[10] However, most qualitative researchers justify their claim to authority by the complexity of their method and the thoroughness with which it was executed.

This section introduces five different qualitative approaches and suggests situations in which each might be used. This in no way implies that one type of research should rely exclusively on one research method. In summary, grounded theory is commonly used to encapsulate processes by which clients experience services or comprehend their own difficulties; discourse analysis is more likely to be used to explore sociopolitical influences, perhaps on exchanges between health professionals and clients or on the construction of new ideas like 'risk management'. Recent interest in narrative therapies suggests that narrative analysis will become a useful research tool for clinicians. Ethnography has been used in health care settings from Goffman onwards, to explore the way that specific groups of people fare in particular social settings; while more recently phenomenology has been reintroduced to provide detailed and alternative descriptions of experience.

Glaser and Strauss (1967) created grounded theory as a reaction to the dominance of two 'grand theories' which sociologists endlessly tested empirically. They felt that research should originate in human experience not in theory: theory should be a consequence not the starting-point. This looks like naive empiricism at first glance, the idea that if a researcher collects enough butterflies they will learn something important about the natural world. Grounded theory is distinguished from empiricism by the centrality of theory-generation, by its de-emphasis of heaps of facts in favour of developing theory iteratively. It is not sufficient to describe what occurs: grounded theory uses the description to provide a theoretical statement about what is occurring in the process under study. This requires the researcher to move between reflection, reading, and collecting different types of information.

Glaser and Strauss led a resurgence of qualitative field studies in sociology against the post-war dominance of analytical and experimental methods. More recently, Layder's (1990) exposition of grounded theory advocates research which draws together and theorizes on the basis of many different types of knowledge. These holistic accounts should be contrasted with research purporting to use grounded theory which describes unconnected themes that 'emerged' out of one person's reading of a small set of interviews, themselves obtained by convenience rather than from consideration of the matter at hand. The main problem about such studies is that they describe rather than create a theory. Hanley-Maxwell et al.'s (1995) study is a typical example: they describe the experiences parents encounter when their child with a learning disability leaves school, but there is no theoretical development of the data. To reiterate Hamel et al. (1993), a good qualitative study distinguishes the purpose of the study from the case selected to illustrate it. Although researchers such as Hanley-Maxwell et al. state their research method as grounded theory, its failure to develop either concepts or theory makes it a pallid contribution to the psychological knowledge of human experience.

Grounded theory research is exemplified by Charmaz's (1991) study on ways that people manage subjective time in living with a chronically disabling condition. One problem in drawing from this tradition in clinical research is that sociologists produce books, not the short research articles which are more usual for researcher-practitioners. The focus on large, comprehensive studies also makes it difficult for clinicians in training to master the techniques in short research projects. Our research encapsulating influences which help or hinder the development of supportive relationships between professional carers and clients (Clegg et al., 1996) is an example of a partial account, one giving a 'slice' through the process of caring. Eventually this should contribute to a grounded theory of the way that meanings are negotiated in care provision for dependent clients, but such an account could not possibly be provided within a journal article. Henwood and Pidgeon (1995) give an admirably concise introduction to grounded theory, identifying component parts of a grounded theory study which can be carried out by postgraduate researchers, and perhaps by clinicians:

- Basic taxonomy development: creating a taxonomy of relevant features in a corpus of data through coding and defining, which secures the breadth of a grounded theory study.
- Focused conceptual development: exploring a limited number of concepts until all aspects seem to have been included and related to one another. This is 'saturation', and provides depth of vision.
- Cycles of interpretation: opening up a section of a study to the challenge of negative cases by pursuing them and reading around the ideas, to increase the theoretical scope of the work.

Examples of discourse analysis in clinical practice include Harper's (1994) exploration of reasons for making a diagnosis of paranoia, and Siperstein et al.'s (1994) examination of multidisciplinary reviews. Both situations provide texts that are amenable to the deconstructive techniques familiar to discursive psychologists, who treat texts as sufficient in themselves and therefore do not look beyond them. In that sense discourse analysis is similar to conversation analysis, using the same notational conventions and analytic techniques. However, they serve different goals. Antaki and Rapley's (1996) conversational analysis of a semi-structured interview between a psychological researcher and a person with a learning disability merely describes common tendencies, for example that when a question is not answered it is almost always rephrased away from multiple – to single – choice, and offers a choice that is biased towards a positive response.

By contrast discourse analysts are concerned to use texts as vehicles that reveal societal power. Their research is more likely to explore the position of the parent in a multidisciplinary review, to show that shared decision-making is more apparent than real; or to deconstruct the processes by which hierarchies of power are softened within multidisciplinary teams, yet remain unchanged. Exploring power structures can challenge existing structures and therefore be threatening, and resistance to discourse analysis within clinical research is often construed as such. However, such research can also contain no curiosity and be transparently deployed to support an opinion – commonly that medical doctors are psychologically incompetent and psychologists should have more power. It presents assessors with difficult ethical questions about the spirit with which research is or should be done: is the researcher curious to develop new knowledge, or merely concerned to 'expose' the power held by medical doctors in health service decision-making, yet again? What psychological knowledge would be developed by so doing? And how would such a research project defend the ethical position it constructs between researcher and researched?

Of course, critiques of decision-making and procedures perform an immensely useful job. Boyle's helpful description of changing views about women's sexuality this century has already been mentioned extensively; Rose's identification of discourses of blame in professional settings is another powerful example.[11] Walsh-Bowers's (1995) 50-year study of the relationship between psychologists and their participants up to 1989 provides another use of history; not classical discourse analysis, but certainly textual analysis within a Foucauldian tradition. Walsh-Bowers shows how participants were used as data sources only, with virtually no report of procedures for consent, debrief or feedback given; how participants but neither data collectors nor settings were described; and how participants were rarely acknowledged. Attending to his critical history should help all contemporary psychologists to mend their ways, because it keeps on centre stage the research relationship and the social-ethical nature of psychological knowledge.

Despite these real achievements, there is growing concern that critical approaches such as discourse analysis are inappropriately destructive, certainly for clinicians, whose primary purpose is deploying psychological ideas to improve people's lives. Protagonists such as Gergen (1994) now argue that critical research should also take responsibility for building new ideas. Certainly, my response to hearing that clinical reviews involving parents are imperfect is to return to the adage that democracy is the worst possible form of government, with the exception of all the others humankind has managed to develop so far.

Narrative analysis also lies within the constructionist tradition, spanning the boundary between literary criticism and social science. Reissman (1993) represents narrative production and consumption in five levels, while emphasizing the interactive and recursive nature of analysis. The first level concerns the focus of the study: here sources or influences on the researcher are identified, issues originally highlighted by Foucauldian scrutiny of why some topics are researched frequently, others not at all. At the second level the narrator tells and retells their story with chosen audiences, whose responses and comments co-create the account. Stories are altered as they are related to the researcher, whose angle of interest has already been foreshadowed by the way the relationship was established. Transcription alters the narrative once again because its conventions, and the amount of detail given, influence future interpretations. The researcher or team then create a metastory out of these transcripts, which goes through a final transformation when meaning is once again dislodged by reader predilections.

For Reissman, narrative sequences are discrete and detachable from the surrounding discourse. Meanings may be consequential (what caused the next thing to happen) or episodic (diversions to describe sub-themes) rather than chronological, but their order cannot be changed without changing the story's meaning. Her own research shows that white Western interviewers expect temporally sequenced narratives and have difficulty hearing accounts that are organized episodically. This points up the huge differences in expectation generated by culturally different narrative forms.

Locating narratives, and identifying their beginning and end, is a complex interpretive process. Some people develop distinctive ways of signalling they are going into narrative, seeking permission from the listener before starting. Others use similar words or metaphors at the beginning and end, or may signal an unfinished narrative by starting with a vague statement – 'I'm walking around waiting to decide' – using the same statement of uncertainty to close the narrative about an experience which itself is unfinished.

Analysis often depends on structural assumptions more prevalent in the 1970s. Both Reissman (1993) and Alasuutari (1995) cite six narrative elements originally described by Labov:

- an opening abstract that summarizes the main point and signals the start of a story;
- orientational information – time, place, situation, participants;

- some complicating action;
- an evaluation of the meaning of the action;
- a resolution or outcome;
- a coda which returns the discourse to the present.

The evaluation of meaning constitutes the soul of the narrative, because it identifies why the person is telling it. Reissman goes beyond Labov to identify other narrative genres: those with a set of protagonists, inciting conditions and a culminating event; habitual narratives, which repeat connected events but have no peak of action; or hypothetical narratives – if that were to happen, then. . . .

Some narratologists focus on oral as well as verbal aspects: changes in pitch, repetitions, pauses and other features which punctuate speech and add meaning. Reissman argues that assistants may prepare a complete transcript but the tape must then be studied by the researcher, who should re-transcribe sections containing narrative sequences: here detail about pauses and inflections is added, alongside tonal features which identify groups of words as poetic stanzas. The final transformation into poetic stanzas involves removing detail, creating an ideal realization of the text so that the aural quality of rhythm and connection can be appreciated. Reissman suggests this is sometimes useful for sections that look and feel like narrative but that cannot be analysed structurally.

A brief example of somebody narrativizing an important experience usually arises from the to-and-fro of conversation. The following example is drawn from research into bereavement. Here the sister of a man with a learning disability describes how he came to live with her:

> *What actually happened was, it was one Saturday last May and my daughter and her husband had gone to visit my Mum, and apparently she was flat out on the settee, she had a flour bag in her hand and the flour dropped, and they said she was really ill, and they got the doctor and he came and said she had had a slight stroke, and what they did was they got B's clothes, and they brought him here. They wanted to take him with them, they said did he want to go home and he said he wanted to come to me. Now, this is funny you see, he had been going nearly every night to see them, mind you it was one bus straight from X to them, and he liked their little girl, and he was going every night, but he wanted to come to me, you know, to live, he wouldn't go back with them at all, he says 'no', and they tried to persuade him and he says 'no, I want to go to K's'. He settled in straight away. . . . That shocked me, that's something I didn't expect, you know.*

She opens to indicate a story is starting: 'What actually happened was . . .' and another sub-story is opened in the middle with 'Now this is funny, you see'. We are quickly oriented to the situation discussed, with people, day, month and situation. The complication comes when Mum drops the flour and seems ill, and the story seems to end with him being brought to her. However, the sub-plot is introduced, and a further linked story describes how they had prepared him to go and live with the narrator's daughter and husband, but that when the time came he refused and chose to live with his sister. The meaning seems to be that he chose her; the outcome is that he settled instantly. The coda that returns the conversation to the present is that the events had all been very unexpected.

In the event, this and other interviews were analysed by using the grounded theory method which fragments the accounts and does not pay specific attention to narratives (Clegg et al., forthcoming). A narrative analysis would have been equally legitimate had we wished to produce a richly detailed account of the experience. We chose to use the management of bereavement as an example of one of many issues where staff and relatives in the learning disability service work together; therefore our final account focuses on complexities at the staff–resident interface rather than purely describing bereavement, although it is an important component of the discussion. Narrative analysis would have been more appropriate if the study of bereavement in learning disability was just being opened up; or if the aim of the study was more open-ended, where the topics that people narrativized would have been less determined by the researchers.

Ethnography has been used in clinical settings for many years. Goffman's ground-breaking investigations of psychiatric hospitals were amongst the first in the area. In learning disabilities this was followed by Edgerton's (1967) study of the way people discharged from hospital cope. In another project from the same stable in California, the self-statements of adults who have learning disabilities were linked with their social relationships and the attitude towards disability held by their family (Zetlin and Turner, 1984). Ethnographic studies are characterized by extensive and close relationships between researcher and researched, described by the term 'participant-observation'. This relationship should not be trivial. Atkinson describes the problems undergraduate researchers encountered during a participant-observation study into the lifestyles of 17 adults with learning disabilities living in the community:

> Some clients who initially had agreed to be observed were then not at home at the appointed time, having broken their own set routines in order to escape their would-be followers. Only five people were actually observed in community activities. . . . 'He refused to walk with me and said I had to walk in front of him – as he walked extremely fast, this was very difficult. We attracted considerable attention as he was walking so fast, directly behind me, and he kept shouting to me that he did not want people to see me with him.' (1985: 35)

Atkinson suggests that people with learning disabilities are only willing to co-operate with participant-observers within their homes, not as they move around the community. She does not consider how Zetlin and Turner (1984) got their information. That study was one of a number that Turner carried out with a group of people he met in the day centre they attended, the one afternoon per week meetings continuing for over 10 years. It is clear that Turner established himself as a trusted confidant, and not a member of staff, before attempting any research with the people.[12] Ethnographic methods may require almost superhuman levels of involvement with wary, vulnerable participants if important information is to result.

Phenomenology is not a new approach to enquiry, having been developed by Husserl in 1913, and studied by Heidegger before he grew critical of its alienating method. It belongs to this 'family' of qualitative research methods because it focuses on individual perceptions of reality or experience, not on groups, and because it does not transform human experience into numerical data. It is concerned with the essence of phenomena, a fundamental understanding that is reached through intuition; phenomenology is described as the descriptive analysis of essences by Honderich (1995). Moustakas describes it slightly differently:

> The scientific study of the appearance of things, of phenomena just as we see them and as they appear to us in consciousness. . . . The challenge is to explicate the phenomenon in terms of its constituents and possible meanings, thus discerning the features of consciousness and arriving at an understanding of the essences of the experience. (1994: 49)

This method is exemplified in seminars with student teachers, who are asked to reflect on the ideal teacher. Moustakas asks the students to note down the nature of the relationship; an episode which illustrates how their own sense of being was recognized and valued; how this person awakened feelings of self-esteem and self-confidence in them; finally adding anything else that was missing from their portrait. Students then work in groups to pool these ideas, weeding out repetitive meanings to produce a composite portrait of the ideal teacher. Moustakas argues that year on year the resulting composite is similar, suggesting that there is an essence of 'good teacher' which can be identified through intuition. This essence is that the teacher recognizes the pupil as an incomparable being, and makes each pupil feel special and unique, by listening accurately and enhancing meaning from the child's frame of reference. Yet this composite can be criticized as a phenomenological description: it seems to owe as much to the questions that prompted it as it does to any essence of the 'good teacher' which existed in the minds of students before the session started.

Phenomenological method apparently enables the perceiver to see what really stands before them, refraining from judgement and avoiding everyday understandings. Phenomena are said to be revisited freshly, naively, in their totality, from the vantage-point of an open self and a pure ego, producing original description. Unlike grounded theory or discourse analysis, phenomenology places little or no emphasis on control of individual biases through critical discussion with peers or members of a research team. Readers must take on trust that phenomenologists have learned to minimize their own subjectivity: attendance at a recognized training course is not required although Husserl considered it a skill requiring intensive training and practice. An example is Smith's (1995) phenomenological account of how women during their first pregnancy experience changes in self-identity, which he suggests counters the prevailing view that this is mainly a time of introspection.

Many philosophers do not believe that we can intuit essences. Social constructionists and hermeneuticists believe that removal of the self from perception is impossible, a naive claim. From this perspective the description of a good teacher given above is the entirely legitimate co-construction of understanding between a teacher and a class, an account of human experience that *assumes* there is mutual influence between questioner and responder. These theorists assume that everybody is situated within a set of social forces: achieving a measure of control over the tendency to impose them on others occurs by making the forces explicit, not by claiming that they do not exist.

Yet there is an attraction to phenomenology: its methods echo the reflectiveness and awareness of biases that are central components of therapeutic supervision. Even in a constructionist world we need to make some effort to unscramble which ideas arise primarily within ourselves and which primarily from the person we are talking to, otherwise there is a clear risk that all my research will do no more than confirm my prejudices. What processes do constructionists and hermeneuticists adopt to minimize their subjectivities? Declaring biases is one way, but it is insufficient to expunge them. Paradoxically, I suspect that phenomenological method has value for researcher-practitioners, although I doubt its epistemological claim to identify truth and essences.

Conclusions on Qualitative Research

This picture of qualitative research has been painted rather by numbers. There is growing concern that discussion of method has become too prominent, that it has become 'methodolatry'. Mair observes that some psychology resembles badly taught French: it gets students through exams but is no help in their efforts to engage with people when they visit France. Exponents of qualitative approaches such as Orford (1995) and Henwood and Pidgeon (1995) are as much concerned with scholarship as they are with the methods by which interviews and other sources of information are turned into texts or raw information for research.

Before these exciting innovations dazzle judgement too much, it may be instructive to return to the research which opened the chapter. Tizard's (1964) research with children who moved to live in the 16-bedded Brooklands house had three aims: to apply and adapt care and educational policies for non-disabled children for 'imbeciles' and study their effect; to compare the development of experimental children and matched controls who stayed in the institution; and to explore the administrative and social implications of this model of care. Tizard explicitly states that the first and third aims were qualitative and his main focus of interest. Data concerning the second aim showed that Brooklands children made significant gains on verbal but not non-verbal IQ over the two years. Since their non-verbal IQ was the higher to start with, these gains were of far less interest to him: 'It was regarded as inevitable that most of the data on Brooklands would be qualitative and evaluative rather than quantitative' (1964: 130). He wrote glowingly about changes in the children's physical appearance and the growing affection for staff which enabled them to become less, not more, dependent. The children became busy, interested, able to play with other children and to maintain interest in activities without staff having to be present to steady them. Tizard was in no doubt about the success of the experiment and unconcerned that there were few numerical data to describe it; the subsequent power of the study demonstrates how significant qualitative research can be.

Similar combinations of qualitative and quantitative outcomes are reported for the Headstart project. This was introduced in 1965 to divert poor North American children from the negative spiral of school failure and identification as retarded: since then varying opinions about its success have been expressed according to the types of data cited. Headstart comprises six elements although only the first is commonly described, that of free provision of pre-school education for children defined as being at risk. However, equally important are health screening, mental health services, nutrition education and hot meals, social services for child and family, and the requirement that parents become involved. Current evaluations of the effect of the project on children who first entered it suggest that initial IQ gains wore off a few years later, but that the children were less likely to become single parents as teenagers, were healthier, and had parents who remained in touch with education services. In addition, the presence of a Head Start programme enhances a community's capacity to meet local needs (reviewed by Zigler and Styfco, 1994). These studies serve as reminders that all 'new' approaches have some history that is worthy of attention, even though qualitative aspects of these studies would now be regarded as rather atheoretical and eclectic.

Criteria for assessing qualitative research in psychology continue to evolve in an environment where postmodern conjunctions abound. For example, Smith's (1995) study into motherhood mixes data from a repertory grid with interviews interpreted phenomenologically, somehow yielding a grounded theory acount. Said to be triangulation, it feels perilously close to a postmodern montage with little conceptual coherence. However, there are few clear guidelines for acceptable research practice in this area. Ferguson and Halle describe their difficulty in editing a special issue on qualitative research:

> Each of these articles challenged our editorial process and our reviewers in various ways. Some were reviewed multiple times, in one case by as many as 10 different reviewers. More than for most articles that follow familiar formats and practices of quantitative research, the reviewers' responses to and recommenda-

> tions about these articles often seemed contradictory. . . . The rules for evaluating the use of qualitative methods across studies . . . are much less clear and concise. But such rules are needed. (1995: 2)

Turpin et al. (1997) propose some rules for clinical psychologists in training; while creating safety for learners and contributing to clarity amongst reviewers, they are not universally welcomed. There is concern that qualitative research in clinical psychology has to develop rules and criteria when mainstream quantitative methods have never had to do so; and that it does itself no good by being constantly on the defensive. Boyle (1997) points out that business leaders are willing to put money into focus groups and other qualitative methods that describe experience, and commit resources according to the results of such studies: so what is it about these methods that makes most academic psychologists so afraid?

Ethics

Recent debates about research ethics will probably be welcomed by clinicians, who are often discomforted by the requirements of research methods. One source of difficulty arises from investigations where results criticize participants or are in some way to their disadvantage. The ethical dilemma is whether the significance of such results legitimizes their publication, or whether publication is always a betrayal of trust. Other concerns arise when the methods themselves could upset or demean participants: insensitive observational studies have been criticized in this area, as have those that ask confused people to do a battery of tests which they mostly fail. The relationship between researcher and participant can create many complications, ethical entry to situations and responsible leave-taking being two examples. Finally, dilemmas may arise at the end of projects: how much information should be shared or negotiated with whom at the end of a study?

Cohorts of people contributing to longitudinal studies usually describe the research as helpful to them.[13] It clarifies their thinking about the problem or disability they are living with, it gives them contact with knowledgeable researchers who may be able to provide them with information, and it respects their experiences and difficulties. However, a few have more negative experiences. Bussell et al. (1995) debriefed participants in their study of family functioning. Nearly half (43 per cent) were proud that they had contributed to knowledge, most found it enjoyable (70 per cent) and interesting (88 per cent), and 90 per cent were willing to take part in a follow-up study. However, 4 per cent felt let down for two reasons: either they were offered no help with troubles they revealed, or the study changed their family in ways that they could not have predicted when they agreed to participate. Since this included an increased frequency of arguments, they felt the researchers should have helped them to overcome a problem that the process seemed to have generated.

Yet Oliver (1992) argues that research on disability has had little influence on policy and no positive effect on the lives of its subjects. Moreover, the process of being researched alienates people with disabilities from researchers. He asserts that disability research has largely skewed perceptions towards the view that disability is an individual problem when he construes it as neither that nor a social problem, but a political one. Thus he makes common cause with feminist researchers whose epistemology requires the research relationship to be reciprocal, to contribute towards the empowerment of participants and relevant political change. Oliver advocates changing the social relations of research production to an 'emancipatory research paradigm'. This assumes that disability research should assist disabled people in their struggle against oppression. The slogan 'no participation without representation' was coined to encourage people with disabilities to reject research if they played no part in its design. 'Researchers have to learn how to put their knowledge and skills at the disposal of their research subjects, for them to use in whatever way they choose' (1992: 111).

Kerruish (1995) describes the way these ideas transformed an evaluation of mental health services into a project based on human values carried out with users. We are told that residents 'did not hide things from us' (can any researcher justify such a claim?), that they discussed an enormous range of positive and negative aspects of the service, and that they introduced 'innovative' ideas such as residents wanting to be involved in the selection of support staff – a policy for staff recruitment prevalent in group homes for people with learning disabilities since the early 1990s. If Kerruish was to repeat the research she would want to spend even more time getting to know and recruit people before starting to collect information; she also hopes they would have more involvement in design and analysis – while admitting that her attempts to involve users in analysis during this project were unsuccessful. There is a long and detailed account of the research process: there is no research outcome.

Kerruish questions whether evaluative research should only be commissioned and carried out by users themselves: just as some feminists question whether men can be allies in research into their experience, Kerruish asks whether non-disabled people can ever be allies in research with disabled people. However, she steps back from that precipice to state that all oppressed groups do need allies, so long as those allies recognize their responsibilities. These extend beyond their conduct during the project, to ensure afterwards that information is neither misrepresented nor abused to the detriment of the participants.

That people have been harmed by social and psychological research is undoubtedly true. However, it is less clear that guidelines such as those recommended by Oliver will be useful. Are the ever-expanding introductory time periods realistic? What will happen when these close, trusting, ethical relationships are broken at the end of the project – or should researchers stay with the same group for ever? Can any researcher control the way information is used once it is in the public domain?

We do not have to reinvent the wheel: sociologists got there before us. Punch summarizes ethical concerns about qualitative research involving participant observation with various groups of people. These are debates which he describes as part of the folk knowledge of sociologists, rarely written down because some of it seems to be such heresy:

> Entry and departure, trust and confidence, elation and despondency, commitment and betrayal, friendship and abandonment – all are as fundamental here as are dry discussions on the techniques of observation, field notes, data analysis and report writing. (1994: 84)

Punch observes that benefit and harm to both parties are equally probable in any personal relationship; research relationships are no different. Human research revolves around a fundamental dilemma: balancing privacy and protection of the participants against the importance of conducting independent and original research and sharing it through publication. Concerns voiced by critical participants are of having experienced harm, of not consenting or doing so without being fully informed, of deception, of invasions of privacy, of the failure to manage information confidentially, and misrepresentation in the final report. These complaints may be avoided by the emancipatory research paradigm advocated by Oliver and by Kerruish. Yet there is another side.

Punch notes that researchers can encounter obstructional gatekeepers whose personal needs seriously affect what it is permissible to study, while tensions in the field can force the researcher to take sides. Some organizations commission research, confident that their service will be portrayed positively; they want either to turn research that shows otherwise into a celebratory account, or to block its publication. There can be problems between a lone research assistant in the field and a supervisor or research team back at the institution. Assistants often struggle to collect data for their dissertation alongside the project which pays them. Other problems arise from unclear ownership of the project and data, rights of publication, and the implications of differential status and career opportunities within research teams.

Possible problems do not end with Punch's list. Supervisors need to produce multiple publications if they are to keep their jobs at all. A British centre of excellence grants its clinicians one research day a week and expects four published papers per year in return; failure to keep up is reputed to be met with an informal invitation to leave. Such policies encourage people to over-research small populations, losing track of the need for participants to get a payoff that balances the inconvenience or intrusion. A different group of problems is set in motion when senior staff get a once-in-a-lifetime job offer half-way through a project and abandon it; then inexperienced people are left to complete the work as best they can while searching for other posts. Keeping the question 'Why is this research being done?' central in the minds of all involved can help to minimize some of these problems, but they are far from easy to contain.

Nor is it always clear what comprises ethical practice, since guidelines from ethics committees make some field research impossible. The individual watching a riot can hardly wade into its midst to get signatures on informed consent letters before making any observations, although most societies need to understand riots so that they may be avoided or the inequalities which prompted them addressed. Punch notes that anthropologists have similarly complained that gaining informed consent can kill unfolding relationships with people for whom such procedures are quite alien. Concern about informed consent emerged from the appalling abuses of the individual in medical research carried out by the Nazi regime, and is properly a central tenet of all medical ethics committees. Punch merely helps us to see the limits to such arguments, to recognize that situations do exist to which these rules cannot apply.

Anodyne exhortations from emancipatory researchers seem alarmingly naive when the complex web of tensions affecting most research is considered. Both academic and clinical research is increasingly dominated by short-term contracts and job insecurity for all parties, hardly ideal conditions for making long-term commitments to participants. In such circumstances there is nobody present who could prevent misrepresentation of results after the project is complete. As Said (1994) observed, there is no point in conjuring a golden age where independence and ethical behaviour could be assured because most research in the past was done by gentlemen with private sources of income. Western culture militates against intellectual work in myriad ways.[14] Since we cannot stand outside our culture we need to be aware of the pressures it creates and to debate their influence: wishing them away will not work.

However, one aspect of Oliver's critique does merit attention. Discussing preliminary findings with research participants, and sharing results widely with members of the local service, is not only good ethical practice: it is good clinical and research practice. Telling and retelling the story with different audiences allows researchers to know their reactions and perspectives, and to get better at creating a positive perspective on problems experienced by everyone involved. The service also benefits from hearing vivid stories excluded from the final research report. Presenting research to many different audiences seems to have no downside. Since it is obviously good practice, why do we find it so difficult?

Occasionally there are good reasons for avoiding feedback about research when it concerns personally distressing matters such as bereavement; but even then one can provide the opportunity and let participants vote with their feet. However, I suspect diffidence about the value of our research plays a large part; publication gives reassurance and so there is a temptation to wait until a final account has been accepted somewhere. For clinicians doing part-time research, this usually takes 18 months to three years, long after participants actually met with a researcher, and long after clinicians early in their career have changed jobs. The trail seems cold, one fears they will hardly remember. The long wait suggests you have been doing something complicated: yet the method was fairly simple and it seems difficult to justify the delay. It might look as if you troubled them to take part without yourself being concerned to complete the analysis. Another barrier is the need to revise the account for different audiences, when there is pressure to get a new grant and be on to the next topic. One's youthful vow never to treat participants like mushrooms starts to waver.[15]

Yet these are churlish reasons. Conference presentations to anonymous audiences may be daunting and can be criticized, but feedback to participants is altogether different. Once the meeting has been set and invitations sent, even three years later a roomful of people will turn up as long as the address is reasonably prestigious. Outside researchers may need to be hosted by somebody the audience know, but what is required is a reflection of the seriousness of the matter. People are usually generous about results that are far from earth-shattering: they did not think you were Einstein, so it comes as no shock. You have shed light on an issue that concerns them and which nobody else seems to care about. More important, their presence spurs you to find ways to report positively: it is worth doing it sooner rather than later so that the written account benefits from that perspective. And research can be a long and lonely business: everybody needs to stop and celebrate.

Writing as Discovery

Scientific approaches to research generally perceive writing as reporting. Objectified information avoids the first person and is written in the past tense, flatly describing a procedure and its outcome; technical jargon reassures the uncertain that their work is erudite and limits its accessibility – perhaps deliberately? Qualitative researchers have questioned many of these rules; however, their new approaches contain distinct problems.

Alasuutari (1995) describes how postmodern stylistic habits can blur rather than enhance research accounts. The first person singular may emphasize subjectivity and the multivoicedness of human experience, but can be read as overblown arrogance. Lengthy confession of the personal biases that might creep into an account can seem appallingly self-indulgent. Concern to create involvement between reader and text by using the inclusive 'we' may be effective, but can seem patronizing. Clearly, developing new approaches to research texts is not problem-free.

Stake (1994) lists five stylistic options for case-study researchers, to show how author choices can profoundly affect the final account:

- how much to make the case a story;
- how much to compare with other cases;
- how much to formalize generalizations;
- how much information about the researcher to include;
- whether or not to anonymize the case.

Qualitative researchers have achieved a change in emphasis: writing is not merely the report that communicates results to the world, it is an important part of the research process. Ideas are worked and reworked so that they interconnect, and that thinking makes it easier to trace a path through large amounts of clinical information. Writing is a skill that is learned by doing, and it improves continuously given critical reflection. It is learned like any other skill.

Some people find it useful to reread research they enjoyed, focusing the second time on aspects of the author's writing style that added interest to the content. Similar scrutiny of an author whose work you dislike can also be helpful: it reveals not just unpalatable ideas but impenetrable clauses-within-clauses, unimaginative nouns and repetitive use of passive verbs. Such stylistic habits give no sense of a living author communicating through the text: that is more easily learned from writers than from researchers.

One creative writing course taught the maxim 'kill your babies' to a colleague who swears it has stood him in great stead.[16] Whenever a paragraph or page does not quite hang together, the culprit eventually turns out to be the beautifully crafted phrase that he could not conceive of losing but which he finally realizes has to go. Another source of assistance comes from reading poetry, which alerts writers to the rhythm and pace of words. When research accounts contain the words of participants, pace-sensitivity is especially important: changing rhythm by adding quotations can add interest but can also make the work irritatingly fragmented. Reading troublesome paragraphs out loud, even to yourself, is one way to highlight problems that are difficult to identify as you scan visually. This is particularly helpful when correcting a final draft, because reworking often disrupts the original flow of words.

Curiosity about the skills of wordsmiths led me to Goldberg (1986), whose short exercises aim to keep one present in the words so that they live and engage the reader. One can tire of the wisdom of Katagiri Roshi, her Zen teacher, but my writing seems to be clearer and more digestible when I do her exercises regularly. Here are three brief samples of her work:

> It is important to separate the creator and the editor or internal censor when you practise writing, so that the creator has free space to breathe, explore, and express. If the editor is absolutely annoying and you have trouble differentiating it from your creative voice, sit down whenever you need to and write what the editor is saying. . . . The more clearly you know the editor, the better you can

> ignore it. After a while, like the jabbering of an old drunk fool, it becomes just prattle in the background. (1986: 26)

> This is how we should write. Not asking 'why?' but voraciously, letting our minds eat up everything and spewing it out on paper with great energy . . . . (34)

> Right from the beginning, know it [writing] is good and pleasant. Don't battle with it. Make it your friend. . . . It offers me a chance to touch my life which always softens me and allows me to feel connected to myself again . . . writing well is the best trip of all. (110)

Goldberg recommends frequent periods of continuous writing, without pausing or crossing out or separating words into paragraphs. Challenge impossible expectations by stating minimal ones at the outset, knowing that most of this writing will be junk. Leave it in a drawer and read it a month later. Indeed much of it is self-indulgent, self-pitying, and contains the sort of emotional abuse we would be shocked to hear a parent dish out to a child. Ignore the junk and seek out accounts of precious or significant experiences that emerge from the verbiage; they will be described with immediacy and originality that make them your own.

Many authors regard writing as part of taking care of oneself, as well as a means of 'reactivating the truths one needs' (Foucault, 1988: 27). Free writing periods can be the engine for original ideas used in research as well as the vehicle for reflecting on the meanings of clinical conversations, which Hoshmand (1994) recommends as a way to develop reflective practitioner skills. Writing does not replace clinical or research skills: the three support each other like faces of a pyramid.

Yet psychology and sociology do pose specific writing problems that cannot be solved by writers, problems that are not resolved by reading aloud or spewing. Becker (1986) regards writing as a form of thinking: to use its potential we need to understand why human scientists write so ponderously. According to him, clumsy phrases abound not because we know no better but because we have difficulty ascribing agency and causality. He asks whether it is really worse to be wrong and criticized than innocuous and safe, recommending measured boldness such as 'I think A causes B and the study findings support this in these, these and these ways.' The past participle and passive constructions allow us to duck causality, but this safety-blanket threatens to smother social science altogether.

Becker describes a seminar on writing skills that he developed for postgraduates but which members of staff started to join. The cost was submitting a piece of work in progress, on which they would work: everybody felt theirs would not be good enough. However, the course opened not with their own work but with a first draft written by one of the academic staff. Everyone took it away to comment line by line, attempting not to impose meaning but to clarify the author's: should this be here or elsewhere? can this go altogether? They returned the following week astounded at obvious mistakes made by a published author and irritated by his obfuscation; they were also relieved that the poor sufferer was not present to hear this humiliating discussion.

Becker emphasizes that there is no humiliation. To be a professional academic writer means asking people to read drafts, and being willing to make changes as a result of constructive criticism. Everybody in the academic community takes part in such exchanges with colleagues, both informally and through the peer-review process operated by journals. They build co-operative environments where people respect and facilitate one another's struggle towards new truths.

Once the emotions that accompany giving and receiving comments have been addressed, people are ready to think about technique. This involves recognizing what stage an author has reached and tailoring feedback accordingly. If a writer circles around an idea which is not quite clear in their minds they do not need comments on how to rearrange a paragraph or phrase, they need help to clarify their point so they can drop the rest. Only later will they benefit from suggestions about where to place the strongest ideas so that structure enhances meaning.[17]

Throughout his text Becker exposes the academic throat-clearings that permeate first drafts. Examples include 'it is important to note' when the problem is to show why it is important: showing is more powerful than telling, although much more difficult. 'The question as to whether' is a common filler, as are stating-the-obvious introductions in the third person: 'A comprehensive literature review will be presented' or 'We will argue that the existing streams of research do not shed sufficient light on . . .'. They must be pruned because they contribute no meaning and merely communicate the initial uncertainty most authors feel: they pepper introductions. As one gains confidence that the work has value it becomes easier to identify, excise and replace such phrases with maps of the territory. Producing such maps also helps you to clarify what your findings are and how their implications could affect the field. When you write in the present, using direct verbs wherever possible, the reader can enter the world you are creating without fear of getting lost. Writing then ceases to be the dead hand of reportage; it becomes a process of discovery for author and reader.

Conclusions

Research in the NHS has recently gained administrators' attention because it attracts new funds, resources and ideas into the organization. These bring vital forms of renewal in times of financial stringency, but only when the research is carried out in a host organization that can encompass the disruption it brings. Negotiation is necessary for research to be put into practice, and seeking synergy can be difficult. Change-focused research needs to complement practice but not to be limited to such narrow confines that nothing new can emerge. Given that caveat, far from being the icing on the cake, research presents a bulwark against stagnation.

New methods provide new possibilities: similarities between interpretive, qualitative methods and therapies means that research does not need to be an alien practice incompatible with clinical thinking. However, while qualitative methods are more clinician-friendly, they are also unproven: significant research developments are likely to draw on judicious combinations of both approaches. Qualitative research is often seen as no more than an elaborate pilot study by researchers from a quantitative background. However, the reverse is equally relevant: large-scale data sets can yield anomalous results that need further qualitative research to provide the rich detail required to interpret them.

New methods also bring new dilemmas. Close contact between researcher and researched highlights existing concerns about this relationship, and descriptions of the ethical relationship in qualitative research are underway. Whatever the outcome of those debates, it is clear that making time to feed back and discuss results with participants is central to the idea of research as practice.

Finally, research as practice requires courage. The courage to adopt one set of assumptions about human experience despite knowing that every approach has limitations; giving up the safety of eclecticism to identify an intellectual focus and have some idea why answering this question will contribute to human well-being. The courage to get started, at first with the project and later with the written account of it; knowing that all human experience is interconnected but that the researcher needs to take some slice through it. It requires people to persist in crossing many obstacles: negotiating entry, applying for grants, reporting results that are inevitably far from conclusive, experiencing rejection, seeking critical feedback and using it to change the account – all can seem insurmountable challenges. Yet the struggle to write complements the development of clinical and research skills; in combination they can create and renew and communicate. Few people who make a firm start at being researcher-practitioners want to stop: for them and the services they work with, it provides something precious that neither wants to lose.

Summary

Contemporary issues reviewed here were the need for psychologists to make active pursuit of research a component part of their work, because changing contexts of care now focus on efficacy and audit. Organizations need more clinicians with research skills than ever before, but they need us to negotiate about the type of research that will enhance clinical practice in this context. Five qualitative research methods were reviewed to expand the range of approaches available: they come from sociology, philosophy and the critical theory tradition. Their distinct methods and goals were discussed to counter the tendency towards methodological eclecticism seen in some recent accounts of qualitative clinical research.

When considering research as a form of practice, *a history of the present* would return to Lewin's (1951) action research ideas. The idea appears a decade later in two influential research projects designed in the 1960s, from the USA and the UK respectively: interrupting cycles of disadvantage with Headstart, and research into contexts of care by Tizard. Both combined qualitative and quantitative methods to inform practice and policy at all levels, introducing interventions that remain in place 40 years later. Both projects underline the close links that used to exist between research and practice early in the development of clinical psychology, links that in many places became stretched or broken by the pressure towards professionalism and concern to develop a set of exclusively psychological approaches to intervention.

Intersubjective meanings may develop between clinicians, clients and carers as much from sharing information and debating it as from interventions themselves. This is the basis of a psychoeducational approach to clinical practice pioneered by psychologists working with people who have long-term mental health problems. At best, intersubjective meanings also evolve during research projects, enhanced by confirmatory discussions between researcher and client at the end to check that meanings have been neither misconstrued nor subverted.

Critical thinking about the ethics of the research relationship within clinical settings is lively. Consent is under considerable scrutiny by multi-disciplinary research ethics committees and by professional associations. The radical wing argues that research skills should be made available to service users to enhance their own position, that they should be involved in design, analysis and interpretation, that results should be geared towards user empowerment and their meaning guarded with care. Yet their description of the ideal has relatively little connection to the realities of contemporary research. It will be a rare grant-giving body that funds time to teach service users about research design; staff are employed on short-term contracts and have to ensure their own survival; and clinicians directing the work have to negotiate a path between user need, organizational priorities, and topics that will move contemporary research concerns forwards. Nevertheless, it is essential that researchers acknowledge their participants cannot be treated like experimental animals: participants need to be able to influence results and not be trapped into ready-made boxes, and they need to see some payoff for their involvement. At the very least they should know what the results were, how they were used and where they were published.

These minimum ethical standards make eminent sense to the *reflective researcher-practitioner* who wants her results to improve clinical services for all clients. The problems and concerns that face isolated researchers in clinical settings were reviewed, to encourage people to develop communities of support where drafts are exchanged and commented upon.

Techniques for developing writing skills and overcoming the barriers each researcher faces were considered at greater length, since a constructionist stance makes writing a central component of knowledge-creation. Developing such skills also makes it more likely that policy documents and other proposals will carry sufficient power to affect service-provision.

The organizational perspective on research was discussed to ensure that a *human systems* aspect was incorporated into research planning. This accepts that research creates perturbations that are creative for healthy organizations but destructive to those already sinking into disorder and dissolution. Managers have a responsibility to debate with researchers what type of research they plan, to ensure that it will promote existing service structures. They may also wish to consider the balance between time consumed by the organization and payoff, since the organization remains primarily responsible to the needs of clients. In turn researchers need to identify important questions and not allow them to be constrained by existing assumptions about services. Adapting ideas shown to be useful in other service systems or with other clients creates less earth-shattering results than does discovery research, but also presents less of a challenge to an unstable organization. Adaptation also means that some positive outcome is assured, for the organization and for the inexperienced researcher. Discovery research is harder for the uninitiated and riskier for the organization: it may produce nothing of value, although when there are positive outcomes these are usually significant and relevant.

Notes

1 The numbers in our Trust are probably a little low but instructive: out of 2,200 employees, 80 are doctors, of whom 48 are consultants; seven are clinical psychologists, three of whom are at the consultant grade.

2 For example, Parry and Watts (1989); Rossi and Freeman (1986).

3 This summary is based on the description given by Orford (1992).

4 In the policy statement *Working for Patients* (Department of Health, February 1989).

5 Department of Health (1993) *Clinical Audit: Meeting and Improving Standards in Health Care*. London: HMSO.

6 EL(95)103 is the letter of instruction from the NHS Executive of the Department of Health, issued to every regional and district chief executive.

7 Clegg, Lansdall-Welfare, Andrews and Thurman, research paper under consideration. Apply to the first author for further information.

8 Similar debates also run through history. The relative merits of comprehensive surveys of battles, institutions and government are debated against the value of subjective and personal accounts of what it is like to live in a particular era. The debate is heavily influenced by critiques from feminists and from members of minority cultures who feel that traditional histories minimize or ignore their role and contribution. Hufton (1995) gives a clear summary of this debate in her introductory chapter.

9 Latour (1987); Latour and Wooolgar (1979).

10 A British newspaper review of an edited book on the psychology of work suggests we are not doing too well on this front:

> I wonder what possible use is there for this dull, jargon-stuffed collection, apart from as the raw material for satire. As intelligible as the baying of coyotes across the savannah, and considerably less poignant, I discard it. No correspondence from offended psychologists will be entered into regarding this review. Or even read. (*Guardian*, paperback Review, 12 April 1996)

11 This is covered at length in Chapter 8's exploration of ethics.

12 Personal communication.

13 Personal communication from Cliff Cunningham, concerning his study of a cohort of families who have a son or daughter with Down's syndrome; also from Ron Gallimore concerning his cohort study of the accommodations families make for a neonate who has a learning disability (Gallimore et al., 1989).

14 This assertion was made by Said (1994) and reasons are given for it in Chapter 1 (p. 18).

15 If this very old joke is unfamiliar, mushrooms are kept in the dark and have manure thrown on top of them.

16 Thanks to John Cromby for this tale.

17 For example, I started writing this paragraph with the issue of students acknowledging and receiving comments, but rearranged it so that the main problem – the emotions which accompany this exchange – was given greater prominence by coming early in the first sentence. Becker argues that key ideas should start and end paragraphs; overarching principles should occur in paragraphs at the beginning and end of a section or piece. The way that Schama used structure to enhance historical meaning was explored in Chapter 4 (see p. 66).

8 Ethics: Running against the Walls of our Cage?

The vituperative correspondence about the way psychologists should work in a special hospital which had been condemned by judicial enquiry four years previously, illustrates the emotions stirred by debates about ethics.[1] Yet curiously, psychological ethics remain largely untheorized; and when Lindsay (1995) reviewed the ethical dilemmas described by a random sample of members of the British Psychological Society only 28 per cent responded, 19.5 per cent of whom said they experienced none. What little attention ethics get in clinical psychology, from either psychologists or philosophers, focuses mainly on the therapeutic relationship during one-to-one psychoanalytic psychotherapy even though this is a minority pastime among British clinicians. Naturally, every clinician wants to ensure that their attempts to help some of the most damaged or disadvantaged members of society do not go awry, but it is rarely clear how that can be achieved. Some believe that professional codes will do the trick, but that seems a false hope.

'A series of bald, undefended, unargued, authoritarian fiats' is how O'Donohue and Mangold (1996) characterize the 1992 American Psychological Association's code of ethics: the BPS *Code of Conduct, Ethical Principles and Guidelines* (1997) could be criticized on similar philosophical grounds. Ethics are imposed by rule in such codes and can only provide minimum standards: clinical psychology needs to take a more complex and multifaceted approach to the ethics of practice, by lighting many fires. People need contexts where they can develop the cognitive skills that let them consider multiple perspectives without paralysis; support to create narrative unity within their own practice and the chance to learn from mistakes rather than conceal them; and help to change those aspects of personal history that make us bystanders rather than actors. They also need fora where useful ethical debate can occur, that is, where debate goes beyond the mere raising of problems to describe how the world looks from specific positions and what the consequences of each might be. This interactional approach to ethics suggests that explicit attention to immediate discursive communities is more likely to create beneficial change than publishing ever-longer professional codes.

Before justifying these opening remarks I want to survey ethical terms and ethical theories, to clear the conceptual ground of this chapter. Current conflicts often break out between utilitarian arguments and the defence of individual rights, the latter itself deriving from theories of distributive justice. There seems to be little appreciation that these positions are incommensurable, or that other stances exist that could inform clinicians who struggle to conceptualize and resolve dilemmas. Such muddle encourages people to nail their colours to any banner that promises certainty, and there are plenty of those on offer. Clarkson (1996) observes that to take a position on ethical matters is to risk being wrong, but that is far preferable to doing nothing. Nevertheless, blind assertion of indefensible positions is not quite what she means by taking an ethical stance.

In adopting an ethical position we accept responsibility for understanding both its grounds and its implications; otherwise the position is mere posture. Yet some clinicians decide to hold an ethical torch for clients, feeling entitled if not enjoined to identify the wrongdoing of other professionals or to expose the iniquitous way that past clinicians misused clients or research participants; there is little reflexive questioning about the origin of such certainty. Others cling to a simple notion of confidentiality, enjoying the crusade against demands for access to files and information-sharing that are mainstays of risk management. Another banner to march behind is the aim of helping groups that seem weak and excluded to assert their rights for more resources and to take their 'place' in society, without theorizing what this means or what social reform is being resisted. Current pressure-group politics automatically resists all change as bad, irrespective of the conceptual muddle that is our welfare state: such clinging to the wreckage is based on fear, not ethics.

The first section of this chapter introduces key terms, before outlining the main ethical theories and their relation to one another. This puts dominant topics such as utilitarianism and rights assertions in their place, alongside the less familiar conception of ethics as a virtue theory. It introduces recent perspectives: pragmatism, feminism, pluralism, and returns to twentieth-century virtue ethics. These ideas inform ethics in practice, which forms the second half of the chapter, concluding with a description of dilemma in practice and one possible response.

Theories of Ethics

Defining Terms

Books on the ethics of psychological practice tend to be edited collections with no intellectual plane to link the separate issues explored:[2] one notable text describes itself as an hors-d'oeuvre to whet the appetite. The ethics presented in these collected discussions of problematic areas not only lack the intellectual coherence necessary for serious debate, but also exemplifies the problem of casuistry. Casuistry is the attempt to study and teach ethics by assessing individual cases against extant principles or laws. Such case discussions were originally intended to illustrate ethical theory, but sometimes casuistry becomes an end in itself: it then prevents evolution of theory, principle or law. It also turns ethics into the exclusive study of misconduct, rather than the elaboration of virtue or the identification of social goods.

Editors exhort dissatisfied readers to study medical ethics for further information. Yet medical ethics texts generally explore a small number of topics, primarily genetic engineering and abortion, living wills and euthanasia. These problems have little connection with the dilemmas clinicians encounter in services for people with disabilities or mental health problems; moreover they are discussed predominantly by utilitarians, by people who adopt the distant, analytical stance of the scientist. Most medical ethicists discuss issues within a set of absolute principles – nonmaleficence (do no harm), beneficence and so on – not discussed by moral philosophers; the appropriateness of using such rules while ignoring emotions and personal reactions to a situation is criticized by many philosophers (e.g. Singer, 1994). Apparently culture-free and certain, classical medical ethics ignore the very contexts that create our moral horizons.

Singer (1994) describes 'ethics' and 'morals' as deriving respectively from the Greek and the Latin words for custom, and thus being in some sense interchangeable. Ethics is the term generally preferred by social scientists. It is often used as if there are agreed, value-free standards that apply to us all, even though there is constant change in standards of behaviour considered to be exemplary at different times and in different societies. Clinicians who question the scientific model of psychology currently have to re-examine how we can guarantee that members of the public will not be harmed: if we paint ourselves neither as analytic nor as scientifically 'rigorous' but as subjective and like them, where does safety lie?

Small wonder there is increasing interest in ethics and focus on ethical codes. Written by people who offer their time and energy to protect recipients of psychological services, such work does stop blatant malpractice. However, descriptions of ethical and unethical behaviour are not sacrosanct, they are attempts at social promotion and social control and should be scrutinized as such.

Wittgenstein thought that ethics challenges the rest of philosophy:

> Now I want to impress on you that a certain characteristic misuse of our language runs through all ethical and religious expressions. All these expressions seem, prima facie, to be just similes. . . . As soon as we try to drop the simile and simply to state the facts which stand behind it, we find there are no such facts. . . .
>
> I see now that these nonsensical expressions were not nonsensical because I have not yet found the correct expressions, but that their nonsensicality was their very essence . . . the tendency of all men who ever tried to write or talk Ethics or religion was to run against the boundaries of language. This running against the

> walls of our cage is perfectly, absolutely hopeless. . . . But it is a document of a tendency in the human mind which I personally cannot help respecting deeply and would not for my life ridicule it. (1929, reprinted in Singer, 1994: 143–7)

Wittgenstein observes that ethical concepts such as value derive their meaning from our understanding of monetary value, but the added something which occurs when applying the term to humanity cannot be defined. The enterprise remains shrouded because the words we have available are inadequate for the task, but this does not mean we should avoid tackling it. It has emotional as well as cognitive meaning. Lacey and Schwartz (1996) give a full description of the variety of ways that 'value' may now be used: these include value as a person's ultimate reason for action, a quality that gives worth to their life, and a fundamental standard for their own behaviour and for that of others. The issue of to whom an ethical code or theory should apply – ourselves, our community, or everybody – starts to emerge as needing consideration too.

Wittgenstein sees ethics as part of our wonder at existence, as part of a miracle which neither science nor language can capture fully.[3] He followed the classical system of separating aesthetics from ethics: aesthetics is concerned with the appreciation of style and beauty as inherently good or right in an immediate sense, while ethics concerns ways of behaving with other persons over time. Kierkegaard argued that the aesthetic way of life concerns the attempt to lose self in the immediacy of present experience (an idea central to Buddhism), while the ethical life binds present with past and future experience.[4] This intertwining of the right thing to do, with other people, over time, was a meaning of 'ethics' lost during the Enlightenment when the term started to describe single acts of responsibility or duty. The Enlightenment sense of 'ethics' is in general use now, limited to this restricted meaning.

Traditional Ethics

Traditional approaches to ethics are summarized in Figure 8.1. Deontological ethics states that certain acts are always ethical, regardless of their consequences. They may derive from the handed-down word of God, but other ethical systems of thought have also been developed based on reason or intuition.[5] As has been discussed, rationalists such as Kant assumed that reason should take the position formerly occupied by God, and that analytical philosophy can determine what are right acts. Kantian philosophers such as Hare (1989) see this as focusing on duty, that the verb 'ought' is the verb of ethics: contemporary legislation about the 'duty of care' that professionals owe to vulnerable clients originates in this thinking. Debates around principles such as 'You must never take an innocent life' illustrate how no deontological principle survives undented when taken to extremes; that all ethical principles reach limits in some situation. Moreover, Gardiner (1996) summarizes Foucault's successful challenge to

Deontological	Teleological	Virtue
Divine command Rationalism, e.g. Kant Emotivism, e.g. Hume	Consequentialism, e.g. utilitarianism Justice theories, e.g. Rawls	Greek Christian

FIGURE 8.1 *Traditional ethical theories*

deontological ethics by demonstrating that external moral codes are intertwined with prevailing structures of power: philosophical logic does not necessarily give privileged access to the 'right' action after all.

Hume's emotivism countered rationalism by saying that ethical judgements originate in emotion, not reason. Contemporary emotivists (e.g. Mackie, 1977) give a place to principles such as impartiality which filter or limit the desires we can count as ethical; but their main focus remains on cultivating the understanding which allows us to distinguish moral from immoral acts subjectively. This is a position that MacIntyre (1985) regards as unnecessary if one takes an Aristotelian perspective on virtue, because emotional contact and insight into the needs of others is part and parcel of ancient virtue theories. However, feminist philosophers such as Held (1990) regard Hume's philosophy as a good basis for contemporary ethics.

Teleological ethics concerns actions which optimize a state of affairs or achieve a goal. For example, consequentialism states that ethical decisions should be based on the predicted outcome of an action: its theories are subdivided into three types. Egoism – that people decide on the basis of self-interest only; Altruism – that they place the best interests of others above their own; and Consequentialism (of which utilitarianism is a subset), when they select the action which brings the greatest good or happiness or benefit (and note these are rarely the same) to the greatest number. Consequentialist arguments are those used by P. Singer (1993) and other medical ethicists to argue for abortion and euthanasia under specified conditions, even though this conflicts with the deontological principle that one should never take an innocent life.

Justice theories are also future-oriented, to increase fairness in society, but their contribution is large enough to require separate classification. Honderich (1995) divides justice theories into two groups, corrective and distributive. Corrective justice theories ground legal systems: they provide a conceptual frame for laws applied to people who transcend agreed boundaries. By contrast, distributive justice concerns the attempt to share resources more equitably across society, although whether 'resources' refers to satisfaction, good things or opportunity remains at issue. Statements of rights affecting clinical services for the past 15 years, for example the 1977 UN Declaration of the Rights of the Disabled Person, derive from a distributive justice view of ethics and focus on equality of opportunity. Jeremy Bentham, originator of utilitarianism, dismissed the French declaration of human rights as 'nonsense on stilts': they are clearly positions at odds with each other.

Rawls's social contract theory (summarized in Honderich, 1995) is a powerful contemporary example of a theory of distributive justice. It is a rationalist approach because the principles derive from reason. Here theorists imagine an ideal state where we do not know socially significant facts about ourselves or others. Under this 'veil of ignorance' they decide what principles should drive a society of which they are a part. Rawls argues that his veil of ignorance ensures that justice is driven by the avoidance of the worst possible ends and the amelioration of socio-economic inequality. His theory is also opposed to utilitarianism, because the greatest good to the greatest number results in unacceptable conditions for a small minority: the 'veil of ignorance' helps theorists to remember that they could be members of that minority.

Midgley (1983) challenges Rawls's theory on two grounds. Firstly, like utilitarianism it is intensely individual in nature. It assumes that the autonomous contractarian is dealing with another autonomous person in deciding issues of justice and rights. Social contract theory ignores every person's embeddedness within a set of allegiances: to family, to colleagues at work, to spiritual or political community, to animals, or to a landscape which they call their fatherland. When this complexity is admitted, arguments about 'rights' become obscure, because listing and specifying what they are is so much harder than merely demanding them. She notes that the idea is further complicated by the way legal implications and wider political meanings are intertwined within discourse on rights. Midgley suggests the word 'right' be dropped entirely, observing that rights language is more useful as a slogan than as a conceptual tool.

Secondly, Rawlsian contract theory does not encompass the weak and the inarticulate. Here Midgley emphasizes that this is not a criticism of the theory *per se*, which in its own sphere has been of enormous value. She is criticizing its use as a comprehensive theory of social justice. Rawls touches on the question of human beings whom he describes as permanently irrational or retarded, saying that they present a difficulty which he cannot examine. Midgley shows how he minimizes a problem which excludes large numbers of people from his theory's purview.

Virtue plays a role in most theories, since ethical theories need to assume the existence of people who are motivated to act in ethical ways. However, approaches which rely entirely on the person as a human being rather than exclusively as a human actor are described as virtue theories, because virtue is seen to be the source of all good experiences between people. Virtue is a term with such Victorian associations in Britain it can be difficult to take the ideas seriously: however, it has an important part to play in any discussion of ethics. Interest in virtue started with Aristotle and has been continually adapted since then. Ancient Greeks focused on four virtues (Geach, 1977; see Figure 8.2).

Temperance is the fundamental virtue since it facilitates all others. The Greeks did not mean the permanent abstinence from alcohol and other stimulants which came to be known as the temperance movement in the

Prudence	Justice	Fortitude	Temperance
Respect, practical wisdom, propriety, ability to see good, alertness, openness to learning and counsel.	That which enables people to give to each other what is their due. Acting not just properly but to acknowledge and confirm the other.	Strength of purpose; promoting hope; bravely challenging injustice (presupposes vulnerability).	Harmony within the body by ordering turbulent emotions and appetites, to achieve the serenity necessary to enact the other virtues.

FIGURE 8.2 *Greek virtues*

Victorian era. Rather, the intention was for people to learn how to rule their appetites through periodic fasts, thus preventing those appetites from dominating their lives. A concept of justice occurs in both teleological and virtue ethics, but they consider different aspects. Teleological justice theories concern the just society; justice as a virtue concerns how to deal with others at the individual level.

Prudence is often described by the Greek term *phronesis*, the practical wisdom which achieves excellence when matched with sophic or theoretical wisdom. Its focus on practical judgement and acting on the world makes it attractive to constructionists such as Shotter (1993). Prudence is notable for matching the qualities of an expert counsellor, teacher or architect described by Schön (1987).

These virtues were subsequently adopted by the Christian Church, which added the familiar values of faith, hope and love[6] to their list. Although I am surveying Western values, it is interesting to find two similar values commended by Buddhists (Hanh, 1995). One concerns generating the will to inhibit evils which have not yet arisen and to cause an increase in good, ideas similar to the virtue of fortitude. The other is mindfulness: this is both a self-possessed way of dwelling in the body so that covetousness and dejection are controlled, and a careful way of dealing with the social and physical world. It is similar to the virtue of temperance.

Contemporary Ethics

As was discussed earlier, Mead's version of pragmatism descends from William James and continues beyond him to Bruner: it is characterized as 'reformist'. Rorty's challenging advocacy of pragmatism derives from Nietzsche and Foucault, and is characterized as 'revolutionary'. Pragmatism is frequently misunderstood, addressed by Rorty:

> 'Relativism' is the traditional epithet applied to pragmatism by realists. Three different views are commonly referred to by this name. The first is the view that every belief is as good as every other. The second is the view that 'true' is an

> equivocal term, having as many meanings as there are procedures for justification. The third is the view that there is nothing to be said about either truth or rationality apart from descriptions of the familiar procedures of justification which a given society – ours – uses in one or another area of inquiry. The pragmatist holds the ethnocentric third view. But he does not hold the self-refuting first view, nor the eccentric second view. (1991: 23)

Rorty is not saying that all knowledge is relative to something else; he is making the negative point that the traditional distinction between opinions and reality should be dropped because the relationship is unknowable. The pragmatist has no theory of truth and so cannot have a relative one, much less the opinion commonly ascribed to pragmatists that for them 'true' has different meanings in different societies and that each belief is equally valid.

Pragmatist	Feminist	Pluralist	Virtue
Mead (1934); Rorty (1991, 1993)	Gilligan (1982); Benhabib (1992)	Habermas (1992); Benhabib (1992); Taylor (1989, 1991)	MacIntyre (1985)

FIGURE 8.3 *Four contemporary ethical stances*

Rorty conceptualizes human progress as increased creativity, where people can do more interesting things and become more interesting people. Pragmatic ethics concerns expanding the range of solidarity, enlarging human sympathies to expand the number of people described as 'we'. Dilemmas occur because most people belong to more than one group, a phenomenon that increases with education and more complex civilizations; when the beliefs of one group conflict with those of another, we do not want to exclude ourselves from either. People use narrative and dialogue to find a way out of such dilemmas, perhaps by trying to expand the sympathies of one of the groups: for Rorty, logic is of little use here.

In his 1993 Oxford Amnesty lecture, Rorty argued that continually polishing our rhetoric will not in itself produce social change, because it speaks to the deaf. Just as Jefferson could compose a bill of rights while owning slaves, so the Serbs did not see that they were violating *human* rights. Declarations about 'people' tend to be read as 'people like us'. Rorty knows that people want to tear down warlords and perpetrators of sexual abuse, to impose justice by confronting evil, but he argues cogently for persuasion. The way that narrative and critique support ethical clinical practice across a community of practitioners was demonstrated by Fulford et al. (1993) when they investigated abuses of psychiatry in the USSR. Examination of academic and samizdat publications found that, contrary to popular belief, abuses did not occur through misclassification but through excessive faith in the science of psychiatry: problems arose from there being no debate about subjective aspects of psychiatry and the limits of applicability. They argue that psychiatry's scientific discourse needs to be exposed to the narratives of non-medical specialists and service users, and the evaluative component of diagnosis kept visible, to reduce psychiatry's vulnerability to abuse to an acceptable level.

Feminism provides the second ethical position. Gilligan's (1982) critique of theories of moral development in psychology argued against the universality of Kohlberg's six-point scale of morality, because girls and women were virtually absent from his research. Gilligan observed that we had a psychology of the moral development of men, focused on justice and fairness: her study of the dilemmas facing women identified problems arising from conflicting responsibilities, not competing rights. The resolution of these dilemmas required a narrative and contextual approach, not the formal and abstract logic favoured by many men.

Held (1990) develops this theme. She notes that masculinity has, throughout history, been defined by rejection of whatever is construed to be feminine at the time. The split between reason and emotion is a familiar philosophical dichotomy, played out in these allocated gender roles; it was elaborated in Campbell's (1993) explanation of why young white men rioted in 1991, and in Goldner et al.'s (1990) development of systemic family therapy for couples who are violent. However, Held argues that if one starts with women rather than men the dichotomy does not reverse: women's ethical decisions turn out not to be more emotional but more socially contextual. Women are concerned to maintain actual relationships with others who have embodied histories, and to express care in the way they resolve ethical dilemmas. Held follows other feminists in arguing for an ethic of care to set beside the ethics of justice which dominate contemporary literature.

These points are interesting and Gilligan's critique of Kohlberg overdue, but Benhabib (1992) has reservations about such essentialist feminism. She notes that debate has missed Gilligan's central insight: that we are children before we are adults and that our ability to nurture and care for others depends on the degree to which we have received it ourselves. As adults, then, we enter ethical debates as embodied beings:

> Modern moral philosophy, and particularly universalist moralities of justice, have emphasized our dignity and worth as moral subjects at the cost of forgetting and repressing our vulnerability and dependency as bodily selves. Such networks of dependence and the web of human affairs in which we are immersed are not simply like clothes which we outgrow or like shoes we leave behind. They are ties that bind. (Benhabib, 1992: 189)

What Gilligan wanted to show was that ethical debates look different when some women are brought into the account: the debate is then no longer neat and unitary. Just as early feminist historians showed how eras characterized as episodes of progress for men were accompanied by status loss for women, so Gilligan wanted to introduce difference, stereoscopic vision, counterpoint. Nevertheless, her focus on an ethic of care is justly criticized for recreating a feminine stereotype of weakness, and ignoring earlier work by men of many faiths who promoted neighbourly love.

Habermas confronts the problem of social justice in a plural word by focusing on the discursive unification of people's wills (McCarthy, 1992). To achieve such unification he needs to postulate the Ideal Communicator. This is someone who is truthful; who gives her own interests neither more nor less value than those of other participants; who takes an impartial standpoint which strives to identify common interests; and who puts herself into the role of others so strongly that she can envisage the consequences of each proposed action for every member of the group.

Benhabib (1992) develops the Habermasian position, but argues that general rules of ethical action do need to be determined. Such rules must go beyond the customs of family, synagogue or political group, and need the validity of some standpoint on justice and impartiality. These are the elements of her broad and pluralist conception of ethics:

- Truth is established within discourses of justification, held between people that are both historically and physically embodied and culturally embedded. The moral point of view is achieved interactively.
- The moral point of view involves the cultivation of 'enlarged thinking' by habitually reversing perspective so that we make insight into the other's position paramount.
- Morality encompasses rather than obliterates differences arising from gender, culture and a myriad other sources. Such ethical thinking is embedded in social culture, but not so firmly that members of any culture are entrenched within stereotypes.
- There is a conceptual continuum for considering the other person, ranging from the generalized other to the particular or concrete. Ethics concerning the generalized other treat every human being as worthy of respect. The concrete other, by contrast, describes ethical relationships with people whose lives are merged with one's own: spouse, parents, siblings. Acquaintances and working relationships are scattered between these extremes. Benhabib argues that traditional ethical theories are too limited because they theorize the generalized but not the concrete other, and focus on the legal domain to the exclusion of more relational ethics.

Taylor (1989) offers a different response to pluralism, drawing a number of ethical positions together into a triaxial moral ontology. He criticizes the 'preshrunk moral universe' which is conjured by ethics derived from one position alone, citing the Habermasian focus on ethical discourse as one example, the analysis of power by Foucault as another. These are significant but not sufficient, in his view.

Taylor is concerned that deeply moving aspects of human life, those which have the capacity to inspire or appal us, have been washed out of both analytical philosophy and social science. Subscribing to what he calls 'hypergoods', goods that we make superordinate in our lives along these three dimensions, is epistemologically unsettling: orienting ourself towards them calls into question values that had seemed important previously. There cannot be rational criteria to decide between hypergoods because one of their defining qualities, and the power they confer, is that they move us intuitively. For him they are the sources of ethical acts.

However, responding to the emotional pulls that suffering and injustice exert on us by *doing* good can demean the recipient, is patronizing without an accompanying ethic of *being*, of seeing-good (agape) in the other person. This enables people to connect reciprocally with the good in others while helping them. Taylor exhorts human services to consider whether they have sufficient agape to sustain their ethic of benevolence; if not, they should moderate their aims.

Taylor's triaxial moral ontology balances three sources of ethics: whatever gives meaning to life; the individual valuing of others which clusters around the idea of respect; and a range of societal values about inclusion and justice which he gathers onto an axis of dignity. He includes emotions associated with awe-inspiring ways of being (as opposed to doing) on his meaning of life axis. Taylor describes alternative approaches to meaning which draw on humanism or religion, artistic performance, and/or academic and political activities, although this is not an exclusive list.

The respect axis describes what Taylor believes to be the dominant ethic in contemporary Western societies. This concerns ethics of obligation, a duty deriving from the Enlightenment to treat others as autonomous and as living ordinary lives that are valuable. This affirmation of ordinary life has already been explored as a major component of normalization,[7] problematic in part because it is so difficult to agree what sort of ordinary life one is discussing. Respect also includes the rights which societies such as France and the USA enshrine politically in the autonomous individual.

The third axis revolves around the theme of dignity, which describes those aspects of our selves which command a respectful attitude from others and which enable us to view ourselves positively. Citizenship is a complex of ideas which provide people with dignity: these differ from country to country but revolve around voting rights, societal expectations, membership of different groups, and other conventions which act to include or exclude. The liminal status of many people with learning disabilities living in the community, discussed previously, is an example of our failure to treat this group ethically.

Taylor's 1991 development explores the culture of self-fulfilment. While generally being criticized as individualistic, narcissistic and ultimately nihilistic, the ideal of authenticity – of being true to oneself – can be driven, Taylor claims, by a valid ideal about what a better life might be like. Authenticity need not be narcissistic if it enhances our ties to other people. For example, meditation can be learned to satisfy curiosity about altered levels of consciousness; conversely it can be a strategy used by an ethical clinician to maintain the tranquillity required for them to offer effective therapy.[8] By defining ourselves against the backdrop of being-in-the-world, what is significant becomes so against a moral horizon which emerges from connection to others.

The last position is virtue ethics as revisited by MacIntyre:

> The interminable and unsettlable character of so much contemporary moral debate arises from the variety of heterogeneous and incommensurable concepts which form the major premises from which protagonists in such debates argue. In this conceptual *melange* there are to be found, jostling with such modern concepts as those of utility and rights, a variety of virtue concepts, functioning in a variety of ways. What is lacking however is any clear consensus. (1985: 226)

He argues that ethical ideas must be situated historically to help us see why they occupy different planes of understanding and cannot easily be contrasted during debate: that words like duty, right, good, should be treated as leftovers from previous cultures, with little or no meaning in this one. He reviews a variety of systems to conclude that there are three distinct conceptions of virtue: that it is a quality that enables somebody to discharge a social role; a quality that enables the person to fulfil a particular vision of humanity with others, be it natural or supernatural; or a quality that helps us to achieve earthly or heavenly success. MacIntyre argues for the second idea of virtue as something that contributes toward some transcending goal for humanity, one pursued constantly thoughout a human life. He thus combines the idea of virtue with the idea of teleology from traditional ethics.

MacIntyre shows how the virtues became narrowed to a single division between virtue and vice. In Victorian Britain vice came to be almost solely concerned with the control of sexuality, and virtue with the maintenance of marriage: small wonder that contemporary intellectuals despise the notion. MacIntyre argues that this is a very restricted idea of virtue ethics, but does not avoid the notion of vice: 'It is no part of my thesis that great violinists cannot be vicious or great chess-players mean-spirited. Where the virtues are required, the vices may also flourish. It is just that the vicious and mean-spirited necessarily rely on the virtues of others for the practices in which they engage to flourish and also deny themselves the experience of achieving those internal goods which may reward even not very good chess-players and violinists' (1985: 193).

He also takes on the idea of pluralism, but with a different slant. He notes that ethical actions are difficult to determine because many different types of transaction co-exist between members of the same group. He criticizes game theory solutions to human problems because of this, observing: 'the problem about real life is that moving one's knight to QB3 may always be replied to with a lob across the net' (1985: 98). This is one of four sources of unpredictability in human life he uses to move ethical debate away from either consequence or duty, for these may be unknowable or may compete.

MacIntyre's overarching picture focuses on virtue and the behaviours that express it in itself, irrespective of outcome. It depends on the specific meaning he gives to the term 'practice', a relevant concept for clinicians. He defines a practice as 'Any coherent and complex form of socially established cooperative human activity through which goods internal to that form of activity are realized . . . with the result that human powers to achieve excellence, and human conceptions of the ends and goods involved, are systematically extended' (1985: 187). Thus learning circular questioning or how to develop an advocacy group is not a practice, but a broad conception of systemic methods of intervention is. Practices contain internal goods; they are themselves considered beneficial in their exercise, because they contribute to overarching goals thought to benefit the society in which the practitioner is located. These internal goods are contrasted with external goods such as wealth and success: any society dedicated only to those is doomed to rampant competitiveness. This distinction between internal and external goods is argued at length, in part to show that utilitarianism's failure to take both into account, and to see that they cannot be summed because they are often in conflict, is one of its major weaknesses.

Institutions such as the Division of Clinical Psychology must not be mistaken for practices; practices are learned and carried out only by practitioners, not by institutions. Entering into a practice means engaging in relationships with contemporary practitioners, and with those in the past who developed them and extended their reach. All practices exist within the context of a moral tradition, into which we inevitably enter if only by rebelling against it. The virtues of justice, courage and honesty are prerequisites for learning such practices; without them 'practices could not resist the corrupting power of institutions' (1985: 194).

MacIntyre argues that virtues require some pre-existing account of the social/moral life to which they contribute, against which they become intelligible. His account is one involving relationships with other people and some conception of good being good for all: however, he is critical of communitarians and dissociates himself from their efforts to recruit him to their cause. Virtue according to MacIntyre requires three stages of development, which must unfold in this order: a background account of his conception of practice; another account of the narrative order of a single human life, of an exemplar accepted as being virtuous; and an account of the moral tradition within which it sits and to which it contributes. His clear agenda tells us how groups of psychologists, or groups of people from different disciplines and backgrounds who share common cause, can arrive at a description of ethical practice that they can develop and sustain. The account would be very different from that published in professional codes of conduct.

Lukes (1993) gives a contemporary overview of four utopias: utilitarianism, communitarianism, communism and libertarianism. His caricatures expose the limits of each vision of society. They show that concern for that which is advantageous to society has to be restrained in favour of individual need. That the specific and local practices of every culture cannot develop unbridled; they can only be expressed within a protected space created from some unifying common ground. That any world view must presuppose a set of existential facts about the human condition: that people will always face cruelty, scarcity, injustice; and that there will never be agreement about ways of life, nor conceptions of what makes it valuable, without some political force towards unity. Finally, that libertarian approaches need to be leavened by concern to rebalance society in favour of the worst off.

Lukes ends by discussing a utopia called Egalitaria towards which we should strive. Committed to equal rights which are of equal worth, citizens aim for a political and economic structure which makes everybody better off but which prioritizes improved conditions for the poorest. There is a libertarian constraint on this mirage: no economy functions on altruism and ethical incentives alone. There is also a communitarian constraint: that many people seek strong identification with a social group, which by default implies the exclusion of another group. Egalitaria's problem is to render the terms of that exclusion harmless.

These caricatures clarify MacIntyre's point that 'Morality which is no particular society's morality is to be found nowhere' (1985: 265). Benhabib (1992) makes a helpful distinction between two different standpoints on ethics in society, the participationist and the integrationist. Participationist is her term for societies that avoid being repressive of difference, negotiating a common life together through debate and conflict. She contrasts this with the integrationist stance she associates with communitarians, whose vision of a coherent society is one where shared values are thought to be an achievable goal: she considers this to be incompatible with autonomy and pluralism. Her vision of participationism encourages not reconciliation and harmony but political agency.

Summary of Ethical Theories

Many people engage in motivated suppressing when faced with the complexity of ethical thinking. However, practitioners cannot justify ignoring the problem, particularly those who adopt more subjective and interpretive approaches where ethical behaviour is the only guarantee against the abuse of others. According to Taylor, cramps on ethical thinking include the tendency to focus on single ethical issues and exclude all other goods or stances; a linguistic heritage from science that rejects emotion-laden terms such as courage and integrity that describe ethical acts; and a negative construction of goodness as smug.

Traditional ethics offers footholds on this difficult topic. Utilitarianism underpins many NHS debates, for example about how to ration limited resources; its limitations need to be better known. Rights arguments often counterpoint utilitarian pursuit of the greatest good, seeking instead to distribute opportunity more evenly: yet conceptual limitations make 'right' more useful as a campaigning slogan than as a workable philosophy.

Four contemporary approaches to ethics have been reviewed; most take a slice through the total matrix of ethical thought. Rorty's pragmatic approach is future-focused, concerned not with what is right but with what is effective in increasing solidarity between people: he regards narrative as more likely to contribute to his project than declarations of rights. The feminist critique emphasizes context and negotiation between competing priorities, questioning the role of abstract principles; Benhabib develops the idea of context within a Habermasian concern for public debate, by emphasizing that people are carriers of embodied personal histories which also influence their actions. Taylor's pluralism suggests that hypergoods are worth identifying and striving for, but that each must be balanced by ethics derived from his other two dimensions. Virtue theories focus on character, on the ethical life rather than the ethical act, and on the development and extension of local ethical practice within a social context that values the concept of virtue.

Of these four positions, Rorty's pragmatism takes on a topic many find difficult, that of deciding upon an ethical response to a third party who is acting brutally. Both Benhabib and Taylor concern themselves primarily with ways to balance ethical decision-making in a complex and multiple world, while MacIntyre advocates the development of communities that allow us to define, enact and extend the moral life through a set of locally meaningful practices.

Ethics in Practice

This section draws clinical practice into these philosophies by following MacIntyre's (1985) three orders of the ethical life. The first describes ethical practices: this involves multiple levels of decision-making, debates different ways to frame problems and their influence, and discusses two approaches to balancing different pressures on clinicians and teams in practice. The second order considers narratives of the ethical life: resources provided by other clinicians in their work and lives, and ways that reflection can assist our own ethical development. The third order concerns the moral traditions that contextualize these practices. The chapter ends by discussing institutional contexts of clinical work where prescribed actions are enshrined in law, in professional codes and in local policies; it briefly reviews evidence about moral panics and their effects as a warning, and concludes with an illustrative ethical dilemma.

The Practice and its Background

It is difficult to encapsulate clinical practice in psychology because it is ever-evolving, employs expanding numbers of theoretical frameworks and applies them with increasingly diverse populations. Chapter 1 of this volume describes mainsteam perspectives on models of clinical practice in psychology, and their evolution during this century; Chapters 4 to 7 give the intellectual background to much of its current content. Debates about what it is to practise in an ethical fashion may help us to develop further understanding of ourselves and our practices.

Current studies into ethics focus repeatedly on a small set of concerns: the limits of confidentiality, working with people who are suicidal, informed consent, being an expert witness, the therapist–client and supervisor–trainee relationships. Rarely is there any description of the metaethical position informing these debates, in other words whether the authors are drawing on traditional or contemporary ethical theories or any combination of the two: a deontological theorist may take a very different position from one informed by virtue theory. Some follow the lamentable method of distributing a short vignette to which the author has 'the answer' and asking respondents to complete a questionnaire or checklist. Analysis of returns seems almost inevitably to show that ethical thinking in clinical psychology is minimal and that professionals need more training.

Lindsay's (1995) survey of clinical psychologists described two main types of problem: elements of professional practice such as confidentiality, relationships and competence; and restrictions on ethical practice imposed by employers – a topic never addressed in professional codes. There is also a three-level model of ethical thinking and research on its development by Kitchener (1983). The first level involves formulating problems constructively by identifying the nature of the ethical issues to be considered, relating them to relevant principles or theories, and generating a range of alternative actions which are critically evaluated. A metacognitive perspective on these issues is the second level, while the third is the ability to process problems epistemically – that is, monitoring the processes employed to evaluate alternative solutions. Although Kitchener describes this as a stage theory, she is not suggesting that people replace one way of considering ethical issues with another. She argues that people steadily develop the ability to process dilemmas in all three ways, and to use the information to arrive at a plan of action.

A young woman with mild learning disabilities has experienced a number of phases of acute confusion over the last two years. While in hospital she settles, but fragmented thinking returns whenever there are attempts to rehabilitate her either home or into sheltered accommodation: these are accompanied by increasing talk of divorce or separation from both of her parents.

First-level conceptualization involves listing the ethical concerns. Her level of confusion does not warrant permanent institutionalization, yet it would be unethical to force a return home or a move elsewhere that would make it worse: the professional risks being wrong both by acting and by not acting, one definition of an ethical dilemma. Family-focused work seems indicated, but there are no trained family therapists in the locality and no funds to refer outside: do these circumstances justify the practitioner using a technique he is not competent in?

Metacognitive considerations concern thinking about how to think about this problem. This may involve balancing a personal preference for pragmatic theories against other considerations such as the code of conduct of my profession, sociolegal considerations, and the stance taken by other colleagues involved in the case.

Epistemic considerations would include being aware of recent critiques of structural interventions in family therapy, which in this type of case recommends reasserting parental authority and banning divorce until the young person leaves home successfully. Feminists observe that such interventions reiterate traditional patterns of domination, while constructionists criticize unwarranted use of therapeutic power. The therapist may also risk missing undisclosed abuse. Monitoring the truth value of these and other ideas needs to be incorporated into the evolving plan.

The solution I found was to work together with a peer, to start learning about family therapy, and to get live supervision from a qualified colleague in the early stages of therapy; all this while maintaining active debate with the family and the team about priorities, methods and ethics.

Research suggests that gains in reflective judgement about epistemic issues, the third level of this model, occur over long periods of time. Most young adults on university courses show significant gains over two to four years and nearly all do so over six years. Also, that although sophisticated thinking in this area is dependent on verbal intelligence, analytical thought and formal logic are not the whole story. In Kitchener's model, epistemic cognition involves identifying appropriate criteria for ill-structured problems as well as monitoring the nature of problems and considering what is knowable. It also involves creativity and flexibility, and draws on affective as well as cognitive information. An example of creative epistemic thinking is when practitioners learn how to transform either/or dichotomies into both/and ones, to avoid getting stuck in traditional ways of problem-framing. Sophisticated thinking requires people to stop believing that single correct answer exists for all problems: the practitioner may not be able to 'find' a solution, she may have to generate one.

Problem-framing has been extensively considered, outside psychology, to play a central role in the opinions we develop and the decisions we take. The anthropologist Clifford Geertz first discussed the idea of thick and thin descriptions in 1973: it is a powerful idea which has been elaborated by a number of other writers. Thick descriptions of individuals and peoples include their cultural and historical contexts, their multiple roles and day-to-day variations. Thin descriptions are more abstract: they help us to see common ground with others.

Davis (1991) discusses the effects of using thick and thin descriptions of cases where difficult bioethical decisions had to be made. For her, thin descriptions are the brief illustrations one uses in teaching and research where consent has not been sought; here details are falsified or elements of different cases combined so that no reader would recognize himself within it. However, Davis observes that as the implications of gender, age and ethnicity in the construction of human experience become clearer, it grows increasingly difficult to change personal details without compromising the integrity and usefulness of the case. She is also concerned that thin descriptions tend to be arranged to suit the purposes of the narrator, inhibiting any reinterpretation which the reader might make were more of the detail available.

As ethics moves away from a concern for universal, abstract laws towards concern for individuals embedded within particular communities, thick description becomes more important. Detail makes the issues easier to understand, and helps students to feel a genuine sense of empathy with the players. It also maps more effectively onto life, which is never as simple as textbook vignettes suggest.

The argument for moving to thick description applies equally to clinicians in mental health and disability services, and to researchers with an interest in practical ethics. Davis hastens to defend client confidentiality and the necessity for thin descriptions where consent has not been obtained, but exhorts us to create more examples which use thick description. For her one source is cases that have been discussed in court, where the details are public: however, such cases tend to skew perception and make students feel that all dilemmas are decided by judges. Other sources are fictional examples: the play *Whose Life Is It Anyway?* (Brian Clark, 1972) gives her useful material. Perhaps *A Day in the Death of Joe Egg* (Peter Nicholls, 1967) could be used to open up the experience of parents with a severely disabled child. Finally, biography provides an excellent source of rich description, a route which recipients of clinical services are increasingly pursuing.[9]

Davis also advocates rediscussing cases to help us understand how our thinking about ethics changes, and to reduce the constant search for new material. Most important, she argues that health care professionals should look out for cases which could form the basis of ethical discussion, now and in the future, and be more proactive in seeking the permission of clients and families so that their details may be shared with other professionals.

Kelly and Milner (1996) consider how ethical dilemmas are framed and the influence this has on decisions taken. They studied the way that the Children Act 1989 is working in Britain. This increased the number of professionals involved in child protection and the formality of their meetings, yet data suggest that the Children Act has had no effect on the number of child deaths. They examined transcripts of child protection proceedings in cases where the child subsequently died. Their retrospective analysis suggested that once a decision has been made to leave the child with the parent(s) and add resources to help them cope, professionals found it difficult to reverse the decision despite mounting evidence of abuse or neglect. They conclude that the Children Act frames the debate as one of loss of the child's natural parent, and that framing the discussion this way encourages professionals to act to avoid that loss. Kelly and

Milner challenge the 'avoidance of loss' frame in favour of listing the losses and gains of every proposed action, for each of the family members. That allows the child's gain of a safe, nurturing environment to be laid alongside the loss of a natural parent; the parents' gain of stress reduction and removal of intrusive child protection experts from their home can be laid next to the loss of their child. The authors hope that gains as much as losses will then bear a more appropriate amount of weight in child protection proceedings.

Shotter (1993) makes a different contribution to thinking about the knowledges we draw on when deciding what to do: to the familiar distinction between *knowing how* and *knowing that* he adds *knowing from within*. This emphasizes the personal, hermeneutic understanding of clients – of knowing, for example, that they feel humiliated by the necessity to be escorted across the hospital grounds because they might run off and hurt somebody. It is vital to represent such subjective knowledge within discussions about interventions.

Of course, ethical decisions occur through both formal and informal discussion. Smith et al. (1991) surveyed mental health practitioners in the USA and found that although practitioners refer to ethical guidelines and laws when faced with an issue, they are more likely to prioritize personal values, practical considerations and the opinions of colleagues when determining exactly what to do. Moros et al. (1991) are four professionals drawing on a number of ethical positions, who describe their practice. They note that their most difficult conflicts arise from hidden tension between utilitarian and deontological positions; they propose that people involved in informal ethical debates do the following:

- recognize, identify and classify the ethical issues;
- appreciate the complexity of ethical choices and the inevitability of highly valued principles coming into conflict;
- be able to think theoretically about both ethical issues and ethical conflicts, and to distinguish them;
- recognize that contradictions and discrepancies signal the need for critical re-evaluation;
- focus on the process of taking a decision to act, avoiding merely debating ideas;
- recognize the inevitability of ambiguity and uncertainty.

Moros et al. argue that broad classifications can speed decision-making in ethical situations where people cannot stop to read and take stock; conceptualizing an issue as primarily one of autonomy, or of social justice, or of the principle of beneficence, clears the ground. However, the human context of the debate also needs to be conceptualized, since tensions between different professionals and/or different members of the family clearly influence their views about the debate. Finally, having done the ethical thinking and taken the decision, it is vital to communicate this to others involved in carrying out that decision: in their view this is not mere courtesy but a moral duty.

When different values conflict they suggest rank-ordering, to allow circumstances to decide the relative priority of 'I should never lie' against 'I should not cause distress without good cause'. Kitchener (1984) also suggests that professional bodies assist members by weighting different values. However, it is not always easy to agree ranked priorities because values differ across cultures such as those expressed by profession, faith or ethnicity. Another helpful tactic to sidestep all-or-none debate is to ask about quantity: how much information creates the informed client? Is the person's competence completely compromised, or are they competent in one area, or competent intermittently? How far should professionals place a relative's interpretation of a client's wishes over their own judgement, if they disagree? This questioning approach to ethical problem-solving is exemplified later in discussion of guidelines published by the Association for Family Therapy and Systemic Practice (see p. 198).

Moros et al.'s focus on doubt and ambiguity is an important development from earlier discussion, which contained the fiction that there is a 'right' answer to ethical discussions and that professionals can be trained to produce it (e.g. Tymchuk, 1986). They pinpoint the discomfort caused by critical thinking by making uncertainty and conflict central, accepting that ethical reasoning cannot guarantee the best decision but that generally it enables people to avoid the worst errors. People who believe they uphold the ethical position within a group can be extremely inflexible and dogmatic and not necessarily helpful to clients: yet endless compromises made by committees do not guarantee ethical care either. Moros et al. argue that in order to sustain the relationships necessary for ethical debate, staff need to extend the principle of fidelity to each other: trust, promise-keeping and loyalty. Despite being couched in traditional ethical conflict between deontological duty and utilitarian effectiveness, this recommendation is not so distant from MacIntyre's (1985) view that people entering into a practice need to display the virtues of justice, courage and honesty.

Woody (1990) offers a different approach to balancing competing pressures. She draws on five different decision bases for resolving ethical concerns about the way to act in clinical practice:

- Theories of ethics
- Professional codes of ethics
- Theories of practice
- Sociolegal context
- Therapist's personal/professional identity

Many clinicians remain dependent upon utilitarianism as the theory of ethics with which they are most familiar, and Woody is no exception, although she leavens this (rather oddly) with a smattering of Rawls's theory of distributive justice. Nevertheless, balancing these dimensions is possible regardless of which theory of ethics is espoused: although I will argue strongly for MacIntyre's position, I do not believe it a sufficient basis on which to resolve every dilemma I will encounter. Woody's model allowed me to see what other influences might, could or should be operating.

Woody makes useful points about the utility of codes of practice in the USA, which she believes to be almost zero as long as practitioners continue to give them no more than a cursory read and assume that *de facto* they must be ethical persons. She emphasizes that ethical principles require thought and practice and discussion if they are to have any chance of being useful when a dilemma presents itself, reiterating a dominant theme. Her own research showed how the theories of practice that clinicians drew on were sometimes given far too much weight: the ethical imperative to be well versed in a theory and to apply it consistently seemed to outweigh any consideration of duty of care, or of risk to others.

The sociolegal context describes cultural influences as much as legal ones. These may include checking the client's system of values in evaluating risks or, if this is inappropriate or impossible, then doing so with somebody who represents the client's culture. Generally she thinks of this decision base as balancing social value against legal reality. It also invites reflection on the degree to which one's setting itself compromises one's therapeutic integrity. Perhaps the therapist is carrying too many competing roles, or the local ethos – for example, to make physically ill people comply with treatment – has become overriding, so that alternative approaches are impossible.

Woody's final decision base is the personal/professional identity. Here vision and beliefs blend with professional integrity and reflective judgements on, for example, one's own competence. Burnout, isolation and life crisis can all compromise the ability to reflect on oneself without undue distortion. A strong professional conscience is necessary as well as exhortations to engage in self-examination. She regards the goal here as being to harmonize personal and professional identities, so that one's integrity and judgement can become available for scrutiny in making ethical decisions. That leads easily into MacIntyre's second order of virtue, consideration of the ethical life.

Narrative Order of the Ethical Life

Making virtue a central component of the ethical practitioner, viewing the ethical person living an ethical life as more useful than casuistic descriptions of the ethical act, challenges psychologists: freedom of personal belief has been a cherished tenet of liberal institutions since religion was ousted by the Enlightenment.

One way to learn about the ethical life is to tell stories about people who exemplify it, but the ahistorical nature of psychological practice makes many people little interested in the lives of past and present practitioners.

Current debate about whether the British Psychological Society may/should/will mark the contribution and death of Hans Eysenck demonstrates the dominance of a 'presentism' that finds it difficult to put contributions into context. There are exceptions: A.M. Clarke and B. Tizard's *Life and Work of Jack Tizard* (1983) gives an inspiring description of somebody with great intellectual range who devoted it to the least of society's members. Tizard advanced our understanding of what affects children and adults with learning disabilities who live in public residential services, what improves their lives, and of how social research itself can be managed to ensure that it has useful effects in practice. We transmit something of the ethics of our practice in the ways we describe people in obituaries: common values celebrated there are helping people at the start of their researcher/practitioner careers as much as they helped colleagues; as being engaged with clients without any hint that they were patronizing them; as placing integrity before self-interest in some controversy. Other histories appear in the journal *History of the Human Sciences* (edited by Stillman and Velody), although clinicians feature but rarely.

Another way to enter ethical practice is to hear experienced practitioners describing their development, the dilemmas they faced and the solutions they found. Skovholt and Ronnestad's (1995) grounded theory study of 100 psychotherapists and counsellors, from recent graduates to practitioners with 40 years' experience, provides an enormously informative description of the therapeutic life. They do not specifically consider ethics but the ethical relationship with clients is discussed by people at all stages, as one that is helpful for the client without using the therapist up.

Dryden's (1985) ground-breaking study of the ethical dilemmas encountered by seasoned psychotherapists describes six different types:

1 Compromise dilemmas (ideals versus practicalities);
2 Boundary dilemmas (self–client; personal–professional; traditional–innovative);
3 Dilemmas of allegiance (to schools of thought that sustain but stunt);
4 Role dilemmas (educator–healer; clinician–researcher);
5 Dilemmas of responsibility (client autonomy/client welfare);
6 Impasse dilemmas (acknowledging stuckness without harming client).

Both Skovholt and Ronnestad, and Dryden, are fascinating but they focus exclusively on the dilemmas of professionals offering one-to-one therapies. Moving beyond that focus to consider the ways that we act and interact with all others is a larger question. Taylor (1989, discussed earlier) raised the question about whether we can see enough good (agape) in others to sustain an equal relationship with them while we are 'doing them good': if not, we patronize and demean. This concern was aired by psychotherapists from the Tavistock, who argue that providers of services for people with a learning disability treat their clients with barely-disguised contempt, an experience that is deeply destructive to them (Sinason, 1992; Symington,

1992). Parents have also noticed a yawning gap between the optimistic rhetoric they hear from people who provide services to their son or daughter with a learning disability, and that service's unfocused and inept ways of working (Beardsmore, 1993). Clearly, we need to think about the professional ethical life in a wide context:

> Ultimately, appropriate professional conduct must expand beyond compliance with standards to enacting values and beliefs about what constitute a good society and measures of progress in our science and practice. We cannot shy away from such questions as what is virtue, what would constitute healthy relationships, what our responsibilities are for the human condition, and how we are to contribute to the common good. (Hoshmand, 1994: 55)

Hoshmand (1994) coherently describes ways to foster an ethical stance. She elaborates Schön's reflective practitioner and Kitchener's research to describe the development and training of the ethical practitioner. This models ethical development as a gradual accretion of the number of perspectives the person can simultaneously hold and process, complemented by a slow expansion in the complexity with which these perspectives can be processed.

Hoshmand argues that practitioners who want to increase the complexity of their ethical thinking need to create time to reflect. Discussing dilemmas and debating case studies can help, but the focus needs to move beyond casuistry to encompass personal ways of knowing and to develop self as knower. Changes are difficult to prompt and they occur over years, not months. Educational input should elaborate abilities at the level students are at, since stage shifts cannot be taught, they can only be facilitated by exposing people to contexts for their development. Experienced practitioners are advised to construct intellectual environments where they can learn from critical dialogue which facilitates reflection after events. Many practitioners do sustain peer supervision groups, but Hoshmand argues that such environments are useless unless members also cultivate the habit of regular personal reflection.

The importance of accepting a commitment to enact ethical decisions was introduced in the review of ethical theories. Clarkson (1996) provides an invaluable exposition of the bystander effect, discussing 12 different excuses we give ourselves for failing to act. She urges us to recognize that moral action is always ambiguous and uncertain and that by acting we automatically run the risk of being wrong: the justification is that history shows that doing nothing is far worse. Clarkson makes extensive use of Latané and Darley's (1970) research into the bystander effect, counterpointing it with Oliner and Oliner's (1988) research into people who acted altruistically towards Jews in the second world war. This suggests that altruism has an experiential component in that those who demonstrate it were brought up to act that way; but also that social and personal factors can facilitate ethical rather than unethical behaviour.

Clarkson proposes antidotes to each of the bystander excuses we give ourselves. At a personal level these include acknowledging our baser motives when we want to gossip or destroy a reputation; accepting the loneliness that can come from questioning and challenging; and putting aside the narcissistic need to see results for our efforts. She suggests we acknowledge that taking care of ourselves occurs by taking care of others; at the least this involves expressing concern, taking an active interest in the grievances of others and informing ourselves about how they came about. Actions spring from accepting responsibility for mediating or de-escalating: exercising the power one has, being creative in finding various ways to intervene, and entering into dialogue to which one remains committed until a resolution is reached.

Finally, the narrative ethical order can be described negatively as well as positively. This whole area remains complex because it involves social control as well as reform, a concern to stop staff acting unethically, even brutally; it is more commonly discussed by committees of enquiry than by texts on ethics. Both volumes of the *Report of the Committee of Inquiry into Complaints about Ashworth Hospital* (DoH, 1992) describe the lack of connection between written policies and actual practice, and the history of a breakdown of clinical care managerially. They also give detailed narrative histories of the way that public services progressively failed to meet the needs of a small group of residents, to counter any tendency to demonize them. Local policies grounded in an understanding of such situations, and which adapt the recommendations of such committees to their context, should succeed in avoiding worst practice.

Moral Traditions Contextualizing Practice

For MacIntyre, moral traditions emerge out of narratives of origin – his moral starting-point – and from combining practices. His sense of tradition incorporates future possibilities engendered by past events. When they are vital they embody dispute, for example, about what the purpose is of a university in a hospital, and traditions decay when they are exercised without virtue. His perspective on the moral life of each person is one spent seeking for the good life of people;[10] therefore the virtues are those required to sustain the institutions – which may be universities or hospitals – that allow men and women to seek for the good together. From this perspective, responsibility for passing on the moral traditions that constitute clinical practice lies on academics who teach, on those who supervise the clinical work of students, and on those who manage their work subsequently.

Nearly all the models of clinical supervision that we have come from psychotherapy and counselling psychology, and concern one-to-one conversations intended to facilitate the growth of others as effective and ethical therapists. Scaife (1995) uses this literature but goes beyond it to talk about the fears, uncertainties and 'compensatory limps' (such as hiding in the library or getting angry with staff) that are inclined to develop when people are closely scrutinized by others. Hers is an admirable contribution to elaborating our moral traditions, both of entering clinical practice and of offering clinical supervision.

We have few models to inform heads of specialties and psychology departments other than those contained in management texts, yet the creation of professional communities is another central aspect of the moral tradition of psychological practice. Drawing on the therapeutic literature leads the manager quickly into burnout once departments grow, yet psychologists are inherently suspicious of hierarchical models of management and prefer to explore others. Some people feel that the research tradition of psychology created an atmosphere of criticism and analysis that was full of conflict, but many innovative and constructive environments have been developed by different practitioners up and down the country. A few are astonishingly successful at retaining staff and ensuring that their contribution is valued by the host organization. Examples are shared and discussed during the admirable course organized by Ann Pattie for the Division of Clinical Psychology, an excellent providential space where moral traditions are both handed on and changed. There is plenty of scope for further development and research in this area, however.

The models we have of ourselves as researchers also come from people and local environments. I do not mean the technical skills of design, method and so on that can be obtained from books with a bit of persistence, but knowing how to judge what sort of feedback is useful to people at different stages of learning. Other aspects of the moral tradition of research practice include discovering the implicit rules that govern book and journal publication, refereeing, lecturing or examining; and developing a way to work with these practices in service of an ethical end, avoiding the temptation to manipulate them cynically. One also needs to work out how to remain so tightly focused on a project that the work gets from conception to completion, while simultaneously contributing to an exciting research environment. Encouraging others and responding quickly to requests to read first drafts is essential; all members of the community flourish with such activities, including yourself.

I have struggled to combine research with practice with little opportunity to learn from others, of necessity picking it up from superficial relationships and observation. For me the task has been to develop sufficient integrity and connection between my research philosophy and my philosophy of practice for the two no longer to fight each other; at that point the combination started to seem synergistic rather than in conflict. Once that is achieved research ideas really do spring from practice, and practice contexts do provide unmissable opportunities to try out new ideas. Some staff want to hear about research only in a nutshell, with no interest in the detail; but there are also many others who are delighted to have copies of articles sent to them or ideas for audit proposed. Their receptiveness again fosters a researcher-practitioner environment from which we all benefit.

Of course, I have learned traditions from people and believe them to be important. This outline sketch of the moral traditions of practice is proposed to be knocked down: no doubt there are others I have yet to learn, and still more that I cannot conceive. MacIntyre's ethical theory sets an important task that would facilitate the researcher-practitioner enormously: that of exploring, elaborating and sharing the moral traditions of our practices.

Institutional Ethics Contextualizing Practice

Dale (1996) discusses ethical communication within her negotiating model of the client–professional relationship. She conceptualizes information and its control as at the core of this relationship, incorporating new legislation that encourages clinicians to be less secretive. Throughout her book Dale acknowledges and balances the problems of clients – who may be unaccustomed to debating assertively with professionals – alongside the professional tensions exposed by open access to records. Despite legislation (Access to Health Records Act 1990) most British psychologists do not inform clients that they have this right, and so it is rare for anybody to request access (Stallard and Hudson, 1994). Moreover, most clinicians do not know the grounds for refusing access, nor where to obtain that information. Such lack of certainty is the breeding-ground of obfuscation. Merely instructing psychologists to routinely inform clients of their right of access (DCP, 1995) will not be enough.

Kitchener (1984) criticizes professional codes of conduct for conservatism, for reflecting professional consensus rather than depicting ideal behaviour. She notes that they have many gaps and contradictions and avoid tackling issues of ethical concern. They provide one level of justification for taking or not taking action, and allow professional bodies to set basic limits and reprimand transgressors: they do provide minimum standards of ethical practice, but standards that should be developed by all practitioners.

The BPS Code (1997) is couched in the familiar language of liberal individualism, the valuing of individual choice and autonomy. It looks at competence, consent, deception, debriefing, right to withdraw, confidentiality, protection of participants, observational research, and giving advice. It also adds sets of guidelines written at different times, concerning the use of animals, advertising, equal opportunities, sexual harassment at work and dual relationships, whistle-blowing when colleagues act improperly and responding to complaints about others. O'Donohue and Mangold (1996) criticize the APA ethical code for having an unclear function, for making no explicit reference to any ethical theory on which it may be based, and for having no evidence on which to base its assertions; all these criticisms apply to the BPS Code.

They are amplified by the BPS Division of Clinical Psychology's *Professional Practice Guidelines* (1995); nevertheless, I wondered quite who or what they were for. They make no claim to discuss ethics, referring practitioners back to the BPS guidelines even though these explicitly cover research and not practice. Confusion of purpose perhaps explains the extraordinary length of these guidelines. The few ethical statements scattered through them are difficult to find in the midst of repetitive demands that staff at all levels of seniority ensure that they have adequate supervision, continuing professional development, opportunities for audit and research and peer appraisal. Enthusiasm for supervision as a guarantor of good practice showed little awareness of Foucault's critique, that such confessional traditions reproduce traditional power in the guise of knowledge and inhibit originality.

By contrast the Association for Family Therapy 1994 *Code of Conduct and Ethical Guidelines* is certainly more concise: the separation of professional requirements from ethical issues is particularly helpful. The Code gives 20 'You must' statements about standards of behaviour expected from family therapists. These list predictable topics, such as informed consent and confidentiality, non-discriminatory practice, prohibition of sexual contact between therapists and clients. It contains one reference to content rather than process: you must be able to demonstrate familiarity with the theoretical basis underpinning your work.

AFT's ethical guidelines follow, not as a set of rules but as 19 questions intended to provoke reflection. These include competence to practise; tensions between viewing families as a group and as a set of individuals; attention to any harm clients may do outside therapy, to one another or to other people; effectiveness audits; and responsibility for influencing public knowledge, or legal and social structures, for the benefit of families. Of course, it is easier to write guidelines for a discrete approach to therapy than for a large profession like clinical psychology which encompasses an enormous variety of activities. Nevertheless, I feel that the AFT's approach is more helpful. Its use of questions such as 'How far have you considered the conflicts and ambiguities within your roles at work which might require you to overrule the wishes of family members?' supports the idea of an ethical professional as one whose thinking develops throughout their career. Since ethical development is prompted by open-ended dialogue and personal reflection, not by the imposition of universal rules, the AFT's ethical guidelines elegantly enact the reflectiveness they recommend.

In addition to ethical codes issued by professional groups, all manner of local policies issued by NHS Trusts and social services are starting to affect clinical practice, and psychologists are writing many of them. A common topic is the prevention of racial or sexual discrimination amongst staff, perhaps missing the point when most overt racism in the service is expressed by clients to staff and to other clients. Other policies aim to ensure that abuses of power are reported and responded to: these stretch from bullying in the workplace to bureaucratic control of disclosures of sexual abuse against children or against adults with a learning disability. Another set of policies intends to ensure equal opportunities in the job market, or (most recently) to advise staff about ways they should act to minimize the risk of violence against themselves. Policies of this type seem to be prompted as much by employers' fears of legal action as by concern for the employee.

The intention behind most of these policies is social reform, but the pragmatist's question 'What is the effect of these policies or committees, and what disadvantages do they bring?' is relevant here. The process of putting together task groups, writing policies, and seeking comments on first drafts raises the profile of various ethical concerns. Yet no Trust can write a policy for every ethical concern; moreover guidelines increase bureaucracy, may restrict clinical independence and compromise client confidentiality, sometimes for no demonstrably good end. Since I have argued that ethical acts arise from interaction between groups of reflective practitioners, and that ethical problems occur in complex and unpredictable worlds, giving simple answers to complex problems in written policies runs the danger of inhibiting the very reflectiveness and flexibility that services need.

Finally, research ethics committees (RECs) are another forum where ethics in the NHS are examined, perhaps one of the longest-standing. Their purpose was enshrined in the 1991 Citizen's Charter to protect members of the public from abuse or undue coercion. Neuberger (1992) researched their functioning. She found that most fell between being research committees concerned with standards and design, and research ethics committees concerned with consent; all were under-resourced, undertrained and hence unable to adopt the more proactive role she envisaged for them. She argued for legislation so that the public would be properly protected, and so that the committees would be both properly resourced and given appropriate powers. Her recommendations include the following:

- There should be a separation between RECs and research methods committees, which are also necessary.
- RECs should not operate only on a case-by-case basis. They should seek to perform an educational role and to be perceived as an essential part of the research machine, not the irritating barrier they often become.
- DHAs should make it a disciplinary offence to conduct research without the approval of the REC.
- RECs should take on vexed ethical questions, such as consent in the mentally disordered, in a more systematic way.
- Members should become aware of current ethical debates. This should occur through induction, regular (at least annual) training, and circulation to all members of the *Bulletin of Medical Ethics*, at least the contents page of the *Journal of Medical Ethics*, and relevant articles from the nursing and medical press.

- A degree of monitoring should be established, such as spot checks on consent and methods of recruitment.

The implications are clear. Ethical decision-making is not an activity for amateurs, nor a place for pursuing casuistry. RECs should comprise a balanced group of people – at least a third of whom should be both non-medical and independent of the DHA – who are properly resourced and properly informed about current ethical debates. And their purposes should include educating researchers, not merely waiting to receive and assess their protocols.

Moral Panics

Perhaps not everything that causes concern needs an answer. The term 'moral panic' was coined to describe moments when concern about a particular social problem grows out of all proportion to its importance or prevalence. Despite criticisms of the idea, it has proved useful as a tool to understand volatile social phenomena and the conditions that host them. Goode and Ben-Yehuda (1994) describe five crucial indicators of moral panic. There is a heightened level of *concern* over the actions of a specific group of people, actions thought to have bad consequences for the rest of society; there is increased *hostility* towards the group in question; there is widespread *consensus* that the threat is real; folk understanding of the size of the threat is *disproportionate* to reasonably neutral estimates, and the generation and dissemination of wildly exaggerated numbers is extremely important to protagonists; and the phenomenon is *volatile*, suddenly erupting and subsiding. Moral panics occur in societies that have relatively fuzzy moral boundaries, usually while they are undergoing rapid social change. Protagonists are difficult to locate, but they are more likely to be people with lower levels of education, living in areas hit by recession, and/or experiencing a serious challenge to their traditional value system such as unemployment or divorce.

Witch hunts were the archetypal moral panic, and historians have noted that they occurred at times of mass social change. Goode and Ben-Yehuda use belief in satanic ritual abuse as an example of a recent moral panic in Britain.[11] It rode on the back of general concern about child abuse, one that led to the urgent allocation of new resources: these increased concern further, because specialized child protection workers carried out more investigations and so detected more abuse. Goode and Ben-Yehuda state that at the start of the 1980s social workers were held in very low esteem by the public but that concern to stem child abuse made their numbers grow faster than that of other similar professionals during the 1990s. The authors argue that the social work profession persuaded government and the populace that they deal with problems that truly menace society, problems they are uniquely qualified to investigate and combat. Conditions were set to spiral beyond child abuse: a conspiracy of satanists who were kidnapping children for sexual molestation, torture and murder was invoked. The popular media in Britain and the USA talked it up, treating it as a new problem: in fact the first known legend of the ritual kidnapping and sacrifice of children by outsiders occurred nearly 2,000 years ago among Romans, who feared that Christians were abducting their children.

Satanic abuse came to a head during 1990, when a series of court cases 'involving baseless allegations on which dubious evidence had been gathered' (Goode and Ben-Yehuda, 1994: 64) culminated in social workers and police making a dawn raid on houses in a remote part of Scotland. Children are said to have been removed from four families without even a familiar toy. When the case reached court the charges were rejected as preposterous, and moral panic about satanic ritual abuse subsided. In spring 1991 the press reacted with a strident campaign against social work as a profession.

These and other issues have created many changes to the ethical boundaries of my working life. Heightened awareness of the possibility of sexual abuse has been important in understanding the difficulties many people face, and the field of learning disabilities has seen an increase in abuse specialists over the last five years. Their activities are implicitly framed within a rights model and, perhaps inevitably, their interests strayed beyond sexual molestation to any action they described as abusive. At the same time police reactions to allegations of abuse in social services establishments moved beyond sexual abuse to anything that might be called abuse. These developments brought an ethical dilemma to a head.

An Ethical Dilemma

Early in August two middle managers in an institution I had stopped working in two years previously asked for an urgent meeting. Their 30-odd staff were all being interviewed by a team of policemen who knew nothing about severe learning disability. The police were investigating unspecified allegations of widespread abuse across the institution, made by a member of staff who had been transferred there from elsewhere in the organization. Morale was low and they hoped I could offer their staff support as they felt the episode was needlessly blaming, upsetting and destructive. They hoped for personal counselling for the three staff most under suspicion, my witness for the anger of the whole team, and that perhaps I would write about their experience to challenge the worst excesses of the anti-abuse culture.

I did not know whether the accusations were founded or not. As is the case in many ethical dilemmas, the institution was not perfect; parents had made a few complaints about lack of focus and failure to follow through in recent years. Although I trusted many staff some had arrived since I left, and I could not indiscriminately support everything that happened there. Lack of recent knowledge made me unsure; yet my distance from the immediate problem also made my support more powerful because self-defence would not be an issue. I found out a little more. That the accuser had already complained internally, with the support of a professional who had spent the previous four years exclusively devoted to identifying and exposing abuse. The senior officer from another locality who investigated could find no evidence to support the allegations. The accuser was also thought to have made unfounded complaints against staff in other parts of the larger organization, hence the free transfer. The three members of staff who were most under suspicion were three he had worked with most closely, never mentioning reservations about their work: they felt they had supported him personally over months and felt betrayed. Prior to the allegations, these managers and local staff were growing concerned at his poor work and were considering how to arrange his transfer elsewhere: perhaps he was aware of that and himself felt betrayed. That was the managers' account.

The dilemma was taking shape. On the one hand a set of staff in an institution with a slightly patchy reputation were faced with what that institution's managers regarded as unwarranted complaint. Many were people I knew and respected, felt were doing their best in difficult circumstances, and did not deserve to carry this sense of shame and blame. Complaints against them had existed in one form or another for the previous six months and that was set to continue; although nobody had been charged, charges were expected. All of the staff faced public vilification, two faced retirement with a real sense that their working lives had been rendered worthless, and all felt that a system intended to care for vulnerable clients had no sense of care for them.

But there is another side. Following enquiries, many institutions have been closed and new resources found to create service change. Many professionals regard enquiries as an effective way to bring the needs of 'forgotten people' to the attention of bureaucrats, and consider the disruption staff experience a fair exchange. Doing nothing to see how the investigation worked out also suited bystanding self-interest. That made me want to avoid being on the opposite side from professional colleagues, and fear airing my concern that the abuse policy had become all-encompassing and was engendering an unhelpful blame-culture. I knew that majority opinion favoured anti-abuse proceedings, believing they brought justice to clients with a learning disability.

Yet I disagree that pursuing conflict through the assertion of rights creates useful social change within effective democracies. Clearly, people should be brought before the criminal justice system when they commit recognizable crimes, but the allegations were not of that nature. I also subscribe to Taylor's view that problems arise when people take an excessively narrow ethical focus, and feel that an isolated professional devoted entirely to the identification of abuse, and staff training concerning its prevention, will in time inevitably become too narrowly focused. I prefer to promote virtue ethics, to create environments where people are strengthened not diminished; where the virtues of care, courage and honour are valued for all, which must include staff; where debate rather than conflict is fostered. I decided that involvement need not be uncritical: that I could hear more about the allegations, and review at each stage whether supporting the staff continued to be an ethically defensible position.

I met the staff as a group to hear their anger and help them to make sense of the complainant's betrayal of their working relationships. We considered practical ways to channel emotion into support by considering how to raise money to cover legal fees should that be necessary. I also suggested that managers clarify how the matter was to be handled in public: the rumour machine was working effectively anyway, and why should the issue remain a dirty secret when staff felt they had nothing to hide? We talked about giving evidence in court: some staff understood that they were being cited as witnesses to an incident involving a colleague without knowing what it was; they feared being tricked into saying something untrue that would harm them. I agreed to offer individual counselling off site and out of hours to any of the accused who wanted to make use of it.

Three staff were told in September that they were to be charged: one knew what the alleged incident was, the other two knew of one allegation but understood there were others and were left casting through their minds what the charges might be. At last in late October they were instructed to report to the police station where they were formally arrested, charged, interviewed, and told not to leave the locality.

One person was charged for one incident that had occurred more than 12 months previously, when the accused member of staff was supervising 50 clients with a colleague and the accuser. A client who cannot speak spat in the accused's face when told he could not leave the room. The accused recalls the incident, recalls angrily telling the client to sit down before leaving to wash the phlegm from his face; he denies striking the client, or any client in eight years working there, though that was the accuser's allegation. The colleague said to have witnessed it could not recall this lunchtime, one of many crowded lunches with no event that would make it stand out for her a year later, nor could she recall having witnessed the accused hit anyone. Such was the accusation that had humiliated and stressed the accused for 11 months. It ended in late November when staff were informed that the Crown Prosecution Service had dropped all charges.

I do not believe that such brutalizing experiences will improve services for adults with a learning disability. We do have to pitch in to improve things when they go wrong, as Rorty argues, to persuade and tell stories and get alongside people, and to make sure that managers and politicans who allocate funds hear some of those stories. Elizur's (1993) work in a home for juvenile delinquents showed how transformation occurred once staff felt understood and cared for: before then they could offer support to neither clients nor relatives. In human services most significant change comes about by humane means.

Conclusions

Ethics may involve running against a linguistic cage but this does not make it pointless. If the range of ideas reviewed here help us to see that there is a debate and it needs to be located within a particular theory, substantial progress will have been made. The ethical statements made in professional codes represent no more than a bottom line; they are insufficient guarantors of ethical practice in an interactional, postmodern cutlure. I have outlined some of the practices, narratives and moral traditions that describe clinical psychology through the lens of MacIntyre's virtue theory. My account will need considerable elaboration and much debate before it could be considered adequate; I hope that others will join the enterprise.

Summary

Giving ethical assurances to people who seek advice, support or information from psychologists is an important *contemporary issue* for those who have stopped claiming to be objective scientists and assume that knowledge of human experience is necessarily interactional and subjective. Yet there is no accepted ethical position; there is confused debate, with unsupported rules asserted in ethical codes and objections to those codes. A pragmatic view of contemporary ethics is that the brutality of third parties cannot be changed by might, only by persuasion; both pragmatists and feminists challenge the Kantian duty ethic and argue that ethics must concern narrative and context. Pluralists like Taylor urge ethics to be considered across three dimensions, suggesting that the narrowness of single ethics is always open to error through distortion. Both Habermasian communicative ethicists and virtue ethicists stress that there is a moral starting-point, that we all come from somewhere with ties that bind and our own history of care or lack of it; any stance towards the ethical life has to take that into account.

These contemporary issues are certainly illuminated by *histories of the present*. Enlightenment ethics – the debate between deontological duty, consequentialism and rights derived from theories of distributive justice – form the backdrop to discussion of twentieth-century perspectives on ethics, including a return to virtue ethics by MacIntyre. His project was to use history to show that ethical debate has become clouded by the presence of so many ideas from different and incomparable planes of thought. The concept of 'ethics' itself is disputed. Some see ethics as the logical analysis of duty or action in a single situation; this is contrasted with the term's expanded, pre-Enlightenment meaning where past and future, ourselves over time and our relationships are brought together to describe the ethical life, rather than the ethical acts.

Intersubjective meaning is assumed by MacIntyre because for him there is no separation between individual and society; my good is intrinsically bound up with society's good because it is disastrous for me to be left standing alone. The intersubjective element of ethical decisions can be cultivated by reversing perspectives, so that before taking a decision I imagine its consequences for each actor and take those into account. Similarly, when engaging in debate I may bear Habermas's description of the Ideal Communicator in mind, someone who enters discussion open-mindedly, willing to be influenced by the contributions of others.

Debates between *critical thinkers* in the philosophy of ethics have been reviewed in detail. This suggested that the 'rights' of disabled or other people is only useful as a campaign slogan, being too all-embracing to be specifiable or usable; that their needs are ignored by both contemporary justice and consequentialist theories; and that we can only consider the needs of people by deciding on our moral position about the good society. Then we can specify what it is to live an ethical life with others that contributes to that good. Critical thinking also requires us to beware of writing local policies that intend social reform but actually inhibit people from reflecting on issues for themselves. Creating fora for discussion, conceptual frameworks and questions for people to discuss may all be more useful in creating ethical communities.

The *reflective researcher-practitioner* was little discussed here, except insofar as reflection makes a fundamental contribution to the development of our ability to think ethically about complex issues. It shapes our understanding of and contribution to the moral traditions that are implicit parts of *human systems*. Human systems contextualizing the ethical choices we make in practice arise from institutions such as the sociolegal system, our profession and our employers. However, more important for our ethical life is learning the moral traditions expressed in the way four key activities are practised: clinical training and supervision, the management of clinical psychologists, research, and jobs that combine the practices of clinician and researcher.

Moral traditions are not necessarily conservative; they arise from debate and dispute, and may be observed as much by challenge as by acceptance. These contexts for action will be more ethical the more thought and coherence go into their creation: they engender an ethical life that has infinitely greater flexibility than attending to lists of codes that determine the ethical act in a few common situations. Elaborating the moral traditions of clinical practice through research is a vital task for those who would promote ethics in action.

Notes

1 I refer to exchanges of letters about the aftermath of the Ashworth hospital enquiry published in *Clinical Psychology Forum* during 1996. The debate could be characterized as evolution or revolution: when is the pace of change so lamentably slow that continuing to be involved legitimizes an unacceptable process?

2 For example, Fairbairn and Fairbairn (1987), Brecher (1988); Crellin and Vetere (1995).

3 This linguistic approach to ethics would be questioned by Fulford. His response to people who argue that concise definitions are necessary for us to be able to use concepts is to ask them to define time (Harris et al., 1993).

4 Kierkegaard cited by MacIntyre (1985).

5 Separating reason and intuition merely plays out the Cartesian subject–object dualism in the ethical field: it is subject to criticisms of this position already discussed in Chapter 6.

6 Elaborated variously as charity, compassion or agape, love having many more nuances in Greek than in contemporary English.

7 See Chapter 5 (p. 89), where Taylor's ontology was briefly introduced.

8 Of course, tranquillity is the virtue of temperance.

9 For example, Bogdan and Taylor (1982) describe the lives of two people with learning disabilities in the USA who left hospital; Rogers et al. (1993) give the perspective of users of psychiatric services.

10 He uses the term 'man' which I have rendered into person and people, I hope without twisting his meaning.

11 They were citing work by P. Jenkins (1992) *Intimate Enemies: Moral Panics in Contemporary Britain*. New York: Aldine de Gruyter.

9 To Boldly Go

Critical exchanges need to develop beyond simple statements of difference and multiplicity to reorganize ideas and identify connections between them. Gregory (1994) urges social researchers to go beyond parochialism, to use their critical thinking skills to evoke different people, places and landscapes in ways that support dialogue rather than separation. The simple assertion of difference and rights is not sufficient to create lasting social change: different voices can only be tolerated if there is accompanying effort towards harmony. Below I draw together core ideas, hopes and beliefs that will influence my agenda over the next few years.

1 Clinical psychologists will become more theoretically coherent in the way they work, eschewing eclecticism as a dangerous muddle that cannot take practitioners in any useful direction because it treats ideas like a plumber's toolkit. By picking out concepts at will from a wide variety of theories and traditions we create the sort of conceptual *mélange* MacIntyre criticizes for scuttling ethical debate. Others agree:

> The preceding discussion is based on the perspective that concepts are meaningful (1) only in terms of their usage in particular contexts, (2) in relationship to other concepts that share a similar background of cultural meanings and practices, and (3) when employed with particular interests in mind. This is an important notion espoused by philosophers since the linguistic turn in the history of ideas. (Hoshmand, 1994: 65)

Eclecticism mixes different concepts: this renders concepts meaningless by taking them out of context and creates a new problem, of needing a metatheory to describe how the different ideas should be combined. Problems in psychological research can often be traced to conceptual rather than to technical limitations. Yet most research carried out by clinicians in training focuses on 'data' and how quickly the person can start to collect it: too little space or time is made for grounding research projects conceptually. This results not only in poor practice and poor research, it also leaves the clinician in an intellectual vacuum which makes uncertainty and pseudodevelopment more probable.

> The crucial moment in terms of development/pseudodevelopment is whether the young professional manages to recognize and bear the unavoidable hardships and challenges that set in after some time. . . . At this point, one becomes

> intensively aware of new complexities. It, therefore, becomes easy to prematurely close and enter the Stagnant Track. (Skovholt and Ronnestad, 1995: 139)

Their survey describes change in therapists and counsellors throughout their professional lives, showing how transitions can divert us from positive development into more defensive or stagnant routes. These are prompted by meeting challenges for which we feel unprepared, or by coping with continued hostility from another professional group. People who take the stagnant track of pseudodevelopment limit their work by concentrating on only one aspect, one method, or on a very restricted set of clients.

Skovholt and Ronnestad contrast these options against genuine professional development, the main content of their book. In summary, they suggest that development occurs when therapists remain open and alert to complexity, and avoid settling for reductionist explanations. An important marker for staying open to development is the ability to tolerate and modulate negative feelings experienced as a result of the inevitable difficulties and disappointments of professional life. The therapists they interviewed reported how helpful it had been when they found or created a conceptual system that anchored their personal, political and therapeutic values within the same position.

2 A corollary of this is that clinical courses will become more explicitly focused on particular positions or theories, abandoning any hope of training eclectic professionals. This will not be a narrow or purist enterprise that will feed the drive towards fragmentation. Plurality is central to the development of new discussions and possibilities that dig us out of stale dichotomies; and as Fulford et al. (1993) showed for the USSR, plural perspectives on topics as slippery as psychiatry provide vital checks on an activity that is easily abused. Their investigation of the abuse of psychiatry concluded that it was not corruption but excessive faith in the science of psychiatry that led practitioners into abusive practices: they were not kept open to alternative discourses by the stream of anti-psychiatry literature which characterizes the West. Accepting the value of pluralism as a bulwark against abuse, we nevertheless need to move towards greater coherence in many areas. We need dialogue about which forms of practice can work together in complementary ways, and which ones start from such different positions that they cannot possibly be used together.

3 If eclecticism is to be condemned but pluralism and openness welcomed, some neat footwork is going to be required. Postmodern interest in a range of contexts of meaning will not diminish, but will become manageable through efforts to create dialogue. Miller's (1996) grounded theory study of teacher and pupil culture exemplifies such neat footwork, combining a metaperspective on systems with a pluralist view of the content of the intervention.

This study investigated changes in the challenging behaviours shown by non-disabled primary school children. It came out of frustration that the bare bones of behavioural or other interventions in educational contexts failed to take the exigencies of each situation into account: they provided no way to predict which alterations to the 'ideal' method would work and which relatively textbook interventions would have no effect. His retrospective study found that in successful cases the intervention included making a new system around the child for a period, comprising the educational psychologist, the teacher and a parent. It also underlined how dysfunctional most school cultures are, in that they maintain problems and ignore success; teachers who succeeded in reducing challenging behaviours described how they protected themselves and the child from negative discourses in early stages of the intervention, and it was rare for any successes to be celebrated. Miller describes the need to understand and address cultural pressures on people in a system before anything can change: he found that chronic situations need new systems to be created before participants can cease blaming each other and work together to develop new solutions.

4 Only 24 children whose behaviour had significantly improved were nominated for inclusion in Miller's study when he approached departments of educational psychology across England; I suspect he would have had a similarly low response had he approached clinical psychology departments. Increasing attention to the outcomes of practical interventions rather than research projects will add to the already gloomy picture emerging from audit: that it is extremely difficult to create change within large institutions such as health services. This will have two effects:

- It will increase interest in systemic theory and therapy.
- It will encourage services to focus their interventions much more clearly, to create coherence from the current set of eclectic interventions tried serially or (worse) simultaneously.

5 Increased knowledge of what can change, and what cannot, will make psychoeducational interventions far more relevant for people with all types of chronic problems, as well as for their relatives and carers. Psychology has a strong tradition in developing and sharing information and this should grow. It also needs to consider how it can contribute to the development of clinical environments where learning occurs mutually between all members.

6 The myth that hospital closure, normalization and community care will solve all problems experienced by people with mental health problems, learning or physical disabilities, or the confused elderly, will be challenged over the next few years. Twigg and Atkin (1994) show how the power of normalization rhetoric – dominant in learning disability services in particular – supports a model of the 'superseded carer'. This model assumes that adults with a learning disability should not be living in the parental home, despite evidence that parents continue to be the main providers of

support and self-understanding; professionals in the service act *as if* the parents were not key stakeholders. Foucault has sensitized us to the hidden powers used by clinicians: here power is used to render people and their opinions invisible. The increasing power held by carers will challenge their erasure.

Moreover, Barclay (1993) suggests that fascination with utopias, with finding an ideal place for men and women in the world such as is defined by normalization, was inherited from the Enlightenment vision that reason would triumph over nature. During the twentieth century idealism apparently shifted from society to individuals, where the person became reconceptualized as 'a finite set of malleable structures which can be changed according to a prior definition of the "good" the "efficient" or fully "rational" person' (1993: 179). Barclay argues that psychologists have been complicit in this process, which started with both Watson's and Skinner's description of behavioural utopias; includes Maslow's view that the 'best' specimens of the human species, the self-actualizers, can be called most fully human; and continues with cognitive theories of human beings as information processors.

New models of service will develop on the basis of common interests and dialogue, rather than common locality; like all aspects of service thinking they will start to explore longer-term interventions and projects than are conceivable or possible while services remain dominated by short-term contracts for superficial episodes of care.

7 Research and practice will reorient itself with regard to time. Not only will service planning move towards a longer vision, psychology as a whole will be affected too. This means that studies in the history of psychology and of clinical psychology will be funded and valued. It also means that we will become more concerned to draw past and future perspectives into the present, in considering both our work and the shape of our careers. The time-frame adopted by local or national employers will also influence practice and these will overlap. Elizur's project (1994) enabling families and staff to join their efforts in supporting young offenders was introduced over two years; the estate-wide reductions in attempted suicides that Holland introduced (1988) took 10 years. Both required bold management and a clinician who made fundholders and participants alike confident that they would remain in post long enough for the project to bear fruit. Maybe it is true that some environments only value short-term interventions; but perhaps clinicians themselves are often insufficiently settled for long-term, preventative work to be an appropriate goal. These changes will go alongside interest in simultaneity theorized by systemic practitioners, the questioning of all manner of Newtonian time assumptions within research, and responsible development of narrative forms of intervention.

8 We will continue to develop our ability to discuss and handle ethics within the subjectivized world of constructionist approaches to practice. This has to go hand in hand with the contexts of our clients and ourselves.

The European Union reported that the gap between rich and poor widened more in Britain than it did in any other EU country between 1983 and 1993. The number of British families living below the poverty line as a proportion of the population rose from 14.3 per cent to 17.2 per cent during that period. Such shameful treatment of almost a fifth of the population contrasts with the situation in Benelux states, where only 5 per cent of people fell below the same poverty line. This EU report also highlights evidence of weakening economic and social cohesion in Britain. McCarthy's (1994) special issue of *Human Systems* explores poverty and social exclusion, providing a world-wide account of different ways to offer therapy that avoids merely adjusting poor people to their state. Papers describe changing therapeutic meanings away from conceptualizing people as deprived and multi-problem to celebrate their survival of a housing crisis they did not make. We need many more imaginative responses to poverty and its effects.

Yet clinicians exist within an environment of increasing blame. Rose (1996) suggests that it is hidden, not manifest powers that impact on professionals, creating a plethora of practices that blame individuals and deflect attention from government responsibility for social problems. He deconstructs risk assessment and management, a 1990s clinical narrative based on the social insurance paradigm, to see it as one of the major tools of the blame culture. Monahan and Steadman (1996) go further to describe risk assessments as virtually impossible. Comparison against base-rate data can be made only in forensic psychology; what little information there is in mental health or learning disability produces the unhelpfully conservative opinion that the strongest predictor of future behaviour is past behaviour. Their paper, 'Violent storms and violent people' makes a playful analogy between weather forecasting and risk forecasting, but one with important lessons for services. They emphasize that despite massive actuarial data and information systems, forecasting is time-limited: weather forecasters are 70 per cent accurate within 24 hours, reasonably accurate over three days, and no better than chance if forecasting beyond six days. Monahan and Steadman note that this is rarely taken into account in the far less certain world of mental health forecasting: 'Courts have held psychologists and psychiatrists liable for inaccurately assessing risk of violence when the violence in question did not transpire until many months after the clinician had made the prediction' (1996: 937). Rose is right to make us wary of new pressures on professionals and new professional practices that purport to respond to those pressures.

Yet professionals have a role too, to take on ethics for themselves and manage the discussion effectively, which means holding it within some theoretical window that offers coherence. The argument was made for sketching in the practices, narratives and moral traditions that would describe clinical psychology through the lens of MacIntyre's virtue theory. Other approaches could be equally valid; what is necessary is the concern to grow beyond adherence to a set of principles handed to us and to respond to the drive for coherence.

Last Words

Miller's research shows us what was obvious but difficult to see. That the human systems in which children and adults with problems are embedded contain so many tensions that change is difficult to achieve. Moreover, clinical professions are beset by factions and rivalries, fertilized if not sown by administrations that create uncertainty and encourage defensiveness by increasing critical scrutiny. Reorganizing these environments in ways that create even greater insecurity is unlikely to provide an answer. The alternative is to move away from structural re-engineering towards the growth of providential spaces in all manner of places, from our own workplaces to the voluntary sector to larger projects, places where differences and commonalities can be discussed in an atmosphere of mutual respect. I hope that the ideas explored throughout this book will engender some of those discussions, and will enable practitioners to identify pragmatic ways forward.

Appendix to Chapter 2: Application of Valentine's Explanations to One Individual

Imagine that a stranger to human variation meets Shahida, a young woman with profound and multiple disabilities. Shahida spends much of her time sitting supported in a glass-fibre mould built into her wheelchair, flicking her fingers before her eyes in a stereotyped manner. The stranger has asked why Shahida spends so much time finger-flicking.

A *classificatory* explanation must go beyond the basic naming preliminary to explanation, to offer new information: it would not explain her actions to say that Shahida finger-flicks because she shows stereotyped behaviour. Classifying Shahida on the recent AAMR system (Luckasson, 1992) as having continuous needs for human support in all areas of her life may help the stranger to understand how little Shahida can do when left alone; this might make finger-flicking more understandable as one of the few options for action available to her, but this is unlikely to satisfy many questioners.

An alternative classificatory explanation might use attachment theory to suggest that she shows the 'avoidant' mode or style of relating. That is, her behaviour is consistent with somebody whose attachment needs have been so chronically unmet that she has developed a way to avoid human contact altogether. To avoid being circular, classificatory explanations need to draw in additional information.

A *correlational* explanation uses probabilistic statements to connect events, in this case the more profoundly disabled people are, the more probable it is that they will have both sensory impairments and show stereotypies such as finger-flicking (Baumeister, 1978). We can deduce from such correlations that she may have a visual impairment, in which case this particular form of finger-flicking may give her visual stimulation which is otherwise unavailable; if she always finger-flicks while facing towards strong sunlight the explanation gains added authority. Nevertheless, correlational explanations carry dangers.

Many newcomers look for *causal* explanations, perhaps the name of a genetic condition which they expect will explain both Shahida's multiple disabilities and her stereotypy. Yet genetic conditions are poor predictors of the range of actions and ways that a person will use their basic genetic composition. The utility and accuracy of behavioural phenotypes – for example dubbing a particular constellation of genes 'the cocktail party condition' because the person is predicted to be not only severely disabled but also chatty and sociable, or seeking a gene for aggression – are disputed by many psychologists. Controversy over a conference about the genetic basis of aggression held in London in 1995 underlines this difference. Supported by the presence of authoritative psychiatrists such as Michael Rutter, it was challenged by radical academics like Nik Rose and Garland Allen who argued that this was bad science and bad politics. Bad science because even eye colour has been shown to stem from interaction between a gene and the environment; bad politics because even if there were a gene for aggression or high intelligence there is no morally responsible way to use this information.

A *functional* analysis of Shahida's stereotypy would involve continuous observation of both environmental events and the occurrence of finger-flicking.

The functional behavioural explanation that could result is that the finger-flicking occurs most during noisy parts of the day, suggesting that noise reduction will result in finger-flicking reduction. However, other theories would also invite us to consider what functions the behaviour could serve within her system: for example, structural family therapists might see the action as part of a complex of behaviours serving the function of maintaining her position as the baby of the family or other social system.

A *neurophysiological* explanation could be based on heart-rate monitoring. Far from being the source of stimulation as people had previously believed, stereotypy seems to block out the external world and be stimulation-reducing (Lewis and Baumeister, 1982). This suggests that stereotypy serves a need by reducing Shahida's physiological and psychological responsiveness, and her arousal level.

Teleological explanations explain the observed event in terms of a future goal, for example that when Shahida flicks her fingers and ignores staff they believe she intends to 'wind them up'; or that by drawing attention to herself her stereotypy serves the evolutionary purpose of ensuring that she gets adequate care. However, that stretches the example somewhat: teleological explanations have greater face validity when applied to people who have speech and more control over events in their world.

A *mentalistic* explanation of Shahida's finger-flicking might suggest that it comforts her in emotionally barren circumstances, if they are barren, in the same way that stereotypies such as rocking comfort people who are deprived or distressed.

References

Alasuutari, P. (1995) *Researching Culture: Qualitative Method and Cultural Studies*. London: Sage.

Anderson, H. and Goolishian, H. (1988) 'Human systems as linguistic systems', *Family Process*, 27: 371–93.

Andrews, B., Morton, J., Bekerian, D., Brewin, C., Davies, G. and Mollon, P. (1995) 'The recovery of memories in clinical practice', *The Psychologist*, 8: 209–14.

Antaki, C. and Rapley, M. (1996) 'Questions and answers to psychological assessment schedules: hidden troubles in "quality of life" interviews', *Journal of Intellectual Disability Research*, 40: 421–37.

Association for Family Therapy (1994) *Code of Conduct and Ethical Guidelines*. Information sheet 5, available from AFT Administration Secretary, 18 Winnipeg Drive, Lakeside, Cardiff CF2 6ET, UK.

Atkinson, D. (1985) 'The use of participant observation and respondent diaries in a study of ordinary living', *British Journal of Mental Subnormality*, 60: 33–40.

Baker, K. (1995) *The Prime Ministers*. London: Thames and Hudson.

Barclay, M. (1993) 'Utopia and psychological theory', *Theory & Psychology*, 3: 173–90.

Barham, P. (1995) 'Making trauma historical', *History of the Human Sciences*, 8: 107–13.

Barlow, D., Hayes, S. and Nelson, R. (1984) *The Scientist Practitioner: Research and Accountability in Clinical and Educational Settings*. Oxford: Pergamon Press.

Bateson, G. (1956) *Mind and Nature*. New York: Fontana.

Baudrillard, J. (1988) *Selected Writings*, ed. M. Poster. Cambridge: Polity Press.

Baumeister, A.A. (1978) 'Origins and control of stereotyped movements in persons with severe handicaps', in C.E. Meyers (ed.), *Quality of Life in Severely and Profoundly Retarded Persons*. Washington, DC: American Association of Mental Deficiency, Monograph 3.

Beail, N. and Warden, S. (1996) 'Evaluation of a psychodynamic psychotherapy service to adults with intellectual disabilities: rationale, design and preliminary outcome data', *Journal of Applied Research in Intellectual Disabilities*, 9: 223–8.

Beardsmore, V. (1993) 'Conductive education: a rejoinder', in J. Swain, V. Finkelstein, S. French and M. Oliver (eds), *Disabling Barriers – Enabling Environments*. London: Sage.

Becker, H. (1986) *Writing for Social Scientists: How to Start and Finish Your Thesis, Book or Article*. London: University of Chicago Press.

Belar, C.D. and Perry, N. (1992) 'National conference on scientist–practitioner education and training for the professional practice of psychology', *American Psychologist*, 47: 71–5.

Benhabib, S. (1992) *Situating the Self: Gender, Community and Postmodernism in Contemporary Ethics*. Cambridge: Polity Press.

Berrios, G. (1995a) 'The history of clinical psychiatry'. Address by guest speaker to the BPS History and Philosophy Section annual conference, in *Proceedings of the British Psychological Society*, 3 (2): 142.

Berrios, G. (1995b) 'Mental retardation', in G. Berrios and R. Porter, *A History of Clinical Psychiatry*. London: Athlone.
Berrios, C. and Porter, R. (eds) (1995) *A History of Clinical Psychiatry*. London: Athlone.
Biklen, D. (1990) 'Communication unbound: autism and praxis', *Harvard Educational Review*, 60: 291–314.
Billig, M. (1987) *Arguing and Thinking: A Rhetorical Approach to Social Psychology*. Cambridge: Cambridge University Press.
Billig, M. (1994) 'Repopulating the depopulated pages of social psychology', *Theory & Psychology*, 4 (3): 307–35.
Billig, M. (1995) *Banal Nationalism*. London: Sage.
Bischoff, R.J. and Sprenkle, D.H. (1993) 'Dropping out of marital and family therapy: a critical review of research', *Family Process*, 32: 353–73.
Blackman, L. (1994) 'What is doing history?', *Theory & Psychology*, 4: 485–504.
Blackmore, S. (1995) 'The revelation of no-self', *Proceedings of the British Psychological Society*, 3 (1): 77.
Blatt, B. (1981) *In and Out of Mental Retardation*. Baltimore, MD: University Park Press.
Bogdan, R. and Taylor, S.J. (1982) *Inside Out: Two First-person Accounts of What It Means To Be Labelled 'Mentally Retarded'*. Toronto: University of Toronto Press.
Bohm, D. (1980) *Wholeness and the Implicate Order*. London: Ark.
Bohm, D. and Hiley, M. (1993) *The Undivided Universe: An Ontological Interpretation of Quantum Theory*. London: Routledge.
Boscolo, L. and Bertrando, P. (1992) 'The reflexive loop of past, present and future in systemic therapy and consultation', *Family Process*, 31: 119–30.
Bowers, J. (1991) 'Time, representation and power/knowledge', *Theory & Psychology*, 1 (4): 543–70.
Boyle, M. (1994a) 'Gender, science and sexual dysfunction', in T.R. Sarbin and J.I. Kitsuse (eds), *Constructing the Social*. London: Sage.
Boyle, M. (1994b) 'Schizophrenia and the art of the soluble', *The Psychologist*, 7: 399–404.
Boyle, M. (1997) 'Resistance to qualitative methods in clinical psychology'. Keynote address to Qualitative Research and Clinical Psychology: Promoting the Interchange conference, University of Wales, Bangor.
Brecher, B. (1988) 'On not caring about the individual', in G. Fairbairn and S. Fairbairn (eds), *Ethical Issues in Caring*. Aldershot: Avebury.
Bretherton, I. (1985) 'Attachment theory: retrospect and prospect', in I. Bretherton and E. Waters (eds), *Growing Points in Attachment Theory and Research*, monograph of the Society for Research in Child Development, 50 (1–2) serial no. 209.
Brewin, C. (1988) *Cognitive Foundations of Clinical Psychology*. Hove: Lawrence Erlbaum.
British Psychological Society (1997) *Code of Conduct, Ethical Principles and Guidelines*. Leicester: BPS.
Bronfenbrenner, U. (1977) 'Toward an experimental ecology of human development', *American Psychologist*, 32: 513–31.
Brooker, R. (ed.) (1992) *Modernism/Postmodernism*. Harlow: Longman.
Brown, R., Bayer, M. and Brown, P. (1992) *Empowerment and Developmental Handicaps*. London: Chapman and Hall.
Brown, S. and Stenner, P. (1995) 'Implicating bodies: Spinoza and the psychology of emotions', *Proceedings of the British Psychological Society*, 3 (2): 142.
Bruner, J. (1990) *Acts of Meaning*. London: Harvard University Press.
Brushlinskii, A. (1987) 'Activity, action and mind as process', *Soviet Psychology*, 25: 59–81

Burman, E. (1994) *Deconstructing Developmental Psychology*. London: Routledge.
Burnham, J. (1993) 'Systemic supervision: the evolution of reflexivity in the context of the supervisory relationship', *Human Systems*, 4: 349–81.
Bussell, D., Matsey, K., Reiss, D. and Hetherington, M. (1995) 'Debriefing the family: is research an intervention?', *Family Process*, 34: 145–59.
Calvez, M. (1993) 'Social interactions in the neighbourhood: cultural approach to social integration of individuals with mental retardation', *Mental Retardation*, 31: 418–23.
Campbell, B. (1993) *Goliath: Britain's Dangerous Places*. London: Methuen.
Chapman, A.J. and Jones, D.M. (1980) *Models of Man*. Leicester: British Psychological Society.
Charmaz, K. (1991) *Good Days, Bad Days: The Self in Chronic Illness and Time*. New Brunswick, NJ: Rutgers University Press.
Clare, I., Murphy, G., Cox, D. and Chaplin, E. (1992) 'Assessment and treatment of fire-setting', *Criminal Behaviour and Mental Health*, 2: 253–68.
Clarke, A.D.B. and Tizard, B. (eds) (1983) *The Life and Work of Jack Tizard*. Leicester: British Psychological Society.
Clarkson, P. (1995) *The Therapeutic Relationship*. London: Whurr.
Clarkson, P. (1996) *The Bystander*. London: Whurr.
Claxton, G. (1994) *Noises from the Darkroom: The Science and Mystery of the Mind*. London: Aquarian.
Clegg, J.A. (1993) 'Putting people first: a social constructionist approach to learning disability', *British Journal of Clinical Psychology*, 32: 389–406.
Clegg, J.A. (1994) 'Epistemology and learning disabilities: invited commentary on Hastings and Remington', *British Journal of Clinical Psychology*, 33: 439–44.
Clegg, J.A. and King, S. (1998) 'Three outcomes of qualitative research in learning disabilities: reconceptualising models, enhancing clinical practice and developing services', *Clinical Psychology Forum*, 114: 7–9.
Clegg, J.A. and Lansdall-Welfare, R. (1995) 'Attachment in learning disability', *Journal of Intellectual Disability Research*, 39: 295–305.
Clegg, J.A., Standen, P. and Jones, G. (1996) 'Striking the balance: a grounded theory analysis of staff perspectives', *British Journal of Clinical Psychology*, 35: 249–64.
Clegg, J.A., Lansdall-Welfare, R., Andrews, C. and Thurman, S. (forthcoming) 'Using grounded theory to develop conceptual clarity in bereavement management'.
Cohen, E. (1997) 'On using systemic theories and techniques in preparing court reports', *Context*, 33: 15–18.
Cole, M. (1995) 'Culture and cognitive development', *Culture and Psychology*, 1 (1): 25–54.
Cooper, C. (1996) 'Clinical audit association'. Paper presented to Forging Ahead with Clinical Audit, the second national conference on audit in mental health services, Royal College of Psychiatrists, Sheffield.
Cox, M. (ed.) (1992) *Shakespeare Comes to Broadmoor*. London: Jessica Kingsley.
Crellin, C. and Vetere, A. (eds) (1995) 'An ethical issue'. Special edition of *Clinical Psychology Forum*, 80.
Cromby, J. (1995) 'Development of self-concept in children with mild and moderate learning difficulties'. Unpublished PhD thesis, University of Nottingham.
Curt, B. (1994) *Textuality and Tectonics: Troubling Social and Psychological Science*. Buckingham: Open University Press.
Dale, N. (1992) 'Parental involvement in the KIDS family centre: who does it work for?', *Child: Care, Health, Development*, 18: 301–19.
Dale, N. (1996) *Working with Families of Children with Special Needs: Partnership and Practice*. London: Routledge.
Dancy, J. and Sosa, E. (1992) *A Companion to Epistemology*. Oxford: Blackwell.

Danziger, K. (1990) *Constructing the Subject: Historical Origins of Psychological Research*. Cambridge: Cambridge University Press.

Danziger, K. (1994) 'Does the history of psychology have a future?', *Theory & Psychology*, 4: 467–84.

Davies, C.A. and Jenkins, R. (1997) 'She has different fits from me: how people with learning difficulties see themselves', *Disability & Society*, 12: 95–109.

Davies, N. (1996) *Europe: A History*. Oxford: Oxford University Press.

Davies, P. (1995) *About Time: Einstein's Unfinished Revolution*. London: Viking.

Davis, D. (1991) 'Rich cases: the ethics of thick description', *Hastings Centre Report*, 21: 12–16.

Davis, N. (1990) *Once upon a Time: Therapeutic Stories*. Oxen Hill, MD: Psychological Associates.

Deleuze, G. and Guattari, F. (1994) *What is Philosophy?* trans. G. Burchell and H. Tomlinson. London: Verso.

Deutsch, J.A. (1960) *The Structural Basis of Behaviour*. Cambridge: Cambridge University Press.

Devlin, B. (1996) 'The national confidential enquiry on perioperative deaths'. Paper presented to Forging Ahead with Clinical Audit, the second national conference on audit in mental health services, Royal College of Psychiatrists, Sheffield.

Dickens, P. (1994) 'Should we be certified?', *The Psychologist*, 7 (12): 545–7.

Dickenson, D. and Johnson, M. (eds) (1993) *Death, Dying and Bereavement*. London: Sage.

Division of Clinical Psychology (1995) *Professional Practice Guidelines*. Leicester: British Psychological Society.

DoH (1992) *Report of the Committee of Inquiry into Complaints about Ashworth Hospital*. London: HMSO.

Doise, W. (1986) *Levels of Explanation in Social Psychology*. Cambridge: Cambridge University Press.

Dosen, A. (1993) 'Diagnosis and treatments of psychiatric and behavioural disorders in mentally retarded individuals: the state of the art', *Journal of Intellectual Disability Research*, 37, (Supplement 1): 1–7.

Dryden, W. (1985) *Therapists' Dilemmas*. London: Sage.

Eagleton, T. (1983) *Literary Theory: An Introduction*. Oxford: Blackwell.

Eagleton, T. (1994) 'Discourse and discos: theory in the space between culture and capitalism', *Times Literary Supplement*, 4763: 3–4.

Edgerton, R. (1967) *The Cloak of Competence*. Los Angeles: University of California Press.

Elizur, Y. (1993) 'Ecosystemic training: conjoining supervision and organisational development', *Family Process*, 32: 185–201.

Elizur, Y. (1994) 'Working with families in institutions for juvenile offenders: an ecosystemic model for the development of family involvement', *Human Systems*, 5: 253–66.

Emerson, A. (1994) 'Facilitated communication'. Paper presented to the Department of Learning Disability's seminar programme, University of Nottingham.

Engeström, Y., Brown, K., Engeström, R. and Koistinen, K. (1990) 'Organizational forgetting: an activity-theoretical perspective', in D. Middleton and D. Edwards (eds), *Collective Remembering*. London: Sage.

Epston, D. and White, M. (1989) *Literate Means to Therapeutic Ends*. Adelaide: Dulwich Centre Publications.

Fairbairn, S. and Fairbairn, G. (1987) *Psychology Ethics and Change*. London: Routledge.

Faulconer, J.E. and Williams, R.N. (eds) (1990) *Reconsidering Psychology:*

Perspectives from Continental Philosophy. Pittsburgh, PA: Duquesne University Press.

Ferguson, D. and Halle, J. (1995) 'Editorial: considerations for readers of qualitative research', *Journal for the Association for Persons with Severe Handicaps*, 20: 1–2.

Feyerabend, P. (1993) *Against Method*, 3rd edn. London: Verso.

Firth-Cozens, J. (1993) *Audit in Mental Health Services*. Hove: Lawrence Erlbaum.

Flynn, M. (1989) *Independent Living for Adults with Mental Handicap: A Place of My Own*. London: Cassell.

Foucault, M. (1980) *Power/Knowledge: Selected Interviews and Other Writings*, ed. C. Gordon. New York: Pantheon.

Foucault, M. (1988) 'Technologies of the self', in L. Martin, H. Guttman and P. Hutton (eds), *Technologies of the Self*. Amherst, MA: University of Massachusetts Press.

Fowers, B. and Richardson, F. (1996) 'Why is multiculturalism good?', *American Psychologist*, 51: 609–21.

Frank, A.W. (1992) 'The pedagogy of suffering: moral dimensions of psychological therapy and research with the ill', *Theory & Psychology*, 2: 467–86.

Frank, A.W. (1996) 'From dysappearance to hyperappearance: sliding boundaries of illness and bodies', *Theory & Psychology*, 6 (4): 753–60.

Freeman, M. (1993) *Rewriting the Self: History, Memory, Narrative*. London: Routledge.

Friedberg, R.D. (1994) 'Storytelling and cognitive therapy with children', *Journal of Cognitive Therapy: An International Quarterly*, 8: 209–17.

Frosh, S. (1997) 'Fundamentalism, gender and family therapy', *Journal of Family Therapy*, 19: 417–30.

Fulford, K.W.M., Smirnov, A.Y.U. and Snow, E. (1993) 'Concepts of disease and the abuse of psychiatry in the USSR', *British Journal of Psychiatry*, 162: 801–10.

Gallimore, R., Weisner, T.S., Kaufman, S. and Bernheimer, L.P. (1989) 'The social construction of ecocultural riches', *American Journal on Mental Retardation*, 94: 216–30.

Gambrill, E. (1990) *Critical Thinking in Clinical Practice*. San Francisco: Jossey-Bass.

Gardiner, M. (1996) 'Foucault, ethics and dialogue', *History of the Human Sciences*, 9: 27–46.

Gardner, R.A. (1971) *Therapeutic Communication with Children: The Mutual Storytelling Technique*. New York: Science House.

Geach, P. (1977) *The Virtues*. Cambridge: Cambridge University Press.

Geertz, C. (1973) *The Interpretation of Cultures*. London: Fontana.

Geertz, C. (1983) *Local Knowledge*. New York: Basic Books.

Gergen, K. (1985) 'The social constructionist movement in modern psychology', *American Psychologist*, 40: 266–75.

Gergen, K. (1994) *Toward Transformation in Social Knowledge*, 2nd edn. London: Sage.

Gilligan, C. (1982) *In a Different Voice: Psychological Theory and Women's Development*. Cambridge, MA: Harvard University Press.

Glaser, B. and Strauss, A.L. (1967) *The Discovery of Grounded Theory: Strategies for Qualitative Research*. Chicago: Aldine.

Gleason, J. (1993) 'The creation of meaning: what persons with severe or profound multiple developmental disabilities do in context', *Australia and New Zealand Journal of Developmental Disabilities*, 18: 157–67.

Goffman, E. (1961) *Asylums*. New York: Doubleday Anchor.

Goldberg, D., Magrill, L., Hale, J., Damaskinidou, P.J. and Tham, S. (1995) 'Protection and loss: working with learning-disabled adults and their families', *Journal of Family Therapy*, 17 (3): 263–80.
Goldberg, N. (1986) *Writing Down the Bones*. London: Shambhala.
Goldner, V., Penn, P., Sheinberg, M. and Walker, G. (1990) 'Love and violence: gender paradoxes in volatile attachments', *Family Process*, 29: 343–64.
Goode, E. and Ben-Yehuda, N. (1994) *Moral Panics: The Social Construction of Deviance*. Oxford: Blackwell.
Grant, G. (1993) 'Support networks and transitions over two years among adults with a mental handicap', *Mental Handicap Research*, 6: 36–55.
Gregory, D. (1994) *Geographical Imaginations*. Oxford: Blackwell.
Gribbin, J. (1984) *In Search of Schrödinger's Cat: Quantum Physics and Reality*. London: Corgi.
Griffin, C. (1993) *Representations of Youth*. Cambridge: Polity Press.
Griffin, D. and Bartholomew, K. (1994) 'The metaphysics of measurement: the case of adult attachment', in K. Bartholomew and D. Perlman (eds), *Advances in Personal Relationships Vol. 5: Attachment Processes in Adulthood*. London: Jessica Kingsley.
Griffiths, R. (1988) *Community Care: Agenda for Action*. London: HMSO.
Grosz, E. (1993) 'Bodies and knowledges: feminism and the crisis of reason', in L. Alcoff and E. Potter (eds), *Feminist Epistemologies*. London: Routledge.
Haack, S. (1992) 'Pragmatism', in J. Dancy and E. Sosa (eds), *A Companion to Epistemology*. Oxford: Blackwell.
Habermas, J. (1992) 'Further reflections on the public sphere', in C. Calhoun (ed.), *Habermas and the Public Sphere*. London: MIT Press.
Hacking, I. (1995) *Rewriting the Soul: Multiple Personality and the Sciences of Memory*. Princeton, NJ: Princeton University Press.
Halpern, A.S., Close, W.D. and Nelson, D.J. (1986) *On My Own*. Baltimore, MD: Paul Brookes.
Hamel, J., with Dufour, S. and Fortin, D. (1993) *Case Study Methods*, Qualitative Research Methods, series 32. London: Sage.
Hanh, Thich Nhat (1995) *Zen Keys*. London: Thorsons.
Hanley-Maxwell, C., Whitney-Thomas, J. and Mayfield Pogoloff, S. (1995) 'The second shock: a qualitative study of parents' perspectives and needs during their child's transition from school to adult life', *Journal of the Association for Persons with Severe Handicaps*, 20: 3–15.
Hare, R.M. (1989) *Essays in Ethical Theory*. Oxford: Clarendon Press.
Harper, D. (1994) 'The professional construction of "paranoia" and the discursive use of diagnostic criteria', *British Journal of Medical Psychology*, 67: 131–43.
Harper, D. (1996) 'Deconstructing paranoia: towards a discursive understanding of apparently unwarranted suspicion', *Theory & Psychology*, 6: 423–48.
Harris, J., Birley, J.L. and Fulford, K.W. (1993) 'A proposal to classify happiness as a psychiatric disorder', *British Journal of Psychiatry*, 162: 539–42.
Harvey, D. (1989) *The Condition of Postmodernity: An Enquiry into the Origins of Social Change*. Oxford: Blackwell.
Hastings, R.P. and Remington, B. (1994a) 'Staff behaviour and its implications for people with learning disabilities and challenging behaviours', *British Journal of Clinical Psychology*, 33: 433–8.
Hastings, R.P. and Remington, B. (1994b) 'Staff behaviour and challenging behaviour: a reply to Clegg's commentary', *British Journal of Clinical Psychology*, 33: 445–50.
Hazan, H. (1980) *The Limbo People: A Study of the Constitution of the Time Universe among the Aged*. London: Routledge.
Held, V. (1990) 'Feminist transformations of moral theory', *Philosophy and Phenomenological Research*, 50: 321–44.

Henwood, K. and Pidgeon, N. (1995) 'Grounded theory and qualitative research', *The Psychologist*, 8: 115–18.

Hermans, H.J.M. and Hermans-Jansen, E. (1995) *Self-narratives: The Construction of Meaning in Psychotherapy*. London: Guilford Press.

Hewitt, H. (1995) 'Identities as a resource: life story work'. Paper presented at Understanding the Social World, Huddersfield University, July.

Hoffman, L. (1992) 'A reflexive stance for family therapy', in S. McNamee and K. Gergen (eds), *Therapy as Social Construction*. London: Routledge.

Holland, S. (1988) 'Defining and experimenting with prevention', in S. Ramon and M. Giannichedda (eds), *Psychiatry in Transition: The British and Italian Experience*. London: Pluto.

Holland, S. (1992) 'Community mental health and community psychology: the White City Project', Abstract published in *Proceedings of the British Psychological Society, 1993*.

Hollinger, D. (1995) *Postethnic America: Beyond Multiculturalism*. New York: Basic Books.

Honderich, T. (ed.) (1995) *The Oxford Companion to Philosophy*. Oxford: Oxford University Press.

Hoshmand, L.L.T (1994) *Orientation to Inquiry in a Reflective Professional Psychology*. New York: State University of New York Press.

Hoshmand, L.T. and Polkinghorne, D.E. (1992) 'Redefining the science–practice relationship and professional training', *American Psychologist*, 47: 55–66.

Howard, G. (1997) 'Discursive psychology from the viewpoint of narrative psychology', *Culture & Psychology*, 3: 231–6.

Hufton, O. (1995) *The Prospect Before Her: A History of Women in Western Europe*, Vol. 1. London: HarperCollins.

Hutton, W. (1995) *The State We're In*. London: Jonathan Cape.

Ignatieff, M. (1994) *Blood and Belonging: Journeys into the New Nationalism*. London: Vintage.

Iwata, B., Dorsey, M., Slifer, K., Bauman, K. and Richman, G. (1982) 'Toward a functional analysis of self-injury', *Analysis and Intervention in Developmental Disability*, 2: 3–20.

Jacobson, J.W., Mulick, J.A. and Schwartz, A.A. (1995) 'A history of facilitated communication: science, pseudoscience and antiscience', *American Psychologist*, 50: 750–6.

Jahoda, G. (1992) *Crossroads between Culture and Mind*. Hemel Hempstead: Harvester Wheatsheaf.

James, W. (1907) *Pragmatism*, ed. F. Burkhardt and F. Bowers (1975), Cambridge, MA: Harvard University Press.

Jay, P. (1979) *Report of the Committee of Enquiry into Mental Handicap Nursing and Care*. London: HMSO.

Jones, E. (1993) *Family Systems Therapy*. Chichester: Wiley.

Jones, R.S.P. and Connell, E. (1993) 'Ten years of gentle teaching: much ado about nothing?', *The Psychologist*, 6: 544–8.

Karmiloff-Smith, A. (1992) *Beyond Modularity*. Cambridge, MA: MIT Press.

Kearney, R. and Rainwater, M. (eds) (1996) *The Continental Philosophy Reader*. London: Routledge.

Keats, J. (1973) *The Complete Poems*, ed. John Barnard. Harmondsworth: Penguin.

Kelly, N. and Milner, J. (1996) 'Child protection decision-making', *Child Abuse Review*, 5: 91–102.

Kent, G. and McAuley, D. (1995) 'Ethical difficulties faced by trainee clinical psychologists', *Clinical Psychology Forum*, 80: 26–30.

Kernan, K.T. and Sabsay, S. (1989/1997) 'Communication in social interaction', in M. Beveridge and G. Conti-Ramsden (eds), *Language and Communication in Mentally Handicapped People*. London: Routledge.

Kerruish, A. (1995) 'Basic human values: the ethos for methodology', *Journal of Community and Applied Psychology*, 5: 121–43.

King, R.D., Raynes, N. and Tizard, J. (1971) *Patterns of Residential Care*. London: Routledge.

King's Fund Centre (1980) *An Ordinary Life – Comprehensive Locally-based Residential Services for Mentally Handicapped People*. London: King's Fund Centre.

King's Fund Centre (1982) *People First: Developing Services in the Community for People with Mental Handicap*. London: King's Fund Centre.

Kitchener, K.S. (1983) 'Cognition, metacognition and epistemic cognition: a three-level model of cognitive processing', *Human Development*, 4: 222–32.

Kitchener, K.S. (1984) 'Intuition, critical evaluation and ethical principles: the foundation for ethical decisions in counselling psychology', *The Counselling Psychologist*, 12: 43–57.

Krause, I. (1995) 'Personhood, culture and family therapy', *Journal of Family Therapy*, 17: 363–82.

Lacey, H. and Schwartz, B. (1996) 'The formation and transformation of values', in W. O'Donohue and R.F. Kitchener (eds), *The Philosophy of Psychology*. London: Sage.

Lasch, C. (1994) *The Revolt of the Elites and the Betrayal of Democracy*. New York: Norton.

Latané, B. and Darley, M. (1970) *The Unresponsive Bystander: Why Doesn't He Help?* New York: Appleton, Century, Crofts.

Latour, B. (1987) *Science in Action*. London: Sage.

Latour, B. and Woolgar, S. (1979) *Laboratory Life: The Social Construction of Scientific Facts*. London: Sage.

LaVigna, G.W. and Donnellan, A.M. (1986) *Alternatives to Punishment: Solving Behaviour Problems with Non-aversive Strategies*. New York: Irvington.

Layder, D. (1990) *The Realist Image in Social Science*. London: Macmillan.

Lazarus, R.S. (1984) 'On the primacy of cognition', *American Psychologist*, 39: 124–9.

Leudar, I., Fraser, W. and Jeeves, K. (1987) 'Theoretical problems and practical solutions to behaviour disorders in retarded people', *Health Bulletin*, 45: 347–55.

Levine, E.S. (1980) 'Indirect suggestions through personalized fairy tales for treatment of childhood insomnia', *American Journal of Clinical Hypnosis*, 23: 57–63.

Levine, M. and Perkins, D. (1987) *Principles of Community Psychology: Perspectives and Applications*. New York: Oxford University Press.

Lewin, K. (1951) *Field Theory in Social Science*. New York: Harper.

Lewis, M. and Baumeister, A.A. (1982) 'Stereotyped mannerisms in mentally retarded persons: animal models and theoretical analysis', in N.R. Ellis (ed.), *International Review of Research in Mental Retardation*. Vol. II. New York: Academic Press.

Lindsay, G. (1995) 'Values, ethics and psychology – the 1995 Presidential Address', *The Psychologist*, 8: 493–8.

Loftus, E. and Klinger, M. (1992) 'Is the unconscious smart or dumb?', *American Psychologist*, 47: 761–5.

Lotman, Y.M. (1991) 'Technical progress as a cultural problem', *Soviet Psychology*, 29: 6–28.

Lovie, P. and Lovie, A.D. (eds) (1991) *New Developments in Statistics for Psychology and the Social Sciences*, Vols 1 and 2. London: British Psychological Society and Routledge.

Luckasson, R. (1992) *Mental Retardation: Definition, Classification and System of Supports*, 9th edn. Washington, DC: American Association on Mental Retardation.

Luepnitz, D.A. (1992) 'Nothing in common but their first names: the case of Foucault and White', *Journal of Family Therapy*, 14: 281–4.
Lukes, S. (1993) 'Five fables about human rights', in S. Shute and S. Hurley (eds), *On Human Rights: The Oxford Amnesty Lectures*. New York: Basic Books.
Lynch, E.W. (1992) 'Developing cross-cultural competence', in E.W. Lynch and M.J. Hanson (eds), *Developing Cross-Cultural Competence: A Guide for Working with Young Children and Their Families*. London: Paul H. Brookes.
Lynch, E.W. and Hanson, M. (1992) 'Steps in the right direction', in E.W. Lynch and M.J. Hanson (eds), *Developing Cross-Cultural Competence: A Guide for Working with Young Children and Their Families*. London: Paul H. Brookes.
Lyotard, J.-F. (1984) *The Postmodern Condition: A Report on Knowledge*, trans G. Bennington and B. Massumi. Manchester: Manchester University Press.
Macann, C. (ed.) (1996) *Critical Heidegger*. London: Routledge.
McCarthy, I.C. (1994) Editorial for special issue on poverty and social exclusion. *Human Systems*, 5 (3 and 4).
McCarthy, T. (1992) 'Practical discourse: on the relation of morality to politics', in C. Calhoun (ed.), *Habermas and the Public Sphere*. London: MIT Press.
MacDonald, C. and MacDonald, G. (1995) *Philosophy of Psychology*. Oxford: Blackwell.
McGaw, S. and Sturmey, P. (1993) 'Parents with a learning disability', *Child Abuse Review*, 2: 101–17.
McGee, J.J., Menolascino, F., Hobbs, D. and Menousek, P. (1987) *Gentle Teaching*. New York: Human Sciences Press.
McGoldrick, M. (1994) 'Culture, class, race and gender', *Human Systems*, 5: 131–54.
MacIntyre, A. (1985) *After Virtue: A Study in Moral Theory*, 2nd edn. London: Duckworth. First published 1981.
Mackie, J.L. (1977) *Ethics: Inventing Right and Wrong*. Harmondsworth: Penguin.
McNamee, S. and Gergen, K. (eds) (1992) *Therapy as Social Construction*. London: Sage.
Madigan, S.P. (1992) 'The application of Michel Foucault's philosophy in the problem externalising discourse of Michael White', *Journal of Family Therapy*, 14: 265–79.
Mair, M. (1989a) 'Still managing to care?' Paper presented to the Division of Clinical Psychology summer school, York.
Mair, M. (1989b) *Between Psychology and Psychotherapy: A Poetics of Experience*. London: Routledge.
Marks, D. (1992) 'Decision-making in case conferences: an example from education', *Clinical Psychology Forum*, 45: 14–17.
Maslow, A.H. (1954) *Motivation and Personality*, 2nd edn 1970. New York: Harper & Row.
Mead, G.H. (1934) *Mind, Self and Society*. Chicago: University of Chicago Press.
Michael, M. (1991) 'Some postmodern reflections on social psychology', *Theory & Psychology*, 1 (2): 203–22.
Middleton, D. and Buchanan, K. (1993) 'Is reminiscence working?', *Journal of Aging Studies*, 7: 321–33.
Midgley, M. (1983) 'Duties concerning islands', *Encounter*, 60: 36–44.
Millard, D. and Oakley, H. (1994) 'Psychotherapeutic communities: the contemporary practice', in P. Clarkson and M. Pokorny (eds), *The Handbook of Psychotherapy*. London: Routledge.
Miller, A. (1996) *Pupil Behaviour and Teacher Culture*. London: Cassell.
Miller, E. (1995) 'Comment on an ethical issue', *Clinical Psychology Forum*, 80: 7–8.
Miller, G.A., Galanter, E. and Pribram, K. (1960) *Plans and the Structure of*

Behaviour. New York: Holt Rinehart and Winston (reprinted by Adams, Bannister, Cox, 1986).

Monahan, J. and Steadman, H.J. (1996) 'Violent storms and violent people: how meteorology can inform risk communication in mental health law', *American Psychologist*, 51: 931–8.

Morawski, J. (1992) 'There is more to our history of giving', *American Psychologist*, 47: 161–9.

Morawski, J. (1994) 'The human kinds in psychology: can we take our observers, phantoms and experimenters seriously?' Guest lecture to the annual conference of the History and Philosophy of Psychology Section; abstract in *Proceedings of the British Psychological Society, 1995*.

Moros, D., Rhodes, R., Baumrin, B. and Strain, J. (1991) 'Thinking critically in medicine and ethics', in B. Almond and D. Hill (eds), *Applied Philosophy: Morals and Metaphysics in Contemporary Debate*. London: Routledge.

Moscovici, S. (1993) *The Invention of Society*. Cambridge: Polity Press.

Mounce, H.O. (1997) *The Two Pragmatisms: From Peirce to Rorty*. London: Routledge.

Moustakas, C. (1994) *Phenomenological Research Methods*. London: Sage.

Nash, C. (1990) Foreword, in C. Nash (ed.), *Narrative in Culture*. London: Routledge.

National Centre for Clinical Audit (1996) *Guidelines for Clinical Audit*. London: BMA.

Neill, A.S. (1968) *Summerhill*. Harmondsworth: Penguin.

Neuberger, J. (1992) *Ethics and Health Care: The Role of Research Ethics Committees in the UK*. London: King's Fund Institute.

Newell, A. and Simon, H.A. (1972) *Human Problem Solving*. Englewood Cliffs, NJ: Prentice-Hall.

Newman, D.W. and Beail, N. (1994) 'Needs assessment', *Clinical Psychology Forum*, 71: 21–5.

Newton, J.T. and Sturmey, P. (1991) 'The Motivation Assessment Scale: inter-rater reliability and internal consistency in a British sample', *Journal of Mental Deficiency Research*, 35: 472–4.

O'Brien, J. (1987) 'A guide to lifestyle planning', in B. Wilcox and G.T. Bellamy (eds), *A Comprehensive Guide to the Activities Catalog*. Baltimore, MD: Paul H. Brookes.

O'Donohue, W. and Mangold, R. (1996) 'A critical examination of the ethical principles of psychologists in the code of conduct', in W. O'Donohue and R.F. Kitchener (eds), *The Philosophy of Psychology*. London: Sage.

Oliner, S.P. and Oliner, P.M. (1988) *The Altruistic Personality: Rescuers of Jews in Nazi Europe*. New York: Free Press/Macmillan.

Oliver, M. (1992) 'Changing the social relations of research production?', *Disability, Handicap and Society*, 7: 101–14.

Ong, W.J. (1982) *Orality and Literacy*. London: Methuen.

Orford, J. (1992) *Community Psychology: Theory and Practice*. Chichester: Wiley.

Orford, J. (1995) 'Qualitative research for applied psychologists', *Clinical Psychology Forum*, 75: 19–26.

O'Sullivan, J.J. and Quevillon, R.P. (1992) '40 years later: is the Boulder model still alive?', *American Psychologist*, 47: 67–70.

Owen, D. (1996) 'Size, structure and growth of ethnic minority populations', in D. Coleman and J. Salt (eds), *Ethnicity in the 1991 Census, Volume 1: Demographic Characteristics of the Ethnic Minority Population*. London: HMSO.

Parker, G. (1993) 'A four-way stretch? The politics of disability and caring', in J. Swain, V. Finkelstein, S. French and M. Oliver (eds), *Disabling Barriers – Enabling Environments*. London: Sage.

Parry, G. and Watts, F. (1989) *Behavioural and Mental Health Research: A Handbook of Skills and Methods*. Hove: Lawrence Erlbaum. Revised 1995.

Peach, C. and Rossiter, D. (1995) 'Level and nature of spatial concentration and segregation of minority ethnic populations in GB, 1991', in P. Ratcliffe (ed.), *Ethnicity in the 1991 Census, Volume 3: Social Geography and Ethnicity in Britain*. London: HMSO.

Perelberg, R.J. (1992) 'Familiar and unfamiliar types of family structure: towards a conceptual framework', in J. Kareem and R. Littlewood (eds), *Intercultural Therapy*. Oxford: Blackwell.

Phillips, D., Watson, A.R. and MacInlay, D. (forthcoming) 'Distress and the micturating cistourethrogram: does preparation help?', *Acta Paediatrica Scandinavia*.

Pilgrim, D. and Treacher, A. (1992) *Clinical Psychology Observed*. London: Routledge.

Polkinghorne, D.E. (1990) 'Psychology after philosophy', in J. Faulconer and R. Williams (eds), *Reconsidering Psychology: Perspectives from Continental Philosophy*. Pittsburgh, PA: Duquesne University Press.

Potter, J. and Wetherall, M. (1987) *Discourse and Social Psychology*. London: Sage.

Power, M. and Brewin, C. (1997) *The Transformation of Meaning in Psychological Therapies: Integrating Theory and Practice*. Chichester: Wiley.

Price-Williams, D. (1989) 'Communication in therapy with emotionally disturbed mentally retarded individuals', in M. Beveridge, G. Conti-Ramsden and I. Leudar (eds), *Language and Communication in Mentally Handicapped People*. London: Chapman & Hall.

Punch, M. (1994) 'Politics and ethics in qualitative research', in N. Denzin and Y. Lincoln (eds), *Handbook of Qualitative Research*. London: Sage.

Rabinow, P. (ed.) (1984) *The Foucault Reader*. Harmondsworth: Penguin.

Reder, P. and Duncan, S. (1995) 'The meaning of the child', in P. Reder and C. Lucey (eds), *Assessment of Parenting*. London: Routledge.

Rees, P. and Phillips, D. (1995) 'Geographical spread: the national picture', in P. Ratcliffe (ed.), *Ethnicity in the 1991 Census, Volume 3: Social Geography and Ethnicity in Britain*. London: HMSO.

Reissman, C. (1993) *Narrative Analysis* (Qualitative Research Methods Vol. 30). London: Sage.

Richards, G. (1996) *Putting Psychology in its Place*. London: Routledge.

Richards, G. (1997) 'Psychology and religion: a suitable case for treatment?' Paper presented to the annual conference of the BPS History and Philosophy of Psychology conference, York.

Rogers, A., Pilgrim, D. and Lacey, R. (1993) *Experiencing Psychiatry: Users' Views of Services*. London: Macmillan.

Rorty, R. (1991) *Objectivity, Relativism and Truth: Philosophical Papers, Vol 1*. Cambridge: Cambridge University Press.

Rorty, R. (1993) 'Human rights, rationality and sentimentality', in S. Shute and S. Hurley (eds), *On Human Rights: The Oxford Amnesty Lectures*. New York: Basic Books.

Rose, N. (1996) 'Psychiatry as a political science: advanced liberalism and the administration of risk', *History of the Human Sciences*, 9: 1–24.

Rosen, A. (1992) 'Community psychiatry services: will they endure?', *Current Opinion in Psychiatry*, 5: 257–65.

Rossi, P. and Freeman, H. (1986) *Evaluation: A Systematic Approach*. London: Sage.

Rowitz, L. (1992) 'Mental retardation in the year 2000', in L. Rowitz (ed.), *Mental Retardation in the Year 2000*. London: Springer-Verlag.

Said, E. (1994) *Representations of the Intellectual*. London: Vintage.

St Claire, L. (1989) 'A multidimensional model of mental retardation: impairment,

subnormal behaviour, role failures and socially constructed retardation', *American Journal on Mental Retardation*, 94: 88–96.
Salmon, P. (1994) 'Is health psychology a profession or can it become one?', *The Psychologist*, 7 (12): 542–4.
Sampson, E. (1996) 'Establishing embodiment in psychology', *Theory & Psychology, Special Issue on the Body and Psychology*, 6: 601–24.
Scaife, J. (1995) *Training to Help: A Survival Guide*. Sheffield: Riding Press.
Schaefer, J.A. and Moos, R.H. (1993) 'Work stressors in health care', *Journal of Community & Applied Social Psychology*, 3 (4): 235–42.
Schama, S. (1990) 'The many deaths of General Wolfe', in B. Buford (ed.), *History: Granta 32*. Harmondsworth: Penguin.
Schön, D.A. (1987) *Educating the Reflective Practitioner*. San Francisco: Jossey-Bass.
Schweder, R.A. and Sullivan, M.A. (1993) 'Cultural psychology: who needs it?', *Annual Review of Psychology*, 44: 497–523.
Shepherd, G. (1995) 'A personal history of rehabilitation', *Clinical Psychology Forum*, 82: 4–8.
Shotter, J. (1993) *Cultural Politics of Everyday Life*. Buckingham: Open University Press.
Sinason, V. (1992) *Mental Handicap and the Human Condition*. London: Free Association Books.
Singer, B. (1993) 'The democratic solution to ethnic pluralism', *Philosophy and Social Criticism*, 19: 97–114.
Singer, P. (1993) *Practical Ethics*, 2nd edn. Cambridge: Cambridge University Press.
Singer, P. (ed.) (1994) *Ethics*. Oxford: Oxford University Press.
Siperstein, G., Wolraich, M. and Reed, D. (1994) 'Professionals' prognoses for individuals with mental retardation: search for consensus within interdisciplinary settings', *American Journal of Mental Retardation*, 98: 519–56.
Skovholt, T.M. and Ronnestad, M.H. (1995) *The Evolving Professional Self*. Chichester: Wiley.
Slife, B. (1993) *Time and Psychological Explanation*. Albany, NY: State University of New York Press.
Slife, B. (1995) 'Information and time', *Theory & Psychology*, 5: 533–50.
Slife, B. and Williams, R.N. (1995) *What's behind the Research? Discovering Hidden Assumptions in the Behavioural Sciences*. London: Sage.
Smail, D. (1995a) 'Clinical psychology: liberatory practice or discourse of power?', *Clinical Psychology Forum*, 80: 3–6.
Smail, D. (1995b) 'Power and the origins of unhappiness: working with individuals', *Journal of Community and Applied Social Psychology*, 5: 347–56.
Smith, J.A. (1995) 'Qualitative methods, identity and transition to motherhood', *The Psychologist*, 8: 122–5.
Smith, T., McGuire, J., Abbott, D. and Blau, B. (1991) 'Clinical ethical decision-making: an investigation of the rationales used to justify doing less than one believes one should', *Professional Psychology Research & Practice*, 22: 235–9.
Soyland, A.J. (1994) *Psychology as Metaphor*. London: Sage.
Stake, R. (1994) 'Case studies', in N. Denzin and Y. Lincoln (eds), *Handbook of Qualitative Research*. London: Sage.
Stallard, P. and Hudson, J. (1994) 'The Access to Health Records Act (1990): A survey of practice and implications for professionals', *Clinical Psychology Forum*, 73: 22–7.
Stansfield, J.H. (1994) 'Ethnic modeling in qualitative research', in N. Denzin and Y. Lincoln (eds), *Handbook of Qualitative Research*. London: Sage.
Steele, H. and Steele, M. (1994) 'Intergenerational patterns of attachment', in K.

Bartholomew and D. Perlman (eds), *Attachment Processes in Adulthood* (*Advances in Personal Relationships*, Vol. 5). London: Jessica Kingsley.
Sue, D.W. and Sue, D. (1990) *Counselling the Culturally Different: Theory and Practice*. Chichester: Wiley.
Symington, N. (1992) 'Countertransference with mentally handicapped clients', in A. Waitman and S. Conboy-Hill (eds), *Psychotherapy and Mental Handicap*. London: Sage.
Szasz, T. (1994) *Cruel Compassion*. Chichester: Wiley.
Taylor, C. (1989) *Sources of the Self: The Making of Modern Identity*. Cambridge: Cambridge University Press.
Taylor, C. (1991) *The Ethics of Authenticity*. Cambridge, MA: Harvard University Press.
Taylor, S.J. (ed.) (1994) 'Editor's introduction to the exchange of opinion on the risks and benefits of facilitated communication', *Mental Retardation*, 32: 299–318.
Tennant, L. and Cullen, C. (1987) 'Working with mentally handicapped people', in J.S. Marzillier and J. Hall (eds), *What is Clinical Psychology?* Oxford: Oxford University Press.
Tizard, J. (1964) *Community Services for the Mentally Handicapped*. London: Oxford University Press.
Tizard, J. (1983) 'Tomas Coram Research Unit: implications of its work for policy', in A.D.B. Clarke and B. Tizard (eds), *Child Development and Social Policy: The Life and Work of Jack Tizard*. Leicester: British Psychological Society.
Todd, S. and Shearn, J. (1997) 'Family dilemmas and secrets: parents' disclosure of information to their adult offspring with learning disabilities', *Disability and Society*, 12: 341–66.
Trent, J.W. (1994) *Inventing the Feeble Mind*. London: University of California Press.
Trevillion, S. (1996) 'Community care: re-thinking the narrative of collaboration', *Journal of Research, Policy & Planning*.
Trierweiler, S.J. and Donovan, C.M. (1994) 'Exploring the ecological foundations of memory in psychotherapy: interpersonal affordance, perception, and recollection in real time', *Clinical Psychology Review*, 14 (4): 310–26.
Turner, J. and Graffam, J. (1987) 'Deceased loved ones in the dreams of mentally retarded adults', *American Journal of Mental Retardation*, 92: 282–9.
Turpin, G., Barley, V., Beail, N., Scaife, J., Slade, P., Smith, J. and Walsh, S. (1997) 'Standards for research projects and theses involving qualitative methods: suggested guidelines for trainees and courses', *Clinical Psychology Forum*, 108: 3–7.
Twigg, J. and Atkin, K. (1994) *Carers Perceived: Policy and Practice in Informal Care*. Buckingham: Open University Press.
Tymchuk, A. (1986) 'Guidelines for ethical decision making', *Canadian Psychology*, 27: 36–43.
Valentine, E. (1992) *Conceptual Issues in Psychology*, 2nd edn. London: Routledge.
Valsiner, J. (1987) *Culture and the Development of Children's Action*. Chichester: Wiley.
Valsiner, J. (1995) 'Editorial: culture and psychology', *Culture & Psychology*, 1 (1): 5–10.
Vetere, A. and Gale, A. (1987) *Ecological Studies of Family Life*. Chichester: Wiley.
Vicari, S., von Krogh, G., Roos, J. and Mahnke, V. (1996) 'Knowledge creation through cooperative experimentation', in G. von Krogh and J. Roos (eds), *Managing Knowledge*. London: Sage.
Vygotsky, L. (1962) *Thought and Language*. Cambridge, MA: MIT Press.
Walsh-Bowers, R. (1995) 'The reporting and ethics of the research relationship in areas of interpersonal psychology, 1939–1989', *Theory & Psychology*, 5: 233–50.

Weingarten, K. and Cobb, S. (1995) 'Timing disclosure sessions: adding a narrative perspective to clinical work with adult survivors of childhood sexual abuse', *Family Process*, 34: 257–69.

Wertsch, J.V. (1995) 'Sociocultural research in the copyright age', *Culture & Psychology*, 1 (1): 81–102.

Wheeler, D., Jacobson, J., Paglieri, R. and Schwartz, A. (1993) 'An experimental assessment of facilitated communication', *Mental Retardation*, 31: 49–60.

White, M. (1989) *Selected Papers*. Adelaide: Dulwich Centre Press.

White, M. and Epston, D. (1990) *Narrative Means to Therapeutic Ends*. London: Norton.

Williams, R. (1983) *Keywords: A Vocabulary of Culture and Society*. London: Fontana.

Wolfensberger, W. (1972) *The Principle of Normalization in Human Services*. Toronto: National Institute on Mental Retardation.

Wolfensberger, W. (1994) 'A personal interpretation of the mental retardation scene in light of the "Signs of the Times"', *Mental Retardation*, 32: 19–33.

Wood, H.A. and Wood, D.J. (1984) 'An experimental evaluation of the effects of 5 styles of teacher conversation on the language of hearing-impaired children', *Journal of Child Psychology Psychiatry*, 23: 295–308.

Woodcock, J. (1995) 'Healing rituals with families in exile', *Journal of Family Therapy*, 17: 397–410.

Woody, J.D. (1990) 'Resolving ethical concerns in clinical practice: toward a pragmatic model', *Journal of Marital and Family Therapy*, 16: 133–50.

Zajonc, R.B. (1984) 'On the primacy of affect', *American Psychologist*, 39: 117–23.

Zetlin, A.G. and Turner, J.L. (1984) 'Self-perspectives on being handicapped', in R.B. Edgerton (ed.), *Lives in Process*. Washington, DC: American Association of Mental Deficiency Monograph 6.

Zigler, E. and Styfco, S. (1994) 'Head start: criticisms in a constructive context', *American Psychologist*, 49: 127–32.

Index